THE

Forgot

B-1

And the Integration
of the Modern Navy

by Alex Albright

For Rose,
with best wishes,
This jazzy tale of a not so
distant past

Alex Again

17 April 2014
Greenville NC

R.A. Fountain
Fountain, NC

Published in the United States by R.A. Fountain

P.O. Box 44

Fountain, NC 27829-0044

www.rafountain.com/navy

Catalog information

Albright, Alex, 1951-

The forgotten first: B-1 and the integration of the modern Navy.

Includes notes, endnotes, sources, afterword.

Index and chronology at www.rafountain/navy

ISBN 0-9842102-2-9 paperback

1. African Americans—World War, 1939–1945—U.S. Navy—North Carolina, Virginia, Hawaii—Race relations—Musicians.

2. World War, 1939–1945—African Americans—Musicians.

3. U.S. Navy—African Americans—U.S. Navy Music Program—Race relations.

4. Greensboro (N.C.)—North Carolina Agriculture and Technical University—World War, 1939–1945—Bands—Race relations.

5. Chapel Hill (N.C.)—United States, Navy, Pre-Flight School—University of North Carolina at Chapel Hill—Race relations.

6. Norfolk (Va.)—Naval Base—World War, 1939–1945—Race relations.

7. U. S. Navy, Naval District, 14th, Naval Station Pearl Harbor—Pearl City (Hawaii)—Race relations—Military bands.

Printed by Morgan Printers, Greenville NC

on Neenah Classic Crest

Composed in Hoefler & Frere-Jones Sentinel

Design by Eva Roberts

First edition published October 2013

Dedicated

to the bandsmen of B-1
and their families,
especially
their grandchildren,
for whom
this book is written

Moon 3/6W

Raymond Petford
(104)
1502 Ashe St.
Greensboro, N.C.

Maurice "Stubby" Miles
1st trump.
804 Boone Place
Dayton Ohio

Jewitt L. White (trumpet)
2613 Mass. St.
Gary, Ind.

O. Carlean
706 Cassel St.
High Point, N.C.

Millie Judkins (Sax)
710 Linwood Ct.
Durham, N.C.

Abe Thurman (Tpt.)
326 Ridgewood Ave.
Newark 8, N.J.

Otto Bellard
615 Nantucket
Greensboro, N.C.

Aaron Y. Butler Mus. ¾
732 West 25th Street
Winston-Salem, North Carolina.

Whitmore Haith   "Krup"
400 Stewart St. (Drums)
Greensboro, N.C.

Robert Andrew "Joe" Holland
224 Boyer St.
Dayton Ohio

James B. Scott
147 West McCullough St.
Greensboro, N.C. (Pop Charlie)

James C. Maurice mus. ¾ (Beer-Belly)
668 Clinton Ave.
Newark, N.J.

Table of Contents

General Benjamin O. Davis Sr., inspecting general from Washington, D.C., reviews Area 6 soldiers during recent visit to Camp Wolters, Texas.

TALMADGE SEEKS RE-ELECTION ON "HATE PLAN" AIMED AT NEGROES

SATURDAY, AUGUST 7, 1943

Unreconstructed Southerners Revive Civil War Issues as Democrats Seek to Reelect Race-Baiter for Governor.

N.C. Woman, Beaten By Cops, Convicted By Court

WILMINGTON, N. C. — (ANP) — Mrs. Mamie Williamson was given a 30-day suspended sentence in recorders court last week by Judge H. Wendell Smith, upon her conviction on charges of violating the race separation law, assault and battery and resisting arrest. Mrs. Williamson before her arrest was dragged from the bus, kicked and beaten by police officers while 60 bus passengers looked on.

Attys. C. J. Gates of Durham and Aaron Goldberg of Wilmington, contending that the state failed to prove its case, asked leave to appeal which was granted by the court. Machinery was immediately set in motion to prepare for redress before the Hanover County Superior court.

Charges were brought against Mrs. Williamson by J. D. Holloway, driver for the Tidewater Power company who was transporting passengers to the ship docks to witness launching of the Liberty ship John Merrick, named for the founder of the North Carolina Mutual Life Insurance company.

According to Holloway, Mrs. Williamson refused to give a seat to a white man when ordered to do so. He summoned Officers N. S. Wolff and William Leitch who threw the women from her seat into the street, and while each held an arm, pummeled her into a state of near unconsciousness. They then took her to the local jail. Mrs Williamson was forced to remain behind bars for more than a half hour pending arrangement for $500 bail.

Witnesses to the affair claim that the well known woman was the victim of the prejudice of the driver. According to their testimony the following actually occurred:

Mrs. Williamson boarded the bus along with 30 or 40 other persons en route to the launching ceremony and occupied a seat behind the driver. Later other passengers were picked up including four white persons all of whom had to stand because the vehicle was crowded.

The driver, observing the white people standing, ordered Mrs. Williamson to give her seat to a man, but she refused to do this stating that there was no seat for her to occupy. Turning off the main high-

Other passengers who attempted to leave the bus after the incident were ordered back at gun point by one of the officers and told to proceed to the shipyards. Approximately 10 of the terrified passengers complied with the order and arrived at the yards just in time to see the crowd attending the cere...

Capitol City Policeman Acquitted In New Hearing On Brutal Arrest of Soldie

Army Forms 2 Jim Crow Units, And New Air Squad

WASHINGTON, D. C.—In the face of bitter protests from Negro editors and publishers whom it invited to Washington recently for a conference, the War Department Thursday announced that it had completed plans for two jim crow divisions, in the United States Army.

In order to get together the two jim crow outfits which will be based at Fort Huachuca, Ariz., and Fort Knox, Ky., a large number of new recruits will be needed.

This will solve, temporarily at least, the problem the army has faced of having to pass over Negro selectees because all existing jim crow units were up to full strength. To solve another knotty problem, a second jim crow air squadron will be formed to be known as the 100th Pursuit squadron. It will be organized along the same lines as the existing 99th Pursuit squadron now in training at Tuskegee institute in Alabama.

The new divisions will be known as the 6th Armored Division and the 93rd Infantry division. The former will be composed of 10,000 men and officers.

A. and T. Supplies 13 Musicians For Navy Aid School

Thirteen of the 45 negro musicians to be stationed at the navy pre-flight training school at the University of North Carolina at Chapel Hill have already been recruited for service from the ranks of the A. and T. college band by the Greensboro navy recruiting station, it was announced yesterday.

The negro bandsmen sent from here have been passed by the district recruiting station at Raleigh and the other recruits will be located at the Chapel Hill negro community center and will make up the official band of the pre-flight school.

Musicians recruited here are as follows:

Warmth Thomas Gibbs, Jr., Robert Emmons Brower, Walter Franklin James Clarence Young, Roger Franklin Holt, and Charles Lewis Woods, all of Greensboro; Alton Verne Butler, Jr., of Winston-Salem; James Daniel Morgan, Jr., of Comfort; Willie Evans Currie, Jr., of St. Paul, N. C.; Dorsey Clay, of Roxboro; route Jr.; William Edward Skinner, of Gary, Ind.; and Thomas Jeff Gavin, Jr., of Lumberton.

NAVY, MARINES NEED THOUSANDS

...erty Mexican Heat Powder. It ...one kind of medicated powder containing four ingredients recommended by specialists for these miseries. Yet this soothing, cooling, comforting powder costs little, and there's even greater savings in the large sizes. Like millions of tiny sponges it absorbs moisture on skin, a frequent cause of irritation. Keep it always handy. Sold everywhere. Ask today for a season's supply of Mexsana.

...Jee 'Eye To Eye'

be "undivided by senseless distinctions of race, color or theory."

At Marshalltown, Iowa, Mr. Landon called for a more sympathetic approach to America's own racial problems and added that "the war has removed many limitations on the Negro, which will never be replaced."

"Navy, Marines Need Thousands."

Pittsburgh Courier 30 May 1942: 1, 4.

For other headlines in collage

see Works Cited.

Introduction

"The best, most talented musicians
in North Carolina."

—JAMES B. PARSONS

Historians have in recent years begun suggesting that World War II transformed the South more than the Civil War did, which, especially for white Southerners, may seem a stretch. But for many black Americans, World War II became a watershed event in the march towards the rights of full citizenship. As the war progressed, and once its black veterans returned home, it would become increasingly difficult to attend under-funded "colored schools," to move to the back of a bus, to eat out in a segregated world—in short, to be content with a politically expedient "gradualism" that kept promising equality even as it denied integration. (1)

World War II brought economic, political, and social change to the entire home front. Nowhere were those changes more dramatic than in the South, which FDR often represented as the nation's number one economic problem. His administration sought to solve the South's economic woes by placing defense industries throughout the region and by using its surplus manpower—its large numbers of unemployed and under-employed—to fuel the rapid growth of the U.S. defense industry in the South as well as in the West and Northeast.

Although the Civil War had brought legal freedom to slaves, its end saw a continuation, ultimately, of the same economic system in the South, which remained reliant on cheap labor for its farms for decades of sharecropping. World War I made race relations a national issue, especially for black Americans, and its aftermath made the problems of living together in the same society more "urgent and menacing." Post-war riots—at least 26 throughout the U.S. in 1919 alone—showed that the South's "color psychosis" was spreading throughout the nation. But it took World War II to upset the regional balance of America's race problem. (2)

Beginning in 1940, a new industrialization accompanying the build up to war brought with it mobility and thus the ability for many, especially those tied to sharecropping and domestic work, to choose better jobs, with the option to relocate to secure them. The intransigent if inconsistent dualism that dominated the South when World War II broke out was still in place at its conclusion, but World War II set in motion a mix of forces leading to the conflicts and policies that would ultimately bring that system down. None of these forces was greater than a worker's ability to imagine a better life, in a better place, where perhaps Jim Crow would not be so pernicious.

We already know that in North Carolina, the impact of World War II was dramatic on both the battle and home fronts. More troops from North Carolina—8,910—died in the war than from any Southern state except Texas. And by 1943, more men were being trained in North Carolina than in any other state. In several key ways, the massive influx of trainees—and the construction boom that preceded them—created stresses in and around the communities hosting each of the state's 24 training camps. First, by sheer numbers of new residents, local infrastructures were strained even as economies were boosted. At Camp Butner, which opened on 40,000 acres in August 1942—at about the same time as B-1 was arriving at its first duty station, in Chapel Hill—250,000 troops, including 7,500 African Americans, had an economic impact on Granville, Durham, and Person counties estimated at millions of dollars a year. (3)

Additionally, each base had a large civilian population at work on and near it. Historian Charles D. Chamberlain notes that migrant tent and trailer settlements "encircled Fort Bragg," as thousands moved there seeking government work. They came looking for jobs building and expanding the bases and working at businesses feeding off the bases that included Camps Davis, Lejeune, and Sutton; Cherry Point, Seymour Johnson, and Pope Army Field. At each military installation, local communities were ill-equipped to deal with the impacts of these burgeoning numbers, which brought with them sudden increases in housing, transportation, and recreation needs and an inevitable strain in local race relations. In "countless Southern wartime communities" the result was "chaos," Chamberlain writes. (4)

Race relations were tested especially by northern blacks who arrived at training bases in the South unused to the prevalent Jim Crow laws, which were strained wherever publics met: in buses, restaurants, theaters, and on the street. The B-1 bandsmen, however, were veterans of that Jim Crow world: until they left North Carolina for Pearl Harbor in May 1944, the men of B-1 were always transported within that Jim Crow system. Because they understood where they were from, they also knew that what was okay in Greensboro might or might not be okay in Raleigh or Norfolk, Durham, Wilmington, or Chapel Hill, where the law might be different—or simply enforced differently for people "not from here." No one could know the answer to what was okay until it was tested directly—and the answer might well change the next time it was tested. One reason B-1 would successfully complete its tour of duty in two Southern towns and the most exotic of all American ports is that its sailors knew these facts of life and the potential repercussions of testing their limits.

The B-1 bandsmen were among 2.5 million African Americans who registered for the draft; over a million served. North Carolina managed these important distinctions: at Montford Point, near Camp Lejeune, the first African Americans to serve in the Marines were trained, as was the first black Marine band. And the U.S. Navy B-1 Band, organized in Greensboro at North Carolina Agricultural and Mechanical College—now N.C. A&T University— was comprised of the first African Americans to serve in the modern Navy at rank other than messman. They would in the process also become the first band of African Americans to serve that modern Navy. (5)

College campuses felt the impact, too, in varying degrees, as their student bodies were depleted by the draft and enlistment, and their curricula augmented by ROTC and other military support programs. At the University of North Carolina (now UNC-CH), the campus itself was transformed into a training camp when the Navy established one of its pre-flight training schools there and in the process took over many of the university's buildings.

The 48 men who served in B-1 were part of history as well as eyewitnesses to its unfolding, and their individual stories are microcosms of much larger ones that played out throughout the United States from 1942-45. Greensboro, however, was special in the way its black community and colleges nurtured its young, politically as well as culturally. Future B-1 bandsmen worked there with three of the best black classical musicians of the 20th century—Nathaniel Dett, Bernard Mason, and Warner Lawson, whose lives and careers were likewise restrained by the racist times in which they tried to flourish.

B-1 was part of the initial mobilization effort that led its volunteers to break not only the Navy's color barrier, but also racial barriers on the UNC campus and in Chapel Hill, where they would become role models for young African Americans like Doug Clark. In Chapel Hill, bandsmen would also integrate a previously all-white Presbyterian church whose congregation included Frank Porter Graham and whose pianist, fellow A&T alum Calvin Lampley, would go on to produce records by Miles Davis, Louis Armstrong, Duke Ellington, Mahalia Jackson, and Judy Garland. They performed with and for white stars such as Kate Smith, Helen O'Connell, Orrin Tucker, Bob Crosby, and Boris Karloff, among many others. They were stars of countless bond rallies and community concerts. They got lost by the Navy, perhaps in Chapel Hill and again as they were being shipped to Pearl Harbor, and then after the war as the records of their service disappeared into unexamined files. They were first-hand witnesses to the explosions that rocked Pearl Harbor in 1944 in one of the largest domestic tragedies of the war. They likely were unwitting tools used by the Navy to calm racial tensions in Hawaii, where they took into their ranks sailors who had been punished for their protests over unacceptable conditions at other postings. They were favorites of three of the Navy's most prominent officers, and at the war's end, they were the stars of the largest VJ parade staged in the U.S. Their bandmaster, James B. Parsons, would become the first African American appointed to a U.S. District Court judgeship, by President John F. Kennedy in 1961. Many of them individually would go on to long and distinguished careers in public education, where they would also counsel new generations of African Americans through the last days of a segregated public education system. Their students would see many of the social changes the men of B-1 could only imagine when they voluntarily answered the call to duty to serve in the U.S. Navy.

: : : :

The U.S. Navy B-1 Band was officially formed on May 27, 1942, when 44 young men—"the best, most talented musicians in North Carolina"—were sworn into service at Raleigh, North Carolina. Soon after their swearing in, they boarded a train bound for boot camp in Norfolk as, collectively, the first African Americans to serve in the modern Navy at any general rank, not as "sea-going bellhops" but as musicians. Although their service throughout the war was as a segregated unit, the establishment of B-1 was a significant move towards integration of the modern U.S. Navy. "The Navy," Parsons recalled, "hid its head from integration longer than even the Marines," whose commandant called the enlistment of blacks at any rank "absolutely tragic." (6)

Sentiment among black leaders was divided at the time as to whether the creation of all-black units such as B-1 was truly an advancement. By October 1940, the Pittsburgh *Courier* had changed from advocating that blacks be allowed access to all ranks in the Army to pushing for full integration of the military. The Army's January 1942 announcement that it was planning "2 Jim Crow" units, the Chicago *Defender* said, came "in the face of bitter protests from Negro editors and publishers." Most black audience newspapers agreed that the Navy's plan to accept blacks at general rank but in segregated units was not an indicator of much progress. After the NAACP praised the announcement and received for itself hot criticism from the black press, its director, Walter White, changed his mind, calling the plan "only a gesture." (7)

B-1 was ultimately forgotten by the Navy and ignored by most contemporary students of American, military, and African-American history. How this band of integration pioneers slipped through the net of history is hard to explain. Their distinction, however, has been generally credited to a different group of musicians, who trained in Chicago. It seems clear that this official history of the Navy's first step out of its dark ages is tied to the dialog which led Secretary of Navy Frank Knox to announce, on April 21, 1942, a plan to train black sailors in Chicago at what has since come to be known as the Great Lakes Training Center. That training could not begin without the military's first building—or securing—an appropriate, meaning *separate* training facility. But Knox, impossibly, seems to have been unaware that already at the time of his announcement the chain of events was in motion that would lead to B-1's formation well before the establishment of Camp Robert Smalls, the first of the Great Lakes training facilities for African Americans. Commander O.O. Kessing had been brought out of retirement to begin the process of scouring the nation's college campuses in search of appropriate space to establish four schools for training Navy pilots, and early plans for those schools indicate that each was to have a 40+ piece regimental band comprised of African Americans. (8)

Yet, somehow, for over 50 years the historical record continued to state that those who trained at Great Lakes were the first African Americans to serve in the modern Navy at rank other than messman.

The official Navy record that claimed for decades that black enlistments at general ranks began on June 1, 1942—four days after the men of B-1 had been sworn in to duty and nearly six weeks after most had enlisted—finally recognizes that by August 13, 1942, when the "first recruits" had finished their training at Great Lakes, B-1 had completed training and was two weeks into service at its first post-training station, in Chapel Hill. (9)

The press, both black and white audience newspapers, recognized B-1's achievement at the time. In the summer of 1942, the two most influential national black newspapers, the Chicago *Defender* and the Pittsburgh *Courier*, and the regionally popular Norfolk *Journal-Guide* noted B-1's formation as "the first all-Negro Navy band" and "the first and thus far only all-Negro band in the navy." The *Daily Tar Heel* called B-1 "the first all colored band ever in the Navy" but within a month had corrected itself, noting it was the first black band to be recruited "since the last war." (10)

Because of such an obvious omission from official Navy records, it's easy to understand why other contemporary historians continued for half a century to grant the distinction of having broken this color barrier to the black sailors who trained at the Great Lakes bases, where in the course of World War II well over 100 bands were commissioned. Further complicating the historical record, a Great Lakes-trained band replaced B-1 in Chapel Hill in 1944; in Hawaii, swing bands from B-1 performed on many occasions with Great Lakes-trained bandsmen; and four fellows who trained at Great Lakes wound up being assigned to B-1 in Hawaii.

Even after the Army-Navy-Marine Corps School of Music honored B-1 in a 1981 program at the Norfolk Naval Amphibious Base Theater that should have righted the history books, no one, it seems, took much notice. The official Center of Military History publication *Integration of the Armed Forces, 1940–1965*, published in 1985, makes no mention of B-1, and it perpetuates the historical inaccuracy that those trained at Great Lakes had broken the Navy's color barrier. But the epitome of historical confusion over B-1's distinction is probably the claim made in program notes to a 2003 celebration in Chicago of the "Great Lakes Experience" that B-1's Roger Holt was part of the "first Black Naval Band Unit at Great Lakes." Holt, then living in Chicago, was never at Great Lakes. Also reprinted with that program and distributed in the celebration packet is Rear Admiral A.E. Rondeau's congratulatory letter to the Great Lakes re-uniters, whom he addresses as "the first United States Navy African American Musicians." [11]

Words of praise written by Terrence Bell in that 2003 program about the musicians who served at Great Lakes might just as easily have been said of B-1: "These musical giants and heroes of yesteryear truly paved the way for today's musicians. . . . They did much more than just play in bands. During that time, this country was still wrestling with the question of integration and these men suffered all the indignities that segregation carried with it. They served their country with honor, and in the process help[ed] to change the landscape of American music." Admiral Rondeau's letter commemorates those "allowed to enlist outside the Steward's Branch, serving our country as Navy Musicians between 1942 and 1945." Rondeau writes that in 1942, the Navy "changed its policies of the past and began the desegregation of the Armed Forces. Now your Navy is an institution with equal opportunity for all and with a deep appreciation for the richness of our diversity. This is due, in part, to your sacrifices and pioneering spirit." [12]

More recently, in November 2010, Michael Bayes wrote "Navy Pioneers: A History of African Americans in Navy Music," a Smithsonian Institute production that officially notes B-1 as having begun its service earlier than the Great Lakes-trained sailors.

He uses for verification the news accounts and Navy documents that were collected for this history.

The first African Americans to serve in the modern Navy at rank other than messman's or steward's, however, were not those praised by Rondeau and Bell and celebrated in Chicago in 2003. Rather, that distinction belongs rightly to the fellows of B-1, who also were the first African-American musicians to enlist in the modern Navy. The historical record, as this story will show, is clear on both points. But the purpose here is not to demean in any way the important service of the thousands of musicians and other African Americans who trained at Camps Robert Smalls, Lawrence, and Moffett in Chicago and subsequently served the Navy honorably at duty stations throughout the United States, its territories, and the Pacific theater between 1942–45. It seeks, instead, to document a remarkable historical journey while re-claiming for the men who actually made this first bold step their place in American history. Their story is made all the more intriguing by the questions that linger over how B-1 was formed and why it could be so thoroughly lost—questions that may never be answered with the assurance of absolute truth. The principals who made it happen are all dead; their archives, where they exist, are incomplete or, as is the case with some Navy records, not cataloged or not available for researcher use. Yet, enough of the historical record exists to say with certainty that B-1's is a true story of distinction that deserves its rightful place in the history of our nation's slow march towards integration and Civil Rights for all Americans. (13)

Briefly, these are the facts:

U.S. Navy B-1 was conceived as one of the 45-piece bands that would each be attached to the Navy's regional pre-flight training schools. The four schools had been selected by the end of February 1942, after a series of inspections of potential sites by Commander O.O. Kessing, who would also become the first commander of the UNC pre-flight school. Nicknamed "Scrappy" from his days as an athlete at the U.S. Naval Academy, Kessing was "one of the best known characters in the Navy," according to historian Samuel Morison, who also notes that he would go on to become the third and last commissioner of the All-America Football Conference, which from 1946–49 challenged the NFL for control of professional football in the U.S. A decorated veteran of the Mexican campaign of 1914, during which he was captured, and a veteran of World War I, Kessing inspected over sixty college campuses before selecting the final four: UNC, the University of Georgia, the University of Iowa, and St. Mary's College. (14)

The pre-flight school bandsmen, the Navy ordered on April 13, 1942, would be "enlisted as musicians, second class, from men of the Negro race only," and promotions for bandsmen would "be accomplished as individuals become properly qualified." The eastern and western regional training schools, located on the campuses of the University of North Carolina, in Chapel Hill, and St. Mary's College, in Moraga, California, were the only two to wind up with all-black bands. U.S. Navy bands were also established at the other two original pre-flight schools, at the University of Iowa and at the University of Georgia. Why neither wound up with a black band is not clear, although given the political climate in Georgia and the dearth of black citizens in Iowa at the time, easy conjectures might be made. A fifth pre-flight school was established later in 1942 at Del Monte, California. (15)

Except for the unique circumstances of its formation, B-1 would likely have trained at the Great Lakes bases, where the St. Mary's bandsmen would be trained. No B-1 bandsmen, despite their qualifications, would gain rank higher than musician first class; in fact, many would lose rank in the process of transferring duty stations, from Chapel Hill to Hawaii. (16)

The original plan for the band to be stationed at Chapel Hill was to recruit musicians for B-1 exclusively from the state of North Carolina. Because of the pressure that would be on them—for performances as well as for behavior, especially when they would be outside the black community in Chapel Hill that would embrace them—it was essential that these recruits be excellent musicians who were intelligent and even-tempered. They would be a band of which, the first UNC pre-flight commander said, "all the people of the state will be justly proud." They had to understand the absolute nature of the color line that dominated social conventions in the Jim Crow South, and—at least on the surface—they had to accept it as a way of life. The B-1 bandsmen knew they were front-line pioneers in the Navy's new policy, announced on April 7, 1942, of accepting black recruits at all ratings, not just the messman's rank, and they knew that many would expect them to fail. (17)

President Roosevelt had suggested, in June 1941, that the Navy "make a beginning" towards integration by placing some "good Negro bands" on board battleships. Earlier that year, the Navy had argued that relegating African Americans to menial ranks was not discriminatory but "a means of promoting efficiency, dependability, and flexibility." By limiting blacks to mess, cooking, and steward duties, the Navy was avoiding the chance that blacks might wind up commanding whites, which Secretary of Navy Knox believed "was a thing which instantly provokes serious trouble." The Navy remained obstinate, at least publicly, for several months in its position that because segregation was impractical, exclusion was necessary. A Navy report in January 1942 concluded that if restriction of blacks to messman's branch was discriminatory, "it was but part and parcel of a similar discrimination throughout the United States." (18)

Many black leaders at the time pinned the cause of the Navy's reluctance to change its policies regarding the service of African Americans as the fault, primarily, of Frank Knox, who said "it is no kindness to Negroes to thrust them upon men of the white race." Samuel Barnes, who became one of the Navy's first 13 black officers—known subsequently as "the golden thirteen"—recalled that Knox died about a month after he and his fellows had been commissioned, and that they all laughed when they heard the news of his death, not meaning to be "unkind," but wondering if their commissions had caused it. One of them then expressed the hope that perhaps their commissioning "sort of expedited it." (19)

The arguments, controversy, and travail that would come to mark race relations in the U.S. and among its military personnel, especially at its home front bases, during World War II were but new versions of the same old stories. Repeatedly, for generations, the U.S. had reneged on promises that African Americans who served in time of war would be rewarded with significant additional rights after the peace was won. Because the latest round of these promises, during World War I, had been the most egregiously broken—and the meritorious service of so many so quickly forgotten—race relations during the build-up to World War II were the tensest they had been since Reconstruction. Black leaders and newspaper editors as well as white military leaders and newspaper editors feared that the war with Japan was being complicated by questions of race. Hitler's own racist regime was an easier one to fight, but even on that front, reports and rumors of black Americans saying they hoped Hitler won were not uncommon.

African Americans by the 1940s knew "far better than those of 1917-18 what their rights" were as citizens and had seen the futility of "appeasement and segregation," wrote Walter White, executive director of the NAACP from 1931–55, in a 1943 article for the *Journal of Negro Education*. White agrees in this article with the Nobel Prize-winning author Pearl Buck, who had in November 1941 written that the "militant restiveness" of African Americans is part of a "global race problem which must be solved if the war is to be won and if future wars are to be averted." White adds that African Americans were now better organized and educated, increasingly more militant, and for the first time, their struggles at home, as people of color, had become linked to those struggles world-wide. (20)

Despite that increasing militancy in both civilian and military environments, the B-1 bandsmen survived over three years of military service as front-line forces in the fight for racial equality, even as they served their country. And, perhaps most remarkable of all their accomplishments, they served without major incident, despite provocation that lurked wherever they went. It remains a testament to their selfless bravery—despite the tensions of these times—that they would not be provoked into actions that would demean their uniform, their service, or their humanity.

INDUSTRIAL HIGH AND
ELEMENTARY SCHOOLS
C. M. EPPES, SUPERVISING-PRINCIPAL

FIFTH STREET SCHOOL
SADIE I. SAULTER, PRINCIPAL

GREENVILLE CITY SCHOOLS
JUNIUS H. ROSE, SUPERINTENDENT
GREENVILLE, NORTH CAROLINA

April 29, 1942.

Hon. J. M. Broughton
Governor of North Carolina.

I am sure that the influence possessed by you, would aid the Negro much if in some way, the "Negro Newspaper" could (know, or) learn that agitation concerning racial discrimination at this time, should cease. It bodes no good for our race, When the War is over, they may appeal to proper authority. I can never forget 1898- and the destruction of the Negro Newspaper in Wilmington, the utterances of the paper caused the riot. We have travelled a long and successful journey Educationally in this state since this time. Your assurances at the sesquicentennial - following Bishop Ransom's great address - was heartening. You would be surprised to know how strong the sentiment is in North Carolina to let well enough alone. For in no state in this Union is the Negro faring as well.

Yours to Command
C. M. Eppes

Backgrounds: Military, Social, Political and Musical

"It goes a long way back. . ."

—RALPH ELLISON *Invisible Man*

Although early colonial militias in the United States made use of "every available man" regardless of race, politicians soon came to fear the threat to domestic order posed by free black militiamen who might become involved in slave revolts, using weapons given to them by the military. This "threat" would linger for centuries: in 1917, Sen. James K. Vardaman of Mississippi called it a mistake to have "called the Negroes of this country to arms," a sentiment echoed again during World War II by his colleagues Sen. Theodore G. Bilbo and Rep. John Rankin. Virginia became the first colony, in 1639, to develop a policy that would exclude blacks from militia service. The fear of slave insurrections, however, was not sufficient to trump the military's eventual need for fighting men and laborers once the Revolutionary War commenced. But when the deposed loyalist governor of Virginia offered freedom to all slaves if they would join the fight on the British side, the U.S. liberalized its own policy, promising the same reward. Once the British military had begun employing Negro troops, the Continental forces began using both slaves and freedmen; about 5,000 African Americans served the U.S. during the Revolutionary War, "often in integrated units, some as artillerymen and musicians." Several thousand slaves were subsequently freed, but the slave system remained in place and the post-war period established a pattern that would be followed into the post-World War II years, as the "services and achievements" of black servicemen were "quickly forgotten." (1)

By the time of the War of 1812, blacks were officially excluded from service in the U.S. military. But once again, the British offered freedom to slaves who would join their fight, and the U.S. followed suit. However, this time most were returned to their masters after the war. The most significant use of black troops came at the Battle of New Orleans, where Andrew Jackson's desperate need for manpower was the basis for the creation of the Louisiana Free Men of Color. His address to those troops is remarkable: "Through a mistaken policy you have heretofore been deprived of a participation in the glorious struggle for national rights in which our country is engaged. This no longer exists." Jackson, however, was wrong: the "mistaken policy" of exclusion was actually still in place when he spoke to his troops and would remain in place until the Civil War. After the U.S. victory, exclusionist policies were relaxed (or ignored) enough to allow, in 1816, blacks and whites to "mess together" on the USS *Java*, a 44-gun frigate. (2)

During the Civil War, 186,000 African Americans served the Union Army in 149 segregated combat regiments; another 30,000 served in the U.S. Navy. After the war, the Army Reorganization Act of 1866 established four segregated black army units. General W. T. Sherman lobbied unsuccessfully for racial distinctions to be "obliterated from the statute book" and for whites and blacks to be "enlisted and distributed alike in the army, as has been the usage in the navy for a hundred years." The Army, however, went with its plan for segregated units—the 9th and 10th Cavalry and the 24th and 25th Infantry—who would serve under white officers. The Navy remained integrated: in the last half of the 19th century, black sailors accounted for 20–30 percent of the Navy's enlisted strength. Although their service was in integrated units, they generally were relegated to the lowest ranks. Still, during the Spanish-American War, black sailors provided distinguished service in major battles at Manila and Santiago. A surge in enlistments in the Army during that war tripled the number of black soldiers, many of whom fought with Teddy Roosevelt at San Juan Hill. But the conflict also helped heighten racial unrest at home, resulting in several incidents of attacks by civilian mobs on black troops. At the conclusion of that war, things only got worse: the troops who had fought so valiantly found on their return home "a more pervasive racism than they had known previously" as the U.S. military aligned itself with the segregationist views that had been affirmed by a series of Supreme Court decisions that culminated in Plessy v. Ferguson in 1896. (3)

The turn of the 19th into the 20th century is in many ways defined by the resurgent racism marked by the rise of Jim Crow legislation and the white supremacy campaigns throughout the South that enforced through threat, intimidation, and violence both a legalized and an informal and confusingly inconsistent system of segregation. The Brownsville, Texas, riot of 1906 was one awful result, and the government's over-reaction to it—all 167 blacks stationed at Fort Brown were discharged "without honor"—only heightened the feeling among African Americans that their military service was not appreciated. The tone of Booker T. Washington's letter to War Secretary William H. Taft regarding the Brownsville incident reflected a kind of reasoned restraint that would, as World War II opened, be difficult for black leaders to maintain: "The race is not so much resentful or angry, perhaps, as it feels hurt and disappointed." (4)

Although official policy still allowed for the recruitment of blacks at the outset of World War I, the Navy very quickly began adopting the informal segregationist practices so increasingly common in civilian life. These attitudes were fostered under Woodrow Wilson's presidency, as segregation within the U.S. government was introduced soon after his inauguration in 1913—a move consistent with his past practices and beliefs and supported by many in his cabinet. While president of Princeton University (1902-10), Wilson had barred blacks from attending, prompting protests from the *Princetonian*. His wife was outspoken in her segregationist views, and five in his cabinet, like him, were Southern. Secretary of Navy Josephus Daniels, who grew up in Wilson, NC, reported that the President enjoyed telling "darky" stories at cabinet meetings. Wilson's allowing of the re-segregation of toilets, lunchroom facilities, and working areas at the Departments of Treasury and Post Office was a "conspicuous reversal" of a 50-year tradition of integrated civil service and an important component of the "national apotheosis of Jim Crow" that his administration sanctioned. He, like many leading whites of his time, conflated modern liberalism with white supremacy, yielding a conflicted policy of liberal internationalism that was tempered by a national segregationist belief defined by white Southerners and codified by the Supreme Court. (5)

But as much as Wilson and his contemporaries wished to believe that segregation and white supremacy were natural laws, African Americans were increasingly troubled by the status quo. For years, the quiet acceptance of Jim Crow laws and conditions by many black leaders, especially in the South, would lead these white leaders to believe that their way was the proper one. For black citizens forced to endure the resultant indignities, however, accommodation was not so easy. Riots in Houston in July 1917, just three months after Wilson's declaration of war, proved much worse than the 1906 Brownsville riot and initiated a 3-year span of civil unrest that would rock the U.S. Despite a lack of evidence as to who might have been responsible, the Fort Logan riots in Houston resulted in the institutionalized lynching of at least 19 black soldiers and the sentencing to life terms in prison of another 63. Congressional protest that evidence against the black men was planted by local white citizens failed to persuade President Wilson to intervene; instead, he took the hands-off approach that would dictate the U.S. government's general policy, until the 1960s, of leaving the resolution of local racial conflicts to local authorities. In a sad foreshadowing of the same kinds of troubles that would plague military bases in the South during World War II, the riot was precipitated by the infusion of black Northern troops into a hot racial climate and sparked by those soldiers' response to local Jim Crow laws. Most of the black troops stationed at Camp Logan were not accustomed to the secondary status so blatantly assigned them by local laws that put them at the back of the bus and tried to make them drink "colored" water. It took just three weeks before the situation exploded. (6)

The Selective Service Act of May 1917 did not exclude blacks; subsequently, 3 million were registered. But soon into World War I, the use of African-American troops and sailors had been so curtailed that in the Army most were in menial occupations—of

400,000 black soldiers, 380,000 were in services or supply regiments, working as stevedores, drivers, and laborers. In all, only 6,750 black sailors (1.2% of the Navy's enlistment) served during World War I, the lowest percentage by far of any previous conflict. In 1919, under Josephus Daniels' direction, the Navy quit accepting black volunteers and began recruiting Filipino messmen. As a result, the "long and honorable history of bravery and heroism" shown by African Americans in the Navy ended with "the blighting of his chances for equal participation." Nelson writes that the reasons for the Navy's "re-segregation" are "complex" and "outside the scope" of his book, but agrees that they were a part of a national social pattern. By 1920, blacks accounted for less than 1/2 of 1% of the total Navy force. (7)

Most black servicemen remained stateside during World War I, and many were trained at camps in the South, where intolerable local conditions were made worse by the military's persistent use of white officers, often Southerners, to command black troops. Complaints about military camps for blacks being located in the South go back at least as far as 1877; neither the trainees nor their hosts were comfortable with their situations, and at least two generals and a major protested stationing of blacks at New Orleans and Little Rock. Without explanation, the Secretary of War answered those complaints by saying President Rutherford B. Hayes (1877-81) continued to believe that "colored troops should be kept on duty in the South." The Army's Quartermaster General later explained that Southern duty stations were best for black troops because "their race is from the tropics." Talmadge Neece, who would be personnel officer at B-1's duty station in Hawaii, said the practice of assigning white Southerners to supervise black troops extended well into World War II: "It was generally considered that white Southerners were the only ones who knew 'how to handle' blacks." General George C. Marshall would admit to a biographer as he neared death in 1959 that "one of the greatest mistakes I made during [World War II] was to insist that the colored divisions be trained in the south." (8)

But Southern officers and training camp environments were only a part of the racial tensions that threatened domestic peace both during World War I and immediately after it. Prior to it, black audience newspapers were already promoting the migration out of the South as the surest way to better living conditions for black Americans. Some Southerners tried to prevent or slow this migration, outlawing labor agents and discouraging the sale and distribution of the Chicago *Defender*, the primary early proponent of migration. As tensions rose and conditions worsened, between 400,000 and 600,000 African Americans would leave their Southern homes for the promise of a better life and job opportunities. But they were not always welcomed: their presence in industrial cities outside the Deep South was blamed for housing shortages, and many whites believed the new labor force would be used as strikebreakers or to create a surplus of labor that would drive wages down. Jobs and housing conflicts led to an East St. Louis riot in 1917 in which 40 blacks were killed, and to dozens of other smaller clashes in New York, Philadelphia, and Chicago, where between 1917-19 over 20 bomb attacks were made on homes occupied by blacks or owned by realtors who sold to blacks. After World War I ended in November 1918, things only got worse, leading to the "red summer" of 1919, when race riots broke out across the country and at least 83 lynchings were recorded. (9)

The aftermath of World War I brought with it much bitterness to America's black community. In the run-up to war, both the progressives like W.E.B. Du Bois and conservatives like Booker T. Washington had been optimistic that blacks would find an expanded role in American democracy as an end result of the international conflict. Before the war, Du Bois was adamant in his insistence on integrating the military; however, as the war began, he capitulated to the belief that segregated units would be okay, for the time being, and the black press echoed his stance, saying that it would support collective efforts to win the war if blacks were given full citizenship rights after it was over. But confronted with the renewed intransigence of domestic segregation at the war's end, a "New Negro" arose, one who began retaliating more readily against white aggression. Cameron McWhirter credits the "red summer" with awakening black America politically, socially and artistically and notes that from then on, segregation was on the defensive. The NAACP, frustrated by its failure to keep *Birth of a Nation* from screening nationwide, was galvanized into action by the deteriorated race conditions at home. In 1919, it published the landmark study *Thirty Years of Lynching in the United States, 1889-1918* and began urging boycotts of Jim Crow facilities. Membership in the NAACP swelled from 9,282 in 80 chapters in 1917 to 88,377 members in 356 chapters in 1920. (10)

At home in North Carolina, tensions in 1919 reflected national patterns. In Raleigh, the Twentieth Century Voters Club put up a slate of black candidates for office, and indications were growing that blacks in North Carolina might not much longer be docile in accepting their conditions. Governor Thomas W. Bickett (1917–21), in turn, warned returning black veterans to "behave themselves or face serious consequences" and reminded them of what had happened to the Native Americans when they refused to accept "white man's law." But even Bickett denounced Klan plans to establish a whites-only community in Richmond County. North Carolina, Bickett said, was the "best place in the world for a decent black man to make a living." The state was doing all it could to promote "friendly feelings" between the races and to secure for blacks equal privileges in industry, education, and religion. The races needed to be kept separate, he added, and whites needed to be rulers. (11)

The state's former superintendent of public schools proclaimed that society in North Carolina was organized according to God's plan: race differences and instinctive prejudices demand segregation. Blacks, he added, were not ready for equality, and any attempt to get it would only be a tragedy. Still, graduates at St. Augustine's College in Raleigh showed signs of "uppitiness." Fearing further trouble on a national scale, Bickett called on Robert R. Moton, president of Tuskegee Institute (1915–35), to help calm blacks in the state and to improve race relations, which, Moton said, would happen only if black citizens would obey all laws, "state, local, and natural." Bickett added that black unrest was stirring up the Klan and warned that Red Shirts would, like in 1898, "again take to the saddle" if blacks did not relent in demands. (12)

North Carolina's black leaders, especially, took such warnings seriously and they cautioned their constituents accordingly. These leaders generally reflected Moton's and Booker T. Washington's accommodationist politics. It is impossible to say how much of what North Carolina's own black leaders proclaimed was out of fear of what might happen to themselves and to their constituents, and how much was said out of respect for the positions of leadership they had been afforded—most at the discretion of the state's white leaders. But what's clear is that by the 1920s black leaders in the state were solidly conservative, and during the next 25 years they would for the most part echo the standard refrain offered by the state's white political leaders regarding the excellent status of race relations in North Carolina. (13)

The 1920 election further polarized race relations: Cameron Morrison, the Democrat elected governor (1921-25) that year, had run as a former Red Shirt leader who was proud of his role as an originator of the White Supremacy movement. The president of Bennett College banned DuBois' magazine *The Crisis*. N.C. A&T's president James B. Dudley wrote an open letter to every major newspaper in the state urging black women to refrain from registering and voting. Despite passage of the 19th amendment, ratified in August 1920, Dudley said "all lawful things are not always expedient." By voting, black women would "increase race hatred, prejudice, and political strife," in the process impeding progress in North Carolina and postponing the eventual coming of political freedom and independence for blacks. The Greensboro *Daily News* endorsed Dudley's letter, adding that if attempts continued to balance power, there would be a return to conditions of 1898. The frequent reminder of what had happened in Wilmington in 1898, when the Red Shirts had led the overthrow of that city's government, was a common thread in most threats made by whites to intimidate the black citizenry of North Carolina. It would be echoed again by Governor Broughton and Frank Daniels during World War II. Among white establishment leaders, few more than Josephus Daniels, editor of the *News and Observer*, fanned the flames of racial unrest. An avowed white supremacist identified in 2005 as the "precipitator" of the 1898 attacks in Wilmington, he warned in 1927 of an impending era of black political domination and the end of white supremacy. When Furnifold Simmons lost the 1928 election for governor—he boasted in the campaign that he had been "general of the White Supremacy Campaigns of 1898 and 1900"—the *N&O* was so outraged that it reprinted a 1901 speech by then-Governor Charles B. Aycock that warned against "social equality or any move towards it." (14)

The tenor of the 1920s was solidly established by Governor Morrison's address to black schoolteachers at their 1921 convention. After touting North Carolina's racial harmony, he praised the state's black population for "behaving better than ever before" and added that they were receiving as much education as they were ready for: once blacks were ready for more education, whites would give it to them. However, the *News and Observer* threatened, the "white man will stand guard at the threshold of his social life," and if blacks try to intrude, they would provoke a repeat of the "terrible days of Reconstruction." President Warren Harding weighed in that blacks should forget about social equality because it was neither desirable nor possible, and that any attempts towards it would be intolerable. (15)

It was in this incarnation of the Jim Crow South that most of the men who would become members of U.S. Navy B-1 were born and nurtured.

:::::

The Navy used Filipino messmen instead of blacks from 1919 until 1932, when it once again began accepting blacks, but as messmen only and in limited quotas. African Americans like Bandmaster Alton Augustus Adams, Jr., who had been in the Navy during the war, were allowed to remain in service during the 1920s and '30; Adams did not retire from service until 1934. Overall, though, the number of African Americans serving in the Navy in the period between the world wars was negligible; Morris MacGregor calls these years "the nadir of the Navy's relations with black America." In 1932, only 441 blacks were enlisted. Quotas remained at 50 blacks per month allowed to enlist until September 1939, when the quota was raised to 250, "to be enlisted as messmen only" within the stewards department. By 1940, 4,007 blacks comprised 2.3 percent of the Navy's total force, and of these, virtually all were enlisted men serving as messmen and steward's mates, what the black press called "seagoing bellhops."

The Selective Service Law passed in September 1940 codified the Navy's policy, ruling that blacks could not be accepted "in any other capacity than mess attendants."(16)

The subsequent build-up to World War II saw an increased push by black leaders nationally and the black press, especially, towards integration in the military, where, it was believed, such a move would open the way for sweeping societal changes. They recalled too clearly the empty promises made to ensure black support for the war effort in World War I. The 1920s and '30s also saw increasing alienation of blacks from mainstream America and the hardening of Jim Crow laws and customs in the South. As W. E. B. Du Bois notes, race segregation in the South was not always a matter of law but often of custom, which varied from complete separation in living quarters to the public mingling of the races in some cities and sections of others, but with class distinctions. In Durham, for example, "whites only" service in restaurants was a custom not formalized by law until 1940, when large numbers of black soldiers, many of whom were from the North and unfamiliar with local ways, began arriving at military bases in the area. A 1962 survey of segregation laws in North Carolina would conclude that most laws compelling private segregation had their origins in partisan politics and were promoted by advocates of disfranchisement and a "sociological theory of total segregation." C. Vann Woodward writes that segregationist laws were not a product of Reconstruction, as was so often claimed by 20th century defenders of Jim Crow, but came after it, beginning in the mid-1890s, although there was "much segregation and discrimination of an extra-legal sort" prior to these first laws. (17)

Nationally, FDR was "nurtured and elevated to power" by the "Southern-dominated and oriented Democratic party," which so successfully played racial issues to its constituencies that the South had become essentially a one-party block of voters. FDR's fear of this Southern bloc "dominated his political strategy." His failure to vigorously champion Civil Rights came out of his "desperate resolve" to maintain "the unholy alliance" he had with this voting bloc. As a result, Southern Democrats were able to foster and protect segregationist "states rights legislation and rule, especially in the Lower South." And in his cabinet, FDR's key military advisers, Secretary of War Henry Stinson, Secretary of Navy Frank Knox, and Josephus Daniels, who in retirement remained a close personal adviser, viewed questions of Civil Rights as impediments to the war effort; they accepted the common notion of many Southern political leaders that blacks were inferior. (18)

North Carolina and Virginia proved in some ways the exception to Southern white-supremacy rule, seeking to attain a semblance of racial equality while maintaining segregated societies. Both had key state political leaders who were advised by prominent educators, black and white, and they generally all worked at keeping a positive tone to their public comments, even when advocating, or resisting, changes. Black educators and white progressive leaders like Frank Porter Graham, who "represented almost everyone's ideal of the quintessential Southern white liberal," were skilled at infusing their public comment with cautions about how bad things could get, using for example how bad they already were in other Southern states. James E. Shepard, president of the North Carolina College for Negroes (now North Carolina Central University), was especially good at using public situations to advance his institution, even when his public stances got for him hot criticism from the black press. Black leaders urged caution as neither a capitulation to white supremacy nor simply a survival tactic; rather, as Christina Greene points out, they "walked a precarious line, particularly those such as Shepard who worked in state-supported institutions." Concessions by white leaders sometimes may have been more to ameliorate the possibility of racial violence than out of a liberal desire to help advance black rights. No matter: whatever concessions were made never threatened the existing separate-but-equal system. They were important advances to black communities nonetheless, and especially as they improved public schools and libraries and brought opportunities for professional education—at Shepard's college, through pharmacy and law schools added in the late 1930s—they were vital in preparing future African-American leaders in North Carolina. (19)

As war drew nearer, the national black press intensified its push towards integration while at the same time linking the international crisis with an increasingly volatile one at home. The

Pittsburgh *Courier's* "Double V" program, first articulated in a January 1942 editorial, called for victory over fascism and imperialism abroad as well as over racism at home. "If we fight two wars, we can win both," the *Afro-American* echoed. "If we fight only one, we will lose both." A. Phillip Randolph, who organized the first black labor union and later a threatened march on Washington that is generally credited with forcing FDR's administration to adopt the Fair Employment Act of 1942, said there was "no difference between Hitler of Germany and [Gov. Eugene] Talmadge of Georgia or Tojo of Japan and [U.S. Sen. Theodore G.] Bilbo of Mississippi." Randolph was one of two national black leaders to oppose World War I. George Schuyler, business manager of the NAACP and a frequent contributor to the *Courier*, said, "Our war is not against Hitler in Europe, but against the Hitlers in America." Subsequently, the *Courier*—which had been calling on the Army to open up all branches to blacks as early as February 1938—was banned on many ships and at some bases. Fifteen sailors were dismissed from the Navy for writing letters to the *Courier* describing conditions. The black press's view of the impending world conflict as a race war was complicated: white Americans had a hard time understanding that for many black Americans, the hostilities building up with Japan were as much about a struggle against white world domination as they were about an impending assault on American democracy. Without enjoying the benefits of democracy at home, blacks increasingly said, it was difficult to support yet another national war effort that was demanding unilateral support while promising advances yet to come, after the peace was won. (20)

Nationally, the black press took increasing aim at the segregationist policies of the U.S. government in an attempt to "embarrass the white liberals into recognizing the paradox of fighting racism abroad while it remained secure at home." Louis Austin condemned the armed forces' Jim Crow policies as "unsafe, unsound and damnable." But until attacks like these began getting coverage by the mainstream press, most white Americans were unfamiliar with newspapers such as the *Carolina Times*, Chicago *Defender*, Pittsburgh *Courier*, and Baltimore

Afro-American. "When a white man first reads a Negro newspaper, it is like getting hit with a bucket of cold water in the face," said the *New Republic*. Gunnar Myrdal, who counted 210 black weekly, semi-weekly, or bi-weekly newspapers publishing in 1942, found that hardly any whites ever saw black audience newspapers; however, he noted, the readers of these newspapers were "the most alert and articulate" at forming opinions on the race issue. Because the papers were passed around within communities, they also had a much larger influence than would seem obvious from mere circulation numbers. (21)

In North Carolina, the leading "Double V" proponent was Louis Austin, editor of the *Carolina Times* in Durham. An Enfield native, he had been educated at the National Training School, the forerunner to North Carolina College, which was founded by Shepard, C.C. Spaulding, and others in 1910. Although he was often a strong supporter of his former mentors' many accomplishments, Austin became increasingly more outspoken as the 1930s progressed, demanding an end to segregation and racial oppression in education, politics, economics, and the armed forces. Governor J. Melville Broughton (1941–45), a steadfast supporter of separate-but-equal, was often the subject of his scorn: "So the Sunday School-teaching governor would perpetuate a system that accepts as right for Negroes inferior schools, discrimination on jobs, a lower wage scale, police brutality, inferior traveling conditions on public carriers, poor housing and a thousand other injustices." Shepard often felt compelled to let Broughton know that Austin did not represent North Carolina blacks, and Austin came to epitomize for Broughton, in the early days of World War II, "the violent and radical Negro press." Austin's "incendiary articles," Broughton said, were "inflammatory" and the black press in general was "the greatest menace to race relations in the nation today." (22)

Austin also wrote that Germany was doing the same thing to small European nations that France and England had done to weaker African and Asian nations. The day before the bombings at Pearl Harbor, the *Afro-American* said that Japan's rise to power was the "first great challenge by any darker race to the whiteman's right to rule the world." The purpose of aggression towards Japan was "to keep intact the idea of Nordic invincibility and to roll back for another century the rising tide of color." (23)

But immediately after the Pearl Harbor bombings, the same paper said, "Mr. President, count on us." Austin, too, would come to support the war effort, though not the way in which it was being waged. "Walk the highway of patriotism," he wrote after the U.S. entered the war, "with human dignity, in the face of insults." Although the black press continued to push for increased levels of participation in the war effort—and, especially, to report on conditions at and around military bases throughout the nation—the immediacy of the war at hand created a wedge between it and black leaders and their approaches to the war effort. A Chicago *Defender* editorial, for example, is scathing in its condemnation of Walter White of the NAACP and John P. Davis of the National Negro Congress for accepting the new Navy plan that would allow units such as B-1 to form, still segregated although at general rank. (24)

Despite its toned down rhetoric, attacks on the black press by the end of 1942 had become "national in scope," coming from the *Saturday Review of Literature, Reader's Digest,* and even the *Atlantic Monthly.* Austin, in Durham, was audited by the IRS during and after World War II. Background pressure throughout 1942 sought to force FDR into indicting some editors of black newspapers for sedition. But by 1943, these attacks would lessen in frequency and intensity as white liberals began reading beyond sensationalist headlines to discover how well most editorials were argued. And with increased racial violence throughout the country in 1943, the black press was finally recognized for its potential to be helpful. (25)

In 1942, the Swedish sociologist Gunnar Myrdal toured the South for the Carnegie Corporation, seeking to conduct an "objective and dispassionate" survey of race relations: "I was shocked and scared to the bones by all the evils I saw, and by the serious political implications of the problem." He reported "thousands of incidents and accidents" that in the South were "being integrated into the old pattern of Southern determination against outside aggression." He found much bitterness and anger among blacks and that the "ordinary white Southerner is tense," the situation "grave," and the white Southern liberal "fearfully timid" on the "Negro question." Myrdal found that "Southern liberalism is not liberalism as it is found elsewhere in America or in the world," but "a unique species" that was "molded by the forces of the region where it carries out its fight." Southern liberals, he pointed out, "originated and carried out the interracial movement" in spite of "formidable drawbacks" that forced them to "tread cautiously around the Negro problem." Repeatedly, the Southern liberal has to explain that he respects the established rules of racial etiquette for fear of earning the epithet of being a "nigger lover," which would reduce his power. (26)

In the South, racial tensions were heightened not only by intense rhetoric from the black press but—as in World War I—also the infusion of Northern black soldiers for training. Violence in and around military camps throughout the U.S. was sometimes caused by the friction created in segregation and discrimination in on-base facilities such as theaters, post exchanges, and canteens, and the friction was worsened by the prejudices of white soldiers, officers, and MPs. Special Services, the Army branch charged with supervising recreation activities, "implanted Jim Crow discrimination where ever it could" and in the process took racial patterns of the South and spread them wherever U.S. troops were stationed. As a result, theaters in Massachusetts were as "jimcrowed" as those in Mississippi. Blacks stationed in the South also had to endure local Jim Crow laws and were subject to insult and attack from whites, often for simply being black and in a military uniform. As in World War I, no official records exist to confirm totals, but one estimate says that "thousands of spontaneous and individual rebellions went unrecorded and unnoticed" and that the War Department suppressed evidence of black revolt, labeling most deaths from race battles as combat fatalities or "motor vehicle accidents." In the South, James Burran writes, at least six civilian riots, over 20 military riots and mutinies, and 40-75 lynchings showed the extent "whites would go to preserve the color line." Conflicts arose over bus service more than any other cause, as most bases were located outside easy walking distance from the nearest town. In 1941, the lynching of a black soldier on base at Fort Benning in Georgia, the beating of a black recruit in Raleigh, and incidents of racial violence associated with bases in Arkansas, Virginia, and Louisiana preceded an August shootout between white MPs and black troops at Ft. Bragg that left a black soldier and white policeman dead. All drew condemnation from the black press as much for the incidents as for the perceived lack of an appropriate pursuit of justice by military and local authorities. (27)

The move towards integration in the military was never embraced by most liberal whites in the South, nor by the region's black leaders. With Eleanor Roosevelt as their figurative leader—the closest and most liberal of FDR's advisers—they collectively espoused a doctrine of patient gradualism, with a continued push towards equality within the separate-but-equal doctrine, without worrying over social equality or the full integration of blacks into mainstream American society, especially not at this time of crisis. Eleanor Roosevelt's essay "If I Were a Negro" reads like a creed for gradualism: "I would not do too much demanding. I would take every chance that came my way to prove my quality and my ability and if recognition were slow, I would continue to prove myself, knowing that in the end good performance has to be acknowledged. I would accept every advance that was made in the Army and Navy, though I would not try to bring those advances about any more quickly than they were offered." (28)

The same black leaders in North Carolina who had been praised by the black press in the 1930s were subsequently criticized for their lack of progressive leadership in arguing for integrating the military. But the idea of integration as pushed by the Chicago *Defender* and Pittsburgh *Courier*, especially, for them was more an intellectual one that linked philosophies of racism with fascism and imperialism. It was an idea not so easily intellectualized in the South, where the threat of lynching was still real and memories of the Wilmington riots of 1898 vivid.

Both black and white leaders in North Carolina increasingly feared that tensions would erupt into catastrophic violence, perhaps worse than in Wilmington. Educator C. M. Eppes, a Greenville African American, typified fears of what an agitating press might stir up when he wrote to Governor Broughton: "I am sure that the influence possessed by you, would aid the Negro much if in someway, the 'Negro Newspaper' could (know or) learn that agitation concerning racial discriminations at this time, should cease. It bodes no good for our race. . . . I can never forget 1898 and the destruction of the Negro Newspaper in Wilmington. The utterances of the paper caused the riot." And Broughton himself invoked the Wilmington riots in a July 1943 speech: "Forty-five years ago . . . blood flowed freely in the streets of this city, feelings ran riot and elemental emotions and bitterness were stirred," he reminded his predominately black audience. The *Carolina Times* editorialized that Broughton's speech "would do Hitler justice." Both James Shepard and C.C. Spaulding wrote the governor notes of apology for the attack. (29)

Governor Broughton also engages in major historical revisionism in this speech when he claims that only one lynching has occurred in North Carolina "in over twenty years," and that there have been no race riots in the state since Wilmington in 1898. Vann Newkirk has documented at least 10 lynchings and several other mob actions directed against African Americans in North Carolina from 1923-43; if Broughton's "over twenty years" parameter extends to 24 years, another 11 lynchings are counted. Frank Tursi and others have documented the 1918 race riot in Winston-Salem; riotous conditions in Chapel Hill prior to World War II are recounted by Daphne Athas, Junius Scales and others. A May 1943 riot in Durham, less than two months prior to Broughton's speech, had erupted after an incident with black soldiers and a white liquor store clerk. August 1941 was especially bad in North Carolina: a race riot in Wilmington arose over protests against black soldiers being billeted at the Marine Hospital there; the Fort Bragg affair had attracted national scrutiny, in the black press especially; and the attempted lynching at the Person County Courthouse was foiled only after police from Durham and Roxboro, the Person County sheriff's office, and the highway patrol drove the mob away several times with tear gas bombs before getting the black man accused of raping a white woman to Central Prison. This incident had provoked the governor's own investigation. So it seems especially disingenuous to be proclaiming in 1943 how virtually nothing of substance had gone awry in the state's race relations in over twenty years. (30)

Still, it seems doubtful that B-1 could have happened in North Carolina without a governor like Broughton, whose political career had been bolstered by his frequent claim to be a true friend to the state's black population. Broughton was also enjoying a political friendship with FDR and was thoroughly behind the war effort. With his wife, Broughton had visited socially with the Roosevelts in Washington, they attended FDR's 1941 inauguration, and they returned to Washington soon after so that Broughton could meet with the President to further discuss the burgeoning defense industry in North Carolina for which he was an active proponent.

At his February 1941 meeting with FDR, the President commended Broughton's war support efforts and the "rapid progress being achieved on military projects" in North Carolina, and he thanked him for the state's "wholehearted cooperation in pushing forward the national defense program." Broughton appointed his own war cabinet in December 1941 and lobbied unsuccessfully for establishing an ROTC program at North Carolina College; he was a strong supporter of the Victory Gardens campaign, and with Josephus Daniels called for the first Win the War rally in the South. Military construction was especially appealing to Broughton, and the promise of help from the Navy to complete construction projects associated with the pre-flight school was no doubt yet another reason for his interest in executing the Navy's order to get an all-black band on the UNC campus. (31)

Governor Broughton lobbied hard for the placement of the pre-flight school at UNC: "[W]e urge the Navy to designate our University" as the site for its east coast facility, and he helped facilitate negotiations with Chapel Hill's black community leaders necessary to establish a housing plan for the bandsmen. Despite the Navy's intention in early 1942 that all-black bands be established at each of its four developing pre-flight schools, such a plan would have been impossible for the one being established at the University of Georgia in Athens, primarily because of its governor's unapologetic racism. Georgia, like North Carolina, had in 1942 a large black population, increasingly educated, from which to draw a black band for its proposed pre-flight school. But in early 1942, Georgia was still roiling from what became known as the Cocking Affair, during which Governor Eugene Talmadge (1933–37, 1941–43) announced that he would fire any one in the state university system who advocated "communism or racial equality." Before it was over, Talmadge would succeed in removing at least ten university faculty and officials, including the University of Georgia's vice-chancellor. Ultimately, the Cocking affair caused Georgia's state-supported schools for whites to lose accreditation. (32)

Talmadge's incendiary re-election campaign in the summer of 1942 remained an exemplar of how bad things could get for race relations in the South. The Pittsburgh *Courier* was outraged at a Georgia State Democrats meeting during that campaign which called for "white supremacy, constitutional rights and the retention of southern traditions." At that meeting, a former Georgia congressman praised Talmadge's attacks on Prof. Walter Cocking and the university system: "I commend Governor Talmadge for what he did. If he hadn't done it, he wouldn't have been fit to be governor. Cocking should not only have been kicked out of Georgia, but out of Dixie." One delegate at the meeting "shouted 'I like Negroes. I like 'em in their place. And their place is in the cotton field, hoeing and chopping cotton.'" Weighing into the national discussion of the Georgia elections, Frank Porter Graham told the International Student Assembly meeting in Washington, DC that "Southern copperheads of the Talmadge . . . breed" are "forces working in behalf of the Axis powers." Their "race-baiting tactics," he said, were "anti-American and unrepresentative of progressive Southern leadership." (The meeting was "highlighted" by a "brilliant address" by Eleanor Roosevelt.) Historians generally credit the Cocking Affair and its aftermath as the cause for Talmadge's defeat at re-election in 1942. (33)

So, in contrast to Talmadge, who publicly attacked Cocking for his association with the Rosenwald Fund's "Jew money for niggers," Governor Broughton was moderate and in some ways progressive, by mainstream Southern standards if not those advocated by the black press. After he was elected in November 1940, he wasted no time embarking on an impressive speaking campaign at North Carolina's black colleges. At Shaw's 75th anniversary celebration, he boasted that North Carolina led the South in appropriations for Negro education "and it didn't take a Supreme Court decision make us do it." He was named honorary chair of the state's Commission on Racial Cooperation, and in 1941-42 alone gave at least ten keynote addresses at black college campuses. He spoke out against lynching, claimed that in North Carolina's "steady progress" in race relations "the old discriminations were being written off," and declared that the "Negro is equal to the white man" in North Carolina "before the law." At the New Farmers of America meeting at A&T, he paid tribute to Booker T. Washington and afterwards, the delegates "pledged their faith in the principals embodied" in Washington's life. (34)

Governor Broughton and UNC President Frank Porter Graham were political allies and staunch FDR supporters. Graham also had a solid and enduring friendship with Eleanor Roosevelt, and they were frequently on the same program at symposia and meetings throughout the South. They both had keen interests in improving race relations, although they also tended toward what UNC sociologist Howard Odum called "gradual liberalism." Odum and Graham were UNC's most liberal voices. Odum, Buell Gallagher wrote in 1938, "represents much that is best in the new South which is steadily moving away from its earlier prejudices, often expressly repudiating them, as in this case." Buell references "in this case" the publication in 1936 of Odum's *Southern Regions of the United States,* which characterized as a "tragedy of error" the false premise that projected the racial superiority of whites. Odum's *Social and Mental Traits of the Negro,* published in 1910, had argued that blacks could not be educated any more than children because of their limited brain capacity; he proposed, then, separate tracks of education for blacks and whites. Founder in 1924 of the Institute for Research in Social Science at UNC (now the Odum Institute), Odum wrote to Governor Broughton in 1942 to offer his "unbounded appreciation for what you are doing in your talks" to blacks in North Carolina and praised the South's "growing balanced economy, and gradual liberalism." Odum's *Race and Rumors of Race* sought in 1943 to catalog the "rumors, tensions, conflicts, and trends" that justified the "conclusion that the South and the Negro, in the early 1940s, faced their greatest crisis since the days of reconstruction." (35)

Although Broughton, like most Southern liberals of his time, was still a defender of the separate-but-equal doctrine that defined the Jim Crow South, race relations were, in fact, better in North Carolina than in most other Southern states—instead of firing white progressive educators, Broughton cultivated their support. In education especially, North Carolina blacks were closer to being equal, at least in spending, than elsewhere in the South. In June 1942, for example, the state announced that to bring salary ranges even closer to equal between white and black public schools teachers, a 5% raise was given to black teachers while whites received no raise. Secretary of the state school commission Nathan H. Yelton proclaimed the "hope to erase all pay differences" between white and black teachers in "about two or three years." A Fisk University representative of its Race Relations Division wrote to Broughton in 1943: "In preparing a brief manual descriptive of some of the best Southern practices in race relations, we come repeatedly upon the fact that in most respects North Carolina is way out in the lead in this area both in its public and in its private practices." Fisk President Dr. Charles S. Johnson called North Carolina "progressive" in "race relations" as well as "in regard to roads, schools, penal and welfare institutions," and said the state was generally "in the lead" in the South in "good citizenship." Myrdal found North Carolina in 1942 to be "fairly liberal." (36)

Broughton was a frequent speaker on black campuses throughout the state, and he got them money for badly needed construction projects. He was championed especially by James E. Shepard and C.C. Spaulding who, from the mid-1920s until their respective deaths, were the most influential African Americans in North Carolina. Both life-long Durham residents, they shared a sunny optimism that conditions would invariably improve for the state's black population, and they were tireless workers and advocates for increased civil rights in an age when out-spoken blacks, especially in the South, could still legitimately fear violent and unlawful reprisals. They functioned as a team: Spaulding could rock the boat, but Shepard would stabilize it, so that in the end they got action "without upheaval." Over their long and distinguished careers, the two were often speakers together and would serve as informal advisers on race matters to six successive governors. Their social and professional visits elsewhere in the country were regularly noted in the black press, in which they were frequently quoted, on questions of race and education especially. Broughton appointed them both to the National Defense Council and championed Shepard to FDR for a national appointment during the war. (37)

North Carolina College, led by Shepard, and North Carolina Mutual, led by Spaulding, were anchors of the thriving black community in Durham known as Hayti. Beginning in the 1920s, the college hosted frequent national, state and local meetings on race, civil rights, and education, and Spaulding was often an active participant. Although he was sometimes criticized by the national black press for not pushing an integration agenda aggressively enough, Shepard had, in fact, mastered the art of fund-raising in the most trying of financial times without sacrificing his strong, if politically conservative, opinions. Editor Austin said that Shepard hopes "for a part loaf rather than no loaf and court action" and added that he "may be able to do more with an olive branch than others can do with branches of law." Shepard's work reflected the opinion of Luther P. Jackson, who was elected secretary-treasurer of the Southern Conference on Race Relations held at North Carolina College in October 1942: "Negro Southerners may strike blows at the segregation laws forever, but final victory can never come until white Southerners unite with them." (38)

In North Carolina, that unity was comprised of Shepard, Spaulding, Governor Broughton, and UNC President Frank Porter Graham, who all shared the belief that the dawn of war and its subsequent beginnings were the wrong times to push towards integration, and that race progress was best promoted through cooperation rather than confrontation. But to successfully establish a band of African Americans at the all-white campus of the University of North Carolina would take the full cooperation and interest of not only the state's governor, its black educational leaders, and the white administration at UNC, but also the black and white community leadership in Chapel Hill, and, especially, the Navy and its leaders at the proposed pre-flight school. Had any of these groups or individuals balked at the developing plan, it might well have never worked. (39)

:: :: ::

Military history, the *Marine Corps Band Manual* states, "has empirically established the fact that bands are an integral part of the military [and] that they greatly increase the morale of the troops" by being "an important stimulus to morale and *esprit de corps*, furnishing the commanding officer and his command a vital link to ceremonial traditions." Formal military bands themselves date back at least as far as 1765 and to Frederick the Great. In the United States, Revolutionary War "field musick" bands, comprised exclusively of drums, bugles, and fifes, were charged with communicating signals to troops as they prepared for and entered combat. "Bands of musick" were soon incorporated with a primary purpose of entertaining officers. George Washington in 1778 appointed the first Inspector and Superintendent of Music to address what he felt was the poor quality of music in the U. S. Army. After the war, town bands became popular throughout the country, with some attached to local militias. (40)

During the Civil War, a May 1861 executive order authorized regimental bands of 24 musicians for Union forces, although few would get up to or maintain that strength. As the war progressed, most became depleted, giving up their manpower to battle, although each company maintained two field musicians. By war's end, bands existed primarily at permanent headquarters, where brigade bands were able to maintain their identity. Still, during the Civil War, over 500 bands served the Union, with 9,000 players. About 155 Confederate bands used 2,400 musicians—including some African Americans, who by order of the Confederate Congress were paid at the same rate as white musicians. Benny Ferguson identifies six Confederate bands comprised of African Americans. Black bandsmen generally served in all-black units, some mixing freedmen with slaves, but at least one integrated band of drummers has been noted; one Alabama regiment bought itself a drummer, for $1,800, as a slave for its general. (41)

The Navy's needs for musicians were always different from the Army's, for the Navy was not concerned so much with battlefield movements and marching troop formations, except in ceremonial situations. The first use of music in the Navy was likely the singing of sea shanties by sailors, helping both to pass the time and to maintain the rhythmic pulse for working together. Musicians were assigned to U.S. Navy ships as early as 1775, and from then on, its primary need for musicians was to entertain troops on ships and shore and to provide ceremonial music. Musicians when available have also been used by the Navy to signal daily activities and to move personnel to battle stations. The first documented Navy band was organized in 1838, with four musicians first class and one second class; the first Naval Academy Band was organized in 1853; and by the next year the Navy was authorizing musical instruments for shipboard bands. As U.S. military might expanded in the late 19th century, Navy band responsibilities began to include performances at diplomatic receptions in ports of call around the globe. By far the most famous Navy musician was LtCdr. John Philip Sousa, who in 1917 became the first musician to be a commissioned officer in the Navy's history; he established a touring band and a training center at Great Lakes, and during the war he organized at least seven bands and one orchestra, ranging in size from 14 to 46-pieces. (42)

Both the Army and Navy had black musicians from their foundings in the 18th century. In the Army, they would serve continuously in segregated units until after World War II. Service of blacks on U.S. ships was always more limited, although evidence suggests that they performed on board, some as early as 1732, when slave musicians would be taken aboard as status symbols for their owners and sometimes organized into bands. At least two African-American musicians—Nimrod Perkins and Cyrus Tiffany—served the Navy during the Revolutionary War and the War of 1812, but few if any were enlisted until World War I. Stateside, blacks were excluded from service in Navy bands until B-1's enlistment, soon after which the Great Lakes camps would begin turning out unit bands for placement at installations—not aboard ships—throughout the U.S. (43)

Establishment of the Navy's first school of music, in 1935, gave rise to unit bands, which would be assigned to ships as self-contained entities. Most were bands of about 20 pieces, with a bandleader in charge. Bands were numbered consecutively as they left the school—the first to graduate, in 1936, was Unit Band #1—and they were supposed to stay together, at least for their first enlistment period. By order, no one was authorized to break up a unit band or to assign bandsmen to other duties. Four types of bands were organized at the school: bands of 23- and 17-pieces assigned to larger ships and bases; 13-piece bands assigned to smaller ships; and 7-piece bands assigned to troop transports. The school itself maintained a 110-piece concert band and a 100-voice chorus for its special performances and concerts. (44)

By the outbreak of World War II, 28 unit bands had graduated. The war itself represented the heyday of Navy music: 6,800 musicians would serve in 285 bands. Over 100 of these bands were comprised of African Americans; all but B-1 were trained at the Navy's Great Lakes Negro school of music, directed by Harry Noble Simms, Musc. 2nd class. The B-1 bandsmen, in addition to being the first blacks to serve at general rank in the modern Navy, were also the first blacks to earn musicians ratings and the only musicians who were not formally trained at a Navy school of music. While most of the musicians trained at Great Lakes would be assigned to the smaller unit bands, three other regimental bands of black sailors—about 44 pieces each—would be organized at Great Lakes, where they would serve for the duration, performing for ceremonies and bond rallies. By 1943, when the Army abolished its regimental bands, converting all of them into division bands, B-1 was the only regimental band serving the military outside the continental United States. (45)

The particular needs the Navy had for musicians also dictated that its bands embrace popular music more than bands in the other branches. Modern Navy bandsmen had to be proficient players in a variety of styles: symphonic works, patriotic pieces, martial music, Americana, and jazz. During World War II, the

Navy made great use of some of the country's most outstanding jazz talents. Black newspapers of the day regularly carried stories about individual jazzmen and sometimes whole bands being recruited, especially for the Navy. Renowned bandleader Artie Shaw and his Ranger Band (Navy Band 501) performed morale-boosting concerts throughout the Pacific Theater, and scores of talented and well-known black jazzmen were recruited and trained at Great Lakes. (46)

North Carolina's contributions to African-American military band history are not, however, confined to the accomplishments of B-1. The U.S. Marine Band, organized in 1798, established its first African-American band at Montford Point, near Camp Lejeune, in 1943, where it was trained by Lt. Robert W. Troup, formerly of the Tommy Dorsey Band. Troup, a white man, was appointed recreation director at the base and soon after organized its band. While at Montford Point, he composed the locally popular tune "Take Me Away from Jacksonville." His most famous composition was "(Get Your Kicks on) Route 66." (47)

James B. Parsons

B-1 bandmaster

This and all subsequent

photos of individual

B-1 bandsmen on following

pages taken from the

U.S. Navy Pre-Flight

School Band yearbook

published in 1944

Wray Herring Collection

Special Collections

Joyner Library

East Carolina University

Roger Franklin Holt
Rt. 6 Box 111
Greensboro, N.C.

Richard H. L. Jones
939½ W. McCulloch St.
Greensboro N.C.

Silas A. James
310 Umstead St.
Durham, N. C. F-8442-1

Joseph H. Sykes
452 1-206 Street
Bayside New York City
Long Island.

Herbert (Duck) Reeder Norven, N.C.

Robert M. Tate "Old Dad"
401 Grant St.
Durham, N. C

Charles Alton McNeils
1715 Lindsay St.
Greensboro. N.C.

Robert Carter
9550 Breckenridge
Overland 14 Mo.
Wabash 1191 W.

Thomas H. Gavin Jr.
"Bake"
905 William St.
Lumberton, N.C.

PROGRAM

. . .

STAR SPANGLED BANNER

FATHER OF VICTORY .... *Ganne*

MARCHE HEROIQUE .... *Saint-Saens*
   This military tone poem was first written for two pianos,
   and later arranged for orchestra. It was composed during the Franco-Prussian war as an expression of patriotic
   sentiments aroused by the heroic resistance of the French
   to the invading Germans. The first theme is vigorous and
   striking, the second is in noble contrast to the first.

DEEP RIVER .... *Traditional*
   Arranged for band by Mr. Parsons

LUSTSPIEL OVERTURE .... *Keler-Bela*
   One of the best known standard overtures of a light and
   spiritual nature. The song "theme" is planned to represent the sweetness, romance and poetic yearning incident
   to the awakening of Nature after the sleep of winter.

WASHINGTON GRAYS .... *Grafulla*

INTERMISSION

BLUES IN THE NIGHT .... *Harold Arlen*
   From the Picture of the same name.
   (My Mama Done Tol' Me) sung by musician 2/c,
   Simeon O. Holloway

WATER BOY .... *Arr. by Avery Robinson*
   S. O. Holloway, soloist

ON GREAT LONE HILLS (Hymn from Finlandia) .... *Sibelius*
   Navy Band Glee Club

BELLS OF ST. MARY'S
   Band and Glee Club

ANCHORS AWEIGH .... *Zimmerman*
   The Official Navy Song

HIP HIP HOORAY .... *Neno-Ebins*
   Band and Glee Club

Formation: Greensboro and A&T College

"They'd have had us all
if we all could've passed the physical."

—HUEY LAWRENCE

The most important ingredient to make everything work was always the band itself. "From a musical standpoint," Bandmaster James Parsons said, "we were an excellent band. These fellows were the best, most talented musicians in North Carolina." But its members not only had to be excellent musicians, they had to be smart, aware of and at least publicly accepting of the separate-but-equal doctrine that would rule their military existence in the same way it had ruled their personal lives, and they had to be exemplary model citizens. For any move towards integration to work, there had to be, first of all, no trouble. It made perfect military sense to recruit young educated men who had avoided trouble and shown themselves to be smart—most were in college or about to enroll; several were college graduates—and, by virtue of their marching band experience, accustomed to taking orders. (1)

By the outbreak of World War II, Greensboro's five colleges were providing a source of cultural and intellectual stimulation that gave the city "an aura of cosmopolitanism," and Greensboro had become prideful of its "reputation for racial tolerance." The 1940 census counted 16,343 African Americans among a population of 59,319 in Greensboro, and they were served by a thriving black business district centered around East Market Street: the Palace Theatre, Varsity Inn, Sanitary Barber Shop, Crystal Tap Room, Skylight Café, Hairston TV Repair, Triangle News, Lou's Frank House, and Reddick's Barbershop among others. During World War II, the Vines family opened the second floor above their dry cleaning business as an informal USO for black troops. (2)

Most cooperative interaction between blacks and whites, however, took place on the city's college campuses. Bennett College and A&T—situated across the street from each other—were centerpieces of cultural and political activities, sometimes for interracial events like the YMYWCA conference in 1939 that brought nearly 100 delegates from black and white colleges in North Carolina to Bennett. Founded in 1873 in the basement of a local church, Bennett had only 10 students when Dr. David Jones became its president in 1926 and it was reorganized into a 4-year college exclusively for African-American women. Jones had graduated from Wesleyan University in 1911. He worked for the YMCA for a decade, most of it in St. Louis, and was prior to his appointment at Bennett secretary of the Inter-racial Commission in Atlanta, "the only member of our race to occupy such a position." Under Jones' leadership, Bennett would aspire to being the "Vassar of the South." Its students became known as Bennett Belles, easily recognizable wherever they went not just for their dress code—hats, gloves, and pocketbooks required whenever they went out—but also for their demeanor: "well-bred and lady-like, the kind of lady who knew how to preside at a tea." The Belles were also politically active: they led a local theaters boycott in 1937, and Jones encouraged them not to do business with shops that treated them disrespectfully, and to walk wherever they went so that they would not feel the sting of second-class status for sitting at the back of a bus. (3)

The concentration of musical talent in Greensboro was evident in the reputations earned by the bands at Dudley High School and A&T. They were highly visible and popular throughout the region and a central component of Greensboro's rich educational and cultural atmosphere for blacks, despite the restraints of its heavily segregated world. Music instruction began at A&T in 1909, when Charles E. Steward was named director of music. A&T's first band, with 50 pieces, was directed by W.E. Lew, who replaced Steward in 1916 and two years later started the band, one of the first at any black college. By the 1930s, band was of-

Robert E. Brower

baritone horn

Greensboro

NC A&T

fered as an extracurricular activity, and until 1940—when North Carolina Central organized its first band—it was the only black college marching band in North Carolina. Greensboro native and B-1 drummer Arthur Guy noted: "Dudley High and A&T had always been famous for their bands. The A&T band had traveled all over the South, up to Washington, Baltimore, Delaware, as early as the mid-1930s." In B-1's narrative, the two bands' histories merge, not just in the nine high school students who joined straight out of Dudley with the ability to compete, musically, with their college and professionally trained peers, but also because of their bandmasters: when A&T's director, Bernard Mason, failed the Navy's physical exam, Dudley's director, James B. Parsons, stepped in as B-1's leader. (4)

But the strength and reputations of these two bands were just part of the cultural life available to African-American students in Greensboro in 1942. The Greensboro *Daily News* played a significant part in publicizing the many activities presented there, primarily on the A&T and Bennett campuses. At Bennett, the nationally renowned composer and pianist R. Nathaniel Dett was in his last year directing the college choir. One of the most influential black musical artists of the early 20th century—and the "first composer to use Negro folk tunes for classical development"—Dett had come to Bennett in 1936 for what would turn out to be the last academic posting of his life. His most significant tenure had been at Hampton Institute, where he made its choir famous throughout Europe and the United States with several successful tours. (5)

Dett was also responsible for Parsons' coming to Greensboro. While working as acting head of music at Lincoln University, Parsons met Dett, a former teacher at Lincoln who had returned for a guest performance. Dett was sufficiently impressed by Parsons' musical skills at performing and transcribing to recruit him for a position at Bennett to assist in re-scoring some of Dett's chorales. That job was short-lived, though, and by 1939 Parsons had taken a new position as director of instrumental music for Greensboro's Negro schools, which had one high school band and one junior high band. He quickly developed a 3-level high school band and began feeder classes in the elementary school, and Dud-

Alton V. Butler, Jr.

clarinet, saxophone

Winston-Salem

NC A&T

ley's band became known throughout the state for its precision marching and expert musicianship. By spring 1942, it numbered nearly 100 in its concert band and over 150 in its marching band. A program for the second annual Dudley band concert, in March 1942, featured 31 clarinet players, 17 trumpet and cornet players, nine saxophonists, and eight trombonists performing patriotic numbers as well as classical pieces by Tchaikovsky, Rossini, and Beethoven; Barnum and Bailey's "Favorite March"; the popular songs "Deep Purple" and "Stormy Weather"; and a medley of traditional spirituals. (6)

John E. Carlson

trombone

Laurinburg

NC A&T

Nathaniel Dett's influence locally was immeasurable. Near the end of his long and distinguished career when he arrived at Bennett, he used his international connections and reputation to infuse the cultural life of Greensboro's black community with high art that also incorporated African and African-American folk songs and motifs. Arlan Coolidge, head of music at Brown University, was among the first nationally known artists Dett brought to campus. Soon after, mezzo-soprano Charlotte Wallace Murray "captivated her audience" with a formal recital at Bennett. Dett and his contemporaries, A&T choir director Warner Lawson and band director Bernard Mason, became a powerful nucleus for attracting world-class performers to Greensboro. Lawson and Dett successfully promoted their institutions' choirs in national radio performances and concert tours throughout the eastern United States. CBS radio commissioned two Dett symphonies that aired in 1938. A&T's a cappella choir, organized in 1936 by Lawson, had given more than 125 concerts by the time it performed on NBC and CBS radio shows in 1940-41, by which time it had achieved and maintained a "standard of excellency rarely reached in college musical organizations." Dett and Lawson and Mason and Lawson performed critically acclaimed duets throughout the Southeast, and Lawson, by 1933 "one of the best pianists," was usually accompanist for visiting artists. The Chicago *Defender* carried frequent notices, between 1936-42, of performances by Dett, Mason, and Lawson. These three musical giants also found an eager promoter in Charlotte Hawkins Brown, whose Palmer Institute for girls at nearby Sedalia provided another venue for artists and lecturers visiting the area. (7)

The faculty and administrators from Bennett, A&T, and Palmer Institute appear to have worked in concert to sustain a variety of cultural activities that frequently emphasized African-American history. In January 1942, James "Billboard" Jackson, one of the giants of early black vaudeville and also one of its most ardent supporters, visited Palmer Institute, no doubt talking about the history of African-American popular entertainment. Frequent piano concerts by visiting artists generally had mixed into their performances works by African-American composers such as William Grant Still with the more traditional classical pieces. William Allen's January 1942 concert, for example, included pieces by Schumann, Ravel, Debussy, Prokofiev, Shostakovich, and Still's "Quit dat Fool'nish." Aubrey Pankey, then "a young Negro baritone," presented a concert at A&T in February 1942 that mixed classical pieces with traditional African-American spirituals. (8)

Most of the future B-1 bandsmen were nurtured in this culturally and intellectually enriched environment that kept a steady parade into Greensboro of the best known African-American musical artists and also many of the leading thinkers—both black and white—on the ever-vexing "race question." A vesper talk by Bishop Clare Purcell of the Methodist Church was attended by "a large number of townspeople." In a major address in February 1942, the Rev. Adam Clayton Powell, Jr., then pastor at Abyssinian Baptist Church in New York, said at A&T, "Democracy will lose its place as a world power unless the negro and other dark races are given equal rights in the peace." A speech by Judge William H. Hastie, civilian aide to the Secretary of War, addressed the alarming rise of race violence that threatened domestic peace in the early days of World War II. (9)

Among the African-American stars performing in Greensboro during this time were Roland Hayes, Louise Burge, Ella Fitzgerald, and the famed Lincoln Players from Chicago, who came to Bennett in January 1942 for a production of T.S. Eliot's *Murder in the Cathedral*. A&T's annual spring festival of music and fine arts showcased its male chorus, choir, choral society, women's glee club, women's ensemble, and a cappella choir, as well as its band. In February 1942, Dett organized what must have been one of the most magnificent choral events ever staged in North Carolina.

Walter F. Carlson, Jr.

trumpet
Laurinburg
NC A&T

At the First Baptist Church of Greensboro, he brought together eight choirs—a mix of all black and all white choirs from the
Greensboro area—for a gala concert. The Sedalia Singers of Palmer Memorial Institute were joined in the performance by the college choirs from A&T, Guilford College, the Woman's College (now
UNC-G) and Greensboro College. Dett's own Bennett College
choir opened the second part of the program, and he led all eight
choirs and the audience in a sing-along for the grand finale of "Lift
Every Voice and Sing." (10)

In April 1942, Bennett College and Dett also hosted the 12th
annual Festival of the Negro Intercollegiate Dramatic Association
that attracted student actors from ten black colleges. Dett delivered the keynote address, "The Future of the Negro in the Theatre," which he said was "bright." He urged his audience to "glorify
the traditions of their own race, to find inspirational expression
in their natural physical endowments, to present the social significance of Negroes in their plays and to rid themselves of the objec-
tives of only playing to Negro audiences." (11)

John D. Clay

clarinet

Roxboro

NC A&T

A&T also maintained an active debate team, traveling to black
colleges throughout the region to argue such topics as "Resolved:
that the federal government should regulate all labor unions in
the U.S." and "Resolved: the Negro should pursue a back-to-the
farm movement." Its drama group was named for one of the best
known black actors in the U.S., Richard B. Harrison, who taught at
A&T from 1922 until 1929, when he resigned to take the role of De
Lawd in the Broadway hit *Green Pastures*. In the last semester in
school for the B-1 bandsmen, spring of 1942, the Richard B. Harrison Players presented a program of four one-acts that included
two of director Charles G. Green's original dramas; in March, the
Players presented, to great acclaim, Eugene O'Neill's *The Emper-
or Jones* for the second year in a row—with future B-1 drummers
Arthur Guy and Filmore Haith in the cast. The A&T choir presented "The Life of Christ" during Easter; and the A&T a cappella choir presented Gilbert and Sullivan's *HMS Pinafore* just prior
to graduation, which the B-1 fellows would miss due to the timing
of their enlistment. (12)

A&T's band, under the direction of Bernard L. Mason, had by
the mid-1930s become nationally renowned and a favorite at local

and regional special events. "The crack A. and T. College Band," the Norfolk *Journal-Guide* called it in 1942, "recognized as one of the finest college organizations of its kind in the country," was "to be the nucleus of the first colored navy band." The marching and concert bands traveled extensively throughout the South and East, and Mason, who was a big part of their draw, was originally slated to lead B-1. But after failing the Navy's physical, he soon followed his former A&T colleague Warner Lawson to Howard University. Lawson was named dean of music at Howard in April 1942, and he appears to have hired Mason soon afterwards. Mason would direct Howard's symphony for many years. (13)

Mason was a "fantastic musician," recalled B-1 trombonist Richard Jones. "He could stand in front of a whole band and pick out the one guy with a bad note." He and the A&T band were why clarinet player William Skinner, a Norfolk native, had traveled to Greensboro to attend college. Skinner had seen them perform several times: "And I'd heard all about Bernard Mason. 'Prof' they called him. That was the best band around, and he was the best violinist I'd ever seen. We used to sit and cry watching him play. He'd be playing 'Ave Maria' and we'd all be sitting there crying. So I went to school there and played in the marching band and the orchestra."

James Parsons had been thinking "Navy" well before B-1 was formed, but it was Mason's failing of the Navy's physical that charted his future. "Between Pearl Harbor and Christmas 1941," he recalled, "I and several friends tried to enlist in the Navy. They accepted us but didn't know what to do with us. Our enlistments were approved in December 1941. I finished out that semester, hopeful that I'd be in the Navy soon after." It seems likely that Parsons and his friends had read, in late December 1941 in the Greensboro *Daily News*, that the Navy was expanding its enlistment targets by encouraging holders of a variety of Bachelor of Arts degrees to enlist as ensigns. Previously it had accepted as ensign recruits graduates in engineering only. "Volunteers must be native-born, single, in good physical condition and of good repute," the paper reported; training would be at Northwestern University in Chicago. No mention was made of race. The Illinois-educated Parsons would not have seen himself excluded in any way

William H. Cole

piano, trombone
Hampton, VA
Hampton Institute

from what the Navy advertised as requiring of its recruits. He had been named "class orator" for the class of 1929 at Decatur High School, the "first race student" to receive such an honor. He was also distinguished by his scholastic ability and activities and was "one of the most popular students in the class." Chicago—its schools, especially—was as integrated as any American city. So the prospect was understandably enticing. "They took our applications for enlistment and sent us home. Nothing happened." Then, in early February 1942, he recalled, "I was contacted by the Navy with the idea of the band." (14)

Nearly half of the future B-1 bandsmen were students at A&T, where the spring semester of 1942 was a mix of rising war-time tension with a growing national race consciousness, tempered with a concurrent attempt at living a typical college life. Despite the abundant cultural life that surrounded the students, the war was coming close to home: a sub was sighted off the Hatteras coast on January 27; air raid alarms were sounding regularly in Greensboro by early February; blackouts were ordered of nonessential lights; and in March, nearly 60,000 gas masks—"15,000 short of need for area"—were allotted to Greensboro by state civil defense officials. Local news reports that gave names of the young men being drafted—on February 11, 1942 it was reported that 58 whites and 38 blacks had been drafted; the next week, another 19 blacks—also helped to make the war all the more real. So the idea of serving in a band, and serving close to home, at the UNC pre-flight school, was of increasing interest to students at A&T. (15)

The first 13 young men to join B-1—and thus the first to enlist in the modern Navy at rank other than messman's or steward's—were announced on May 10, 1942, at which point they had already been accepted for service at Greensboro and approved for it by the Raleigh district recruiting station. All had been in the A&T band: Warmouth Thomas Gibbs, Jr.; Robert Emmons Brower; Walter Filmore Haith; James Clarence Yourse; Roger Franklin Holt; Charles Lewis Woods; Alton Verine Butler, Jr.; James Daniel Morgan, Jr.; Willie Evander Currie, Jr.; John Dorsey Clay; William Edward Skinner; Jewitt Lorenzo White; and Thomas Jeffries Gavin, Jr. (16)

The build-up to war had been affecting the campus in many ways but none so dramatic as the leaving, before semester's end,

Willie E. Currie, Jr.

trumpet

St. Paul

NC A&T

of most of the band for military service. One popular teacher, social sciences instructor J. Archie Hargraves, had taken an emergency management position in Washington in August 1941, and the campus, like the rest of the state and nation, watched the unfolding events leading up to the December bombing of Pearl Harbor with increasing concern. A&T officially set up a civilian defense program in late January 1942, with 14 committees charged with "meeting the problems of civilian defense" for faculty, staff, and community. Future B-1 bandsmen and brothers John and Walter Carlson were among the first to enroll in the college's civilian pilot training program for spring quarter, which had potential pilots attending classes in ground and flight instruction. Both Carlsons hoped to be accepted at the Tuskegee Air Force Training Station for further training as pilots. A&T's agriculture department conducted "victory garden campaigns throughout Greensboro and the state," and an accelerated learning program designed to graduate skilled "technicians, artisans, and educational leaders" more quickly. A&T was one of four black colleges in the U.S. awarded a 4-year ROTC, which came about as a result of a coalition of efforts between college officials and "congressmen, senators and leading citizens of the state." (17)

Thomas J. Gavin, Jr.

saxophone

Lumberton

NC A&T

The chance to serve in the Navy, in a band, appealed to many of those soon to enlist in what would become B-1. But music wasn't always the primary cause for an interest in joining. "I remember some of the guys talking about the Navy band on campus," said French horn player William Gibson. "We figured it would be our best chance of survival in the war. Plus, we all liked the idea of being on the UNC campus because we felt pretty strongly about needing integration in the state's colleges." Trumpeter Willie Currie laughed as he said, "I just wanted to stay out of the Army. They stayed outdoors all the time. I mean they *lived* outdoors."

Several fellows recalled vividly the appearance at their band practice one day of Chief Bandmaster C.E. Dudrow, brought out of retirement for war service, in his Navy blue uniform with gold stripes to "select the bandsmen and supervise their early training." William Skinner remembered Dudrow telling them about the plans for the band: "He said the governor had asked to get all North Carolina men, and that we'd be in Chapel Hill for the duration of the war. Now a lot of us were in ROTC and we could have gone into the Army as 2nd lieutenants and in six months made 1st lieutenant, maybe made captain after that. But we didn't know where we'd be sent. It probably would have been overseas and even though we probably wouldn't be in a fighting unit, we'd be near one, loading trucks or something. So the Navy band seemed like good duty. We wanted to stay together, and Chapel Hill was only 50 miles from where we were then." (18)

Bernard Mason did the primary recruiting, preparing a roster of potential recruits to audition when Dudrow came to campus. The prospective bandsmen were likely evaluated according to the same criteria used for auditioning for the Navy School of Music: sight-reading, technique, tone, attack, rhythm, phrasing, and memory. Saxophonist Thomas Gavin recalled their audition for Chief Dudrow: "We played some marches, scales, and exercises, individually and in groups. Within a few days, I found out I'd been accepted musically. Then I had the physical exam to contend with. I was a sophomore then, I was 18, and I knew everybody would eventually go into service. I thought it a great opportunity to get in the band program." (19)

Warmouth T. Gibbs, Jr.

clarinet

Greensboro

NC A&T

"They wanted to recruit the whole band," said Arthur Guy, "but not all of the fellows could pass the physical." The scope of recruiting expanded, then, to other campuses. Only one recruit was not then currently in school or teaching: cornet player Benny Laikin, an A&T graduate, was running a hat blocking and shine parlor in Salisbury when he heard scuttlebutt about the band's formation. "I thought I'd have to go anyway," he said, "and I liked to play music, so it seemed like a good idea." Laikin had played with swing bands all across the country, including a stint with King Oliver's band, but he had settled down to get off the road.

The nine recruits out of Dudley High's band, directed by Parsons, enlisted for the music and opportunities to serve, as well as for the man. "We were crazy about him as a band director," French horn player Calvin Morrow said. "So it was a routine smooth change for us."

The Carlson brothers remained at A&T after the band left for training, as they awaited slots to open up at Tuskegee. "But we could've been drafted in the meantime," trumpeter Walter Carlson recalled. "Then the band wound up with two openings, and we decided right then to go. I joined in Raleigh and was playing that night for a dance at the Officers Club. We never did take basics. It seemed great to us, to be able to stay together as brothers and to avoid the draft. That was an unusual situation."

Another bandsman, trumpeter Huey Lawrence, was reluctant to leave campus: "I sat under this great tree on campus. It's still there. My parents didn't want me to go. I sat there just thinking about it. Finally, I knew I just had to. Knowing that sooner or later I'd have to go, and that some of my friends were going, that helped a lot to make up my mind." Lawrence, a Pittsburgh native recruited to A&T to play football, was—like most of his friends—acutely aware of the world stage on which his life was being played. "It was my country," he said. "I had no thoughts of a divided system. In Pittsburgh, we swam together, we played ball together. But my background was different from most of the fellows. I went all through high school in an integrated system, even though I was the only black in my elementary school."

William R. Gibson

French horn
Laurinburg
NC A&T

Regardless of the personal motivations that pushed the recruits to join B-1, they were all aware of the importance of what they were doing. Trombonist Nathaniel Morehead thought it a much bigger deal to be headed to the whites-only UNC campus for duty than to be breaking a Navy color barrier. Calvin Morrow said, "We were aware of what was happening, of what we were doing by going into the Navy. Everybody was aware that we were the first to break the barrier." Bassist Charles Woods noted, "I knew there weren't any blacks in the Navy but messmen, so as we went in, I felt history was being made and that I was a part of it."

"It was an experiment in the Navy's preliminary attempt to bring about a little integration," Parsons recalled. "There'd been none there." Parsons would forsake music education for law school after the war, his interest in legal matters heightened when he was chosen as an observer at trials after the Guam riots of 1944, because he was the highest ranking black Naval enlisted man in the Pacific Theater. But in 1941, he was in his second full-time job out of college. "I was working on developing a statewide association of high school bands for the black school districts," he said. But when Mason couldn't pass the physical, "I was called on by a delegation of Navy men and asked if I would go in as bandmaster."

The base publication published at Manana Naval Barracks in Hawaii, where B-1 later completed its duty, reported in 1944, soon after the band had arrived there, that the selection process was straightforward: "The Navy Department sent Chief Bandmaster C.E. Dudrow, USN, to North Carolina to select the best Negro musicians available to form the first all Negro 45 piece band in the Navy. The men selected as qualified by Chief Dudrow were first recommended by a committee" comprised of Governor Broughton, C.C. Spaulding, and three college presidents: Shepard of North Carolina College, Bluford of NC A&T, and J. W. Seabrook of Fayetteville State. They were invited by telegram to Broughton's office on April 17 to discuss "a matter of importance." (20)

John S. Gilmer

clarinet
Greensboro
Dudley High School

William Skinner, one of the oldest recruits into the B-1, also was one of the most curious, at the time, as to how it was coming together: "I talked with some NAACP executives, and to Dudrow and to [UNC] President Graham about how this had happened. The contact from Washington was first made with Dr. Graham, who took the idea to Governor Broughton."

"We all knew about Dr. Graham from Calvin Lampley," Gibson said. "He was the organist at Dr. Graham's church (Chapel Hill Presbyterian, pastored by Reverend Charles Jones), and that was pretty rare to have a black in a position like that." (21)

"They had decided," Skinner added, "they needed people who knew the mores and customs of the state, that they should be from North Carolina or be in school here so they would know how to act. The NAACP, however, resisted the use of blacks as musicians. They wondered if this was a step forward or was it the same old thing?"

In addition to recruiting young men who "knew how to act," it was also essential that the recruits be excellent musicians, and Greensboro A&T and Dudley High were able to supply a core of such recruits: talented, intelligent, and even-tempered musicians, carefully chosen with the idea in mind that they had to be better than any white counterparts and adversaries. Arthur Guy said: "We were all grown young men who didn't fear anything. We were educated, and most of us had been around white people all our lives, so we didn't push it, we didn't shove. I mean, I grew up in Greensboro and I'd always seen those 'colored' and 'white' signs. Didn't bother me."

Huey Lawrence added: "The men that were recruited for the B-1 band were the best. They were the men who knew music. We read it; we could arrange it. Most people back then thought black music was just jamming. But we played the classics, for the officers, the admirals, for dances for the movie stars. We played stocks, concert music, and marching songs."

"They got nearly all of A&T's band," Lawrence said. "They'd have had us all if we all could have passed the physical." Richard Jones recalled that he almost didn't make the cut: "I failed the color blind test, but then I took it again, and I said what I thought it was supposed to be, not what I saw, and I passed."

Eventually, recruits would also come from Fayetteville State Teachers College, North Carolina College, Johnson C. Smith University, South Carolina State, Hampton Institute, and Hillside High School in Durham, where pianist William Cole had been band director. (22)

Arthur W. Guy

drums
Greensboro
NC A&T

Jones, like most of the other recruits, believed their service would be in North Carolina, not far from home, for the war's duration: "They said they were getting up an all-Negro band to be in Chapel Hill for the duration." Dudrow, during initial recruiting, "promised everybody that they would be spending the whole duration of the war on the campus of the University of North Carolina. That sounded good to me." (23)

"The duration," however, would begin in Norfolk.

Mananan masthead and
cover illustration
art by Stafford W. Evans

Courtesy of
James C. Yourse, Jr.

Training at Norfolk: No Day at the Beach

"Keep your damn mouth closed—
you're in the Navy now."

—NAVY DRILL SERGEANT

B-1 became official with the mass swearing in of its recruits in Raleigh, on May 27, 1942. From there, the new enlistees boarded a train for Norfolk for training that was originally supposed to last four weeks. The pre-flight school in Chapel Hill had opened on May 23, so the band's service was actually needed before it had begun training. Delays in completing the Chapel Hill recreation center where they would be housed would double B-1's training time. But as they left Raleigh, all the bandsmen knew was that they were going farther away from home and closer to the action of the war: by January 1942 U-boats were threatening the east coast, and from January to April, the U.S. was losing almost a ship a day to German torpedoes. Just two weeks after their arrival, offshore explosions sank a merchant ship and crippled another when the vessels hit mines Germans had laid at the mouth of the Chesapeake Bay. (1)

The import of what they were doing was not lost on the new recruits. Willie Currie remembered the swearing in vividly: "The day we took the oath, they said if we weren't sure, to step out of line. I'd have stepped out of that line if anybody else had."

But no one did, and with their swearing in, the men of B-1 began their active service in the U.S. Navy; several were traveling out of state for the first time and had never been as far away from home as Norfolk. There, less than a week removed from campus life, they found a city and its Navy base in a wartime routine, with work shifts around the clock. (2)

As the sailors of B-1 mustered into the Navy, their lives became intertwined with several national trends for which their own experiences would be a microcosm. Everywhere, it seemed, the nation was on the move: civilians moving to jobs, spouses traveling to be closer to mates in military training, and military personnel like the B-1 bandsmen traveling first for training and then to duty stations. Resultant housing shortages and heightened competition for jobs were direct results of this national mobilization. All—travel, job and housing searches—strained both the physical resources of the nation and its race relations. Blacks and whites alike found themselves in unfamiliar territory, away from home and the racial codes familiar to them.

W. Filmore Haith

drums
Greensboro
NC A&T

B-1 was but a small part of the 100,000 enlisted personnel, civilian workers, and their families who soon had more than doubled Norfolk's population. The Hampton Roads area was strained to the max: housing was at such a shortage that people rented beds in shifts and schools ran second shifts. During leave, as many as 10,000 to 15,000 enlisted personnel would be on the streets. The bustling economic environment extended to the black community and its active social life on Church Street, which was lined with cafes, pool halls, theaters, churches, and the Plaza Hotel. But as would be their tendency throughout their service, the men of B-1 would for the most part stay on base. "We didn't go to Church Street in Norfolk, Pettigrew Street in Durham, Hotel Street in Honolulu," said Huey Lawrence, ticking off the areas noted for their clubs and nightlife in each of B-1's postings. "We went to the colleges, to the nursing school. We didn't go to those joints—they were rough. We had one or two that might get loud, but they didn't hang around Pettigrew Street—we just didn't go to those places." None recall going to the beaches to swim, where they would have found machine guns manned at the dune line. (3)

The Norfolk Naval Operating Base, one of four bases run by the Navy, had since its beginning in 1917 been one of most important military installations in the world. Even before World War II, it was the largest base of its kind, boasting a naval training station, a receiving station, a supply depot, an air station, a Marine component, and a submarine base. Since 1918, it had served as headquarters of the Fifth Naval District. The Navy had conducted a school for training Filipino officer's cooks and stewards at

Norfolk since 1930. Growth at the base increased rapidly after the authorization in 1940 of a 2-ocean Navy. In September 1939, the base and air station was comprised of 945 acres and 472 buildings; within three months of the outbreak of war in Europe, over $4 million in construction projects were underway on the base. By 1945, 2,300 buildings were in use on 3,500 acres. Active duty personnel increases were as dramatic: from 2,076 in December 1940 to 16,656 in 1943. Soon after Pearl Harbor, the base supply center alone was employing 9,000 civilians and 1,400 officers. At its peak, nearly 8,000 civilians were employed at the Naval Air Station. By June 1942, the shipyard employed over 38,000. (4)

Otto D. Harris

bass, bass viol
Greensboro
Dudley High School

Norfolk was the first site for training black sailors once the Navy began allowing their enlistment in 1932, and prior to construction of the new bases at Great Lakes, it was the only place where black sailors, all at messman's rank, were trained. By 1939, the mess attendant school had moved to a larger part of the base. As the Great Lakes became operational and the Navy began accepting blacks at non-messman ranks, specialized schools were created at Norfolk in electronics, fire fighting, torpedo welding, and compass work. During the war, 8,175 officers and 139,713 enlisted personnel were trained there. (5)

The Naval yard at Norfolk employed a large number of civilian blacks—as many as a quarter of the 9,000 civilians working at the supply center alone. But the black press was reporting in September 1942 that the environment was still rife with race prejudice. "Brilliantly painted signs" throughout the yard told of the "horrors of Hitler, the Japs, and the hell that war is" and urged "each worker to perform his duty by being patriotic to his country." But just as prevalent were the signs "with bolder lettering" that said 'this is for White' and 'this is for colored.'" Racial segregation, both the Chicago *Defender* and Pittsburgh *Courier* reported, was strictly enforced. Further complicating the situation was the large number of "poor whites from the Northern Carolina hills and the backward sections of Virginia, Alabama and Georgia" who brought to the yard their "hates, their fears, their prejudices, and their feeling of superiority."(6)

The B-1 recruits traveled from Raleigh to Norfolk alongside many blacks who had been recruited into the Navy as messmen, "but after we got to Norfolk," recalled piccolo player Abe Thurman, "they went their way and we went ours." B-1 and the mess trainees were housed in a separate part of the base, isolated from the white trainees. B-1 had its own barracks within this segregated section of the base, and its enlistees had little contact with the other black recruits on base.

William Skinner added: "We were in with a lot of other blacks now. They looked at us funny. They'd never seen or even heard of a unit that came in as a solid group. When you bothered one, you were bothering forty people, so we didn't have much trouble. That's the way we operated there, and in Chapel Hill and overseas. But we didn't walk around by ourselves very much. We stayed in groups, for protection. We had no contact with white sailors there. But there was a certain amount of resentment from some of the other blacks, at us being college graduates, and because of our pay [$54 per month]. The white folks would say 'they don't act like heathens, they don't act like those other niggers.'" (7)

Wray R. Herring

baritone horn

trombone

Greensboro

Dudley High School

"I guess some of us thought the Navy was going to be different," Thomas Gavin recalled, "but we'd become used to that stuff. All the facilities were segregated. The Navy was nothing that different. I had just left a segregated school. We rode up on a segregated train; the hotel in Raleigh was on a back street in a blighted part of the city, segregated. It was the same."

"Once we got to Norfolk," Gavin added, "I felt like I'd made a big mistake, just in the regular way recruits were treated. There was very little you could do right. We were met at the bus by a guy screaming at us, cursing, calling us names. I wasn't used to that."

Added Skinner: "And the language they used was awful, the other blacks, our officers, to each other and to us. We'd never heard anything like it."

Walter Turner, a messman who trained at Norfolk, said the drill sergeants there "would call us 'a bunch of dummies,' 'niggers' . . . actually 'nig-a-roes' as in 'All you nig-a-roes, fall in outside the barracks and follow me." (8)

The screaming drill sergeant and countless vaccinations are memories the B-1 bandsmen share with most military veterans. "The shots made some of us sick," said Skinner, "but we had to continue on."

Thomas Gavin remembered that the band was eventually placed under an Irishman who "let us know he was being ostracized for being drill instructor for a black group. He was determined, though, that we would excel at everything. He drilled us very hard. Carried us through rifle training, swimming, gas mask, everything to be combat prepared. We had a lot of confidence in him. When we marched in drill, we'd be marching in the middle of two white units drilling on either side. The guys constantly called him names without opening their mouths, the way they looked at him, their body language. We slept in the area with the mess attendants, Unit X they called it, and trained with the white seamen. After a few weeks, we started to become a group, started to feel pride within ourselves. There was a feeling of closeness to each other, almost like a family instead of a company."

Eventually, Skinner added, the sergeant loosened up: "He changed his tone and started treating us like people. Instead of making us march, he might say, "Let's not go marching in the sun today. Let's go to a movie where it's cool. He came to us after eight weeks and broke down and cried. Said he'd been in the Navy 37 years and had never seen a group of colored men that grew on him like we did."

Simeon O. Holloway

baritone saxophone
Gary, IN
NC College

Although their bandmaster would be Dudrow until a permanent master was named, B-1 went through regular Navy boot camp training, under—for the most part—regular Navy drill instructors. Physical conditioning was of prime importance. B-1 enlistees were given physical exams in Greensboro, Raleigh, Norfolk, and Chapel Hill, with at least one fellow being disqualified after each of these exams. Their Norfolk training included, then, lots of physical conditioning as well as intensive instruction in the Navy's *Bluejackets' Manual*; the use of weapons and hand-to-hand combat; survival skills, especially swimming; and preparation for dress parades at which everyone on base would march in formation for review.

Huey Lawrence said: "Training was tough. I was in condition from football, so the obstacles were no problem. I was surprised at how tough it was, though. We were trained as if we were going to battle—up at 4:30 in the morning exercising, firing guns, as well as continuously practicing our music, with the group or on our own."

Training struck William Skinner as tough, too: "We had a black drill instructor from Portsmouth, Virginia, who was really rough on us. He told us to march and we did. He marched us down to the pool and told us to jump in, and we did. He had a pole he was going to use to help the ones who couldn't swim get out."

"But he'd wait till you came up the third time before he'd offer it," said Wray Herring. This practice, the "sink or swim" method, was not officially condoned by the Navy, which denied that it was used at all. Walter Turner, a career messman, said that "some guys would pay off the swim instructor—five dollars could get you qualified." (9)

Morehead added: "Having grown up in Greensboro where there were no swimming pools open to blacks, I'd never tried to swim. I was so happy to feel that pole to pull me back. Even today I couldn't care less about getting into water."

Saxophonist Raymond Pettiford was one of the few who was already a swimmer: "I'd known how to swim since I was 8 or 9 years old. My grandparents had dammed up a creek for a water hole for us, and then they built a pond to keep us out from under their feet."

"All we did in Norfolk was drill," Richard Jones recalled. "I never did learn to swim. Bob Tate couldn't swim either, but when they asked us, he went with the swimmers. That's what I should have done."

Skinner added: "I adjusted to the routine okay. It was hard, but we knew we'd be done with it and back in Chapel Hill for the duration, so we felt like we could get through Norfolk easy enough. It was hard discipline, though, the marching especially. Before, all the discipline we'd encountered was this ring of keys that Prof Mason would throw at you if you got out of step, but we took that for play. We'd throw the keys right back at him."

Among other lessons B-1 would learn, one of the first concerning the Navy's duplicity came in Norfolk: "We asked [in Greensboro] what type uniform we'd have," Skinner said, "and they told us the same type as officers (known as "service dress blue"): black pants, black coat, white shirt and tie. That sounded just fine. Then in Norfolk, they started throwing us those white uniforms, and we said something. They said 'Keep your damn mouth closed, you're

Roger F. Holt

trombone
Greensboro
NC A&T

in the Navy now.'" The white uniforms being tossed their way were indicative of cook and messman rank and were designed to be "distinguished from all others." (10)

"This is how rotten the Navy was," Calvin Morrow said: "They wanted to get some publicity about the new roles for blacks in the service. They wanted some pictures for it. So they brought in some black stewards and mess attendants and let them hold our instruments for the picture. Now we had a nice looking group and it seems they got the ruggedest people they could find. It would've been so simple to've done it right."

Though in fact training lasted six weeks, B-1's stay in Norfolk was extended another three weeks as they awaited completion of their Chapel Hill barracks. Early news reports on the band's formation had indicated that they would arrive at Chapel Hill by the middle of July, that Parsons would be named bandmaster after Dudrow's re-assignment, and that other officers would be selected from the men of the band, but those were intentions that never materialized. Training for B-1 was one of those experiences that seemed to last much longer than it did: Gavin recalled "13 weeks"; Nathaniel Morehead remembered that it was something like "3 months." Saxophonist Raymond Pettiford said, simply, "I started to think we were going to stay in Norfolk for the whole war." And no one from B-1 would ever make officer's rank. (11)

After their musical instruments arrived, about their fifth week in Norfolk, things lightened up as training became more directed towards performance. "Once we got our instruments," baritone horn player Wray Herring said, "it was a different experience. Dudrow took over most of the direct training, and he conducted our music rehearsals and marching drills." With their instruments in hand, others on the base also realized that the B-1 enlistees really were musicians. Because they were already well trained at marching formations as well as performing, it didn't take long for their talents to be noticed. Before the instruments arrived, they had often drilled for marches in a big field near their barracks; but once their instruments arrived, Dudrow moved their drills to the base's main staging area. "Some people

Silas A. James

clarinet, saxophone
Durham
NC College
Hampton Institute

got mad at him for bringing us out there," said Abe Thurman, "but we out-drilled everybody."

The most grateful sailors for the arrival of B-1's instruments, Thurman recalled, were those in the base band, an all-white unit. "We graduated after six weeks," he said, "and then we started playing for graduation every Saturday, so the base band got to take the weekend off. They kept saying we'd like to keep you guys here, because they got off when we were playing."

Although time away from base was rare, several bandsmen recall their recreational visits into Norfolk. Their resident guide was William Skinner, who had grown up in Norfolk and been attracted to college at A&T by its excellent marching and concert bands. "Being from Norfolk," he recalled, "I was well aware of the social structure, so it felt good to be part of the first group not to be restricted to the traditional roles." Still, off base, he knew the importance of being careful, and because he knew the area, he was able to direct his fellows to places that would be safe as well as entertaining. Because his home was in Norfolk, Skinner was allowed to spend his nights with his family, away from the barracks, but he seldom did so. Instead, he enjoyed showing his mates about Norfolk, taking them to the Booker T Theatre, to the beach for an evening stroll, and to Daddy Grace's church and restaurant. The Norfolk *Journal and Guide* ran a photo of trombonists Roger Holt and Nathaniel Morehead, along with their wives, enjoying "the cool breezes at Norfolk's City Beach." (12)

Huey Lawrence said, "I got out and played some in Norfolk with Skinner. Sometimes we'd get in a spot and have to fight our way out. But we didn't go to much of the rough places. We'd go to movies, the USOs. But we stayed clear of the blood-and-guts places."

"Yeah, you could leave the base for leave," said Willie Currie, "but there wasn't anyplace you could go except for the movies and Daddy Grace's café to eat." Skinner had introduced several of the bandsmen to Daddy Grace when he had come through Greensboro to preach. "He was some preacher," Currie said. "Had them all fooled into thinking that when he died he was coming back, just like Jesus." Grace's United House of Prayer, located just off Church Street, was a safe place for bandsmen to attend when on leave. It featured nightly services that attracted large crowds. A basic tenet of Grace's was that church should never be dull or boring; as a result, House of Prayer services were filled with lively music provided by two bands, and curious visitors were as welcome as members. (13)

In Norfolk, B-1 also got its first experience at what would become one of its primary wartime duties: performing for bond rallies. At the late July 1942 "American Heroes Day," B-1 was photographed in parade to the Booker T Theatre, where the ensuing 4-hour rally featuring B-1 and an Army band of African Americans from nearby Ft. Eustis would raise $12,000 in bonds and stamps for the war effort. (14)

But the departure for their first official posting finally came. Gavin recalled it vividly: "We were getting ready to come to Chapel Hill. The truck driver and seamen were loading seamen's bags. They'd done nearly all of them, and then they saw us and said 'load 'em yourselves.' I didn't pick mine up. Dudrow thought I should've, but I didn't, so he finally put it on himself."

And once again B-1 found itself on a train, this time headed back to North Carolina, where, they all believed, they'd be stationed in Chapel Hill for the war's duration—a Navy promise that would not be broken for nearly two years.

Come dear lady, let's be on our way,

The Manana dance is on this day,

The refreshments are great, the music is fine

I'll need a partner, won't you please be mine?

Date: 24 October 1944

Time: 6:00 PM to 8:30 PM

At : FULLER'S USO, PEARL CITY.

Buses will leave YWCA at 5:30 PM

Transportation will be furnished in our modern convenient bus es.

Wray Herring Collection

CHICKEN DINNERS served on candle-lit tables featured the party given for the station's all-Negro band last week. The tables were arranged in a double V, and a large Ensign all but covered one wall.

Pre-Flight Colored Band Has Made-to-Order Party

It is now three months since the first all-Negro Navy band of this war was welcomed aboard the Navy Pre-Flight School at Chapel Hill. It was a college group, a third of its 44 members being college graduates and almost all of the remainder having at least two years of college work behind them. The colorful group was strictly North Carolinian, too, its members having been recruited from the several Negro colleges of the state.

From the beginning there was a feeling of local pride in the group which was to be housed in a new building started as a community center for the Negroes of Chapel Hill. An attractively planned structure of natural-color rock with walls two-feet thick and a lobby-parlor 80 feet long, it was taken over and completed for the headquarters of the Pre-Flight School's popular all colored band.

Last week, on Thursday, Oct. 15, a party was given in appreciation for the first weeks of necessarily relentless work to which the band was assigned. Under the Captain's orders, the party was to be exactly what the men wanted, with nothing spared in meeting their requests and wishes.

The bandsmen wanted it to be formal. They wanted their guests to be the girl friends they had left behind in college. Accordingly buses were sent to Negro colleges in Durham and Greensboro to pick up the ladies and bring them to the party, and additional buses were provided for the return trip so that their hosts could escort them back to the doors of their dormitories.

The men wanted the party to be a banquet followed by dancing, games, and entertainment. They wanted chicken dinners served on candle-lit tables, and lime-ice punch (unspiked) later in the evening.

All they asked was granted. Lieut.

Frank L. Gillespie, assistant welfare and recreation officer, to whom the Chaplain, Lieut. Eric H. Arendt, had assigned the carrying out of the requests of the band, saw to that. A double coat of wax was rubbed down on the already shining hardwood floor of the lobby, extra tables, chairs, silver, linen were supplied, and the service help was doubled for the evening.

The welcoming committee was made up of E. Willie Currie, Thomas A. Keller, "Lanky" Cole, Lawyard L. Wilson, James D. Morgan, and Simeon O. Holloway, all Mus.2c.

At exactly 2000, the guests arrived and were announced. In a few minutes bandsman and guest, both excited, sat down about tables that were arranged to form a large double V. The colors of the gigantic Ensign, which all but covered one wall of the lobby, reflected in streamers of red and blue down the long white tables. Courtesies and manners went unbroken.

Early in the evening, the Captain of the station, Comdr. O. O. Kessing, and Mrs. Kessing arrived, were acknowledged in correct military manner, and accepted seats at the tables with the bandsmen and their guests. From the moment the Captain entered the room a broad smile of appreciation and respect played on the face of every sailor in the room.

When Chief Bandmaster Dudrow arrived, a cheer of welcome rushed to meet him. He is the band's instructor who recruited the group and guided it through its nine weeks of training and its first weeks of station experience.

See PARTY, page 6

PARTY

(Continued from page 3)

William Henry (Lanky) Cole, Mus.2c, trombonist and swing piano player, the former bandleader at the Hillside High School, Durham, acted as toast-master, provoking laugh after laugh with his natural humor. Comdr. Kessing, Chief Bandmaster Dudrow, and the band's own leader, J. B. Parsons, Mus.2c, were presented to the group, but there were no long speeches. The Captain told of his pride for the band and ordered the men to take the following day off—which every man could be expected to do with enthusiasm.

The band's 16-piece swing orchestra, directed by bandsman Melvin L. Wall, Mus.2c, stomped off into a short but hot program of jive favorites while the tables were cleared for dancing. Lights were dimmed and 44 sailors in dress blues (shoes glistening) guided their 44 dream girls about the room. As the evening spent itself, the couples left the dance floor for the rooms about the lobby to enter table games or to be served punch and soft drinks. At midnight sharp, the dancing stopped, the National Anthem was played, and the entire party loaded into the buses for trips back to Durham and Greensboro. The men wanted it that way.

FOR SALE—Reconditioned Oak Desk, 30"x60"—$18.00. L. D. Lloyd (one mile from town, Durham Road at Creek). Phone F-2916.

Chapel Hill: "The Best of Times"

"All those handsome and talented
young men ..."

—REBECCA CLARK

Chapel Hill in 1942 was still very much a small Southern town, racially segregated and far from the bastion of liberal thought and progressive ideas for which it would come to be known. The 1940 U.S. census counted 2,456 whites there and 1,124 African Americans. The town "makes no pretense of being cosmopolitan," the *Atlantic Monthly* reported in 1941: "It strives rather for an enlightened provincialism" and is "primarily concerned with Southerners and the South." Its all-white police department, headed by W.T. Sloane from 1934-58, had had its share of troubles with blacks, including at least two racial disturbances in the late 1930s, several near-lynchings, and a series of incidents in 1942 chronicled in detail by the *Daily Tar Heel*, which lodged formal complaints against two officers for mistreating blacks both prior to arrest and after incarceration. Chapel Hill's Franklin Street businesses, when not closed to black patrons, were not welcoming. "At Chapel Hill," James Parsons recalled, "there were two little towns together. One town is heavily black in population and [the other] is heavily white. We found that we were not welcomed into the stores [so] the men used to go up to Durham and buy things at the drug store rather than to be insulted in the stores in Chapel Hill." (1)

Paul Green, the Pulitzer-Prize winning playwright and long-time resident, recalled that when Richard Wright visited him in Chapel Hill to work on a stage adaptation of Wright's controversial novel *Native Son,* Wright was not allowed to eat in the restaurants next to the university. "It was back to Jim Crow for Richard Wright when he came to Chapel Hill this summer," Green's assistant wrote. Daphne Athas said that a party planned for Wright was canceled because of a threat to kill Wright. Green recounted on several instances the story of how a local mob of whites led by his cousin, so incensed by Wright's visits to Bynum Hall on the UNC campus for work on the play, planned to come after Wright. Green did not call police because he was certain they would have sided with the mob. He defused the situation by assuring the mob that he would have Wright out of town the next day and then spent a night in a cotton patch, outside the home in which Wright was staying, to keep vigilantes at bay, although they never showed up. (2)

News of the day regularly reported on incidents that reflected heightened racial tensions. As B-1 settled into its Chapel Hill routines, among the biggest stories of recent months had included that of a white woman's alleged rape by a Roxboro black who was nearly lynched (Governor Broughton would grant early parole to four of the five convicted of the attempt); a Fort Dix, NJ race riot; and a Statesville conviction of a black man for allegedly raping a 60-year-old white woman—he was subsequently given reprieve by Broughton after his white employer verified that he had been over 350 miles away at the time of the alleged crime. (3)

The Southern Conference on Race Relations, held at North Carolina College in Durham in October 1942, assessed the current climate as one of "increased racial tensions, fears and aggressions." Included in its manifesto, written by Dr. Charles S. Johnson, President of Fisk University, was recognition that the war had heightened racial tensions and aggressions, especially in the South, making "open issues" of segregation, discrimination, minority rights and democratic freedom. Although the conference agreed to a fundamental opposition to compulsory segregation, it also argued that it was "both sensible and timely" to be more concerned with discrimination and neglect as society evolved towards equality. The push for attendees was to end segregation in education, leaving the military question alone for the time being. (4)

None of the B-1 bandsmen recall the conference or the extensive coverage given to racial incidents throughout the region.

Richard H. L. Jones

trombone
Greensboro
NC A&T

"We didn't know any of that was going on," said Abe Thurman. "We didn't read those newspapers [the *Defender*, the *Courier* and other black audience newspapers]."

Wray Herring agreed: "We paid attention to our work, what we were supposed to be doing. We all knew there was plenty of trouble out there, and doing your job was the best way to avoid it."

Still, the racism of the times was never far away. The *Daily Tar Heel* reported on the same page in June 1942 that B-1 would arrive on campus in two weeks and that a student drama group was staging "an old-time minstrel show," *Are You From Dixie?* set in a "Negro café in Carrboro." At one smoker that featured B-1 and its swing band, the master of ceremonies was a white cadet in blackface who sang "Old Man River." The pre-flight school's newspaper, *Cloudbuster*, regularly ran cartoons with racist caricatures of blacks in minstrel-type situations and dialog, not infrequently on the same page as an article about a band activity. And, Nathaniel Morehead said, "The doors to the University were closed to us. We could practice in the Tin Can, but we had no access to the canteen, the dining halls. And the white merchants never did anything out of the ordinary for us." (5)

Julian B. Jordan

trombone
Charlotte
Hampton Institute

"They hated those Pennsylvania whites from the pre-flight school," Parsons added, "but they let them go into the drug store. They hated us worse."

"We couldn't help but feel restricted," said Thomas Gavin. "Four of us had pilot's licenses and would love to've been cadets. But it wasn't possible, so we tried not to think of it. We knew what we were doing was an advancement, and we had mixed feelings about that."

Walter Carlson, who with his brother John was among those with a pilot's license, added, "I thought for sure we'd be able to sit in on some of the classes. A lot of the time, we were just lounging around during the cadets' class time. So John and I asked about sitting in on one but there was no way, we were told. I remember us standing outside in the hallway listening to an instructor, and I suppose he figured out we were there, because suddenly that door shut."

William Gibson recalled that he and the Carlsons had wanted to go to Tuskegee, to join the 99th Pursuit Squadron that was training there. They had earned pilot's licenses through the Civil Aviation program at A&T, so service at the pre-flight training school, even if with a band, made the young pilots hopeful. "We thought we'd get to sit in on some classes and pick up points on navigation," Gibson added, "but all we ever got to sit in on were a few classes on enemy aircraft identification." (6)

Parsons was acutely aware of how close his men were scrutinized whenever they were in public because they were black and in uniform. He counted on them being smart enough to avoid confrontations with authority—or with the Jim Crow world in which they lived. "Everytime I left campus or later when I'd leave the base," said Abe Thurman, "I was walking around like on eggshells."

Huey Lawrence said, "We were always in our uniforms and we knew people were looking at us."

"There might have been a couple of places where you could eat," Calvin Morrow said. "Certainly not on campus, and not in downtown Chapel Hill. And you certainly wanted to be real careful if you ever left barracks."

"We knew how to act in the white world," said William Skinner. "We knew not to go in a drug store and sit down to order something to eat. But even though we were fully well-conditioned to segregation, we'd accepted it as a way of life, many times we wondered why we couldn't eat in that big dining hall on the campus."

Two of the Navy's "Golden Thirteen," the first African Americans to make officer rank in the Navy, echoed similar experiences in North Carolina. Samuel E. Barnes, who taught at Livingstone College in Salisbury from 1936-41, said, "I avoided situations that could have caused problems. . . I avoided contacts with white people unless absolutely necessary." George Cooper, a Washington, NC native, said, "Jim Crow was the name of the game. Everything was separate; nothing was equal. . . And there was no choice but to accept it. The only 'choice' that you had was to try to make the best of it or get in trouble. Prejudice was something we lived with every day of our lives." (7)

"Yeah, it was tense," Calvin Morrow said. "We were sitting on a powder keg and we knew it. During that time, it was rough, but that was how it was. Nothing really changed until the '60s."

Willie C. Judkins

clarinet, saxophone
Durham
North Carolina College

: : : :

The integration of UNC was proposed as early as 1868, when a resolution providing for admittance of blacks was introduced to the Board of Trustees. The motion was altered before passing as a request that the General Assembly amend the university's charter to provide "equal facilities for whites and blacks" by constructing a college for blacks near Raleigh. For the next 70 years, that separate-but-equal goal was maintained as a way to avoid questions of integration. But on the UNC campus and throughout the university system, by the late 1930s, some things were different and attitudes were changing. The *Daily Tar Heel* relentlessly pursued incidents of alleged racist acts by local police, covered interracial meetings on campus, and frequently commented editorially on the vexing "race problem." Support from university President Frank Porter Graham was no doubt a factor in establishing a more liberal atmosphere on campus than existed in the Chapel Hill community, and he had been gradually opening up the UNC campus to African Americans in a variety of ways. Graham was already outspoken in his nationally known liberal views on the race question when he became UNC's president in 1930, and his tenure was marked by service on numerous national, regional, and state commissions and frequent speaking engagements throughout the South, often at black college campuses. In 1939, Graham's secretary wrote in his stead to the national Negro Congress that UNC "gladly cooperates with the Negroes whenever possible and in every way possible. Our auditorium is freely used by Negro groups at any time when it is not in use by University groups." At one meeting, she noted, "members of both races sat together and appeared together on the program." (8)

Thomas A. Keller

drums

Springfield, OH

North Carolina College

That cooperation was apparent in numerous interracial events on the UNC campus. On-going was the annual Chocolate Bowl, a popular football game sponsored by the YMCA and hosted by Chapel Hill's Orange County Training School on the UNC campus

Roy H. Lake

clarinet

Greensboro

Dudley High School

at Fetzer Field. Bennett College's Theater Guild made national news in the black press for winning a bronze medal in a state-wide drama competition—their plaque presented by Frank Porter Graham. The WPA Chorus of Durham, which had performed on campus for FDR during his 1938 visit and would perform for the Queen of England, was featured in a 1938 Hill Hall concert as part of a literacy program in which 75 UNC students worked with Orange County illiterates. Two children's choirs from local black churches offered a free concert of spirituals in Memorial Hall. An active inter-collegiate network promoting racial cooperation and integration met variously at UNC, Bennett College, and the Woman's College. At an integrated 1939 forum, over 200 participants voted unanimously to request that the North Carolina legislature allow blacks admittance to UNC. In the midst of local tension related to charges of police brutality against three Chapel Hill blacks, the Carolina Political Union sponsored an interracial panel on the role of African Americans in the current war. (9)

Civilian enrollment at UNC fluctuated during the war, from half to less than half of the pre-war enrollment of 4,000. Professional schools were hurt the most: enrollment in the law school plummeted from 120 students before the war to a low of nine in 1943–44. But the strong military presence on campus actually bolstered student enrollment: of 5,300 students on campus in fall 1943, 3,500 were men in uniform. In addition to the pre-flight school, UNC also hosted a Navy V-12 program, a Navy ROTC, an Army geography and language study program, an Army Air Corps meteorology program, and a unit of Marines. But by far the biggest impact of the war on Chapel Hill was brought about by the opening in May 1942 of the Navy's pre-flight school, which trained over 18,700 cadets, including future Presidents George H.W. Bush and Gerald Ford. To accommodate its cadets, the Navy renovated ten dorms, expanded Woollen Gymnasium, improved the acoustics in Memorial Hall, and built a recreation center, an athletic field, Jackson Hall, the ROTC Armory, Nash Hall, Miller Hall, the original infirmary (now part of UNC Hospitals), an outdoor swimming pool, and the Scuttlebutt snack bar, and also expanded Horace Williams Airport, where cadet Gerald Ford crashed two airplanes. (10)

Because physical fitness was such a high priority for Navy pilot training, UNC's extensive athletics facilites were a major reason UNC was selected as the eastern region school. Frank Porter Graham's working relationship with President Roosevelt, as well as his friendship with Eleanor Roosevelt, was also critical in helping secure the Navy presence, which kept the war-time depletion of civilian students from hurting the local economy not only by the presence of so many spenders but by a campus building boom that saw the Navy construct campus facilites valued at more than $1 million, at an actual cost to the university and state of about $126,000. (11)

B-1's arrival in Chapel Hill made it again a part of a much larger national context. Between 1940–45, 15 million Americans moved from one community to another because of war-related opportunites and assignments, creating in the process a society in flux. Like B-1 in Chapel Hill, most black servicemen would remain stateside: by 1943, 425,000 of the 504,000 blacks in the Army were still stationed in the U.S. But for the duration, B-1 avoided being swept up in the turmoil that resulted from the social upheavals plaguing the country, as widespread outbreaks of racial violence in and around military camps were caused mainly by friction created by segregationist practices and discrimination in on-base facilities such as theaters, post exchanges, and canteens. Scholars today still speak of an overall situation worsened by prejudices of white soldiers, officers, and MPs. Southern Jim Crow laws made it even worse wherever blacks were stationed or brought into communities as laborers, and bus service appears to have been a primary cause of conflicts. (12)

The Office of Defense Transportation reported: "One of the most serious problems in cantonment areas is finding room for Negroes. Because in most communities the local Negro population lives under already over-crowded conditions, it is not easy for a Negro family to make way for a stranger." In Chapel Hill, though, the B-1 bandsmen found a home and welcoming community that helped to insulate them from such stresses. Although the bandsmen were not "from there," they were part of the North Carolina experience for African Americans and recognized as being of that larger community. And because of the unique way

Bennie D. Lakin

cornet

Florence, SC

NC A&T

the band would be situated during its stay there, living among the town's black community and working on its whites-only campus, B-1's history is more intricately intertwined with a civilian population than most Navy experiences would allow. B-1's immersion into Chapel Hill's black community was necessitated by the Jim Crow policies that still were maintained in Chapel Hill and the South, and in that sense, B-1's experience was also a microcosm of the national difficulties that went hand-in-hand with the tasks of transporting and housing the large numbers of African Americans mustering into the armed forces in the first months of World War II—but without the resultant troubles. In the South especially, moving troops and civilian workers by bus and train to new locations and negotiating housing patterns would almost always be complicated by Jim Crow laws and customs. (13)

Huey L. Lawrence

trumpet
Pittsburgh, PA
NC A&T

The local black community had begun anticipating B-1's arrival as soon as it became official that its under-construction community center would be completed by the Navy, for the purpose of giving "the colored musicians assigned to the U.S. Naval Pre-Flight Training School" living quarters "comparable with anything on the campus of the University." Completion of that structure would be the biggest physical improvement the Navy would make in the town of Chapel Hill, although construction delays in completing it would ultimately keep B-1 in Norfolk for five weeks longer than its promised four weeks of training. Construction of the community center had stalled in the spring of 1941. "It had gone slow," Chapel Hill historian Roland Giduz recalled. "Most of it had been done on a volunteer basis, until the Navy got involved." About half of the original $26,000 cost of building the center was to have come from the WPA; $4,000 in labor was to have been contributed "in the form of labor by the negroes of the community, engineering services, and use of equipment," leaving $9,000 to be raised. Frank Porter Graham personally pledged $100 towards its completion. As planned, the community center would include a day-care facility, an assembly room that could double as a hall for social gatherings and indoor games, a full kitchen, rooms for meetings, a nurses' headquarters, a woodworking shop, and a large bathroom with showers. Five acres of grounds featured a baseball field that was in use for over a year before construction of the building was completed. Navy construction respected those plans even as it transformed the basement of the center into a barracks, dining room, practice rooms, and recreation center for B-1. Now called the Hargraves Recreation Center, this was B-1's ship, as baritone saxophonist Simeon Holloway fondly termed it. (14)

Until B-1's arrival, the on-going presence of blacks on campus at UNC remained limited to service jobs: Rebecca Clark recalls making $9 a week working at the university laundry. Her husband, John, was a dormitory janitor. Part of what would thrill her so much about B-1's presence in both the black community and on the university campus was the hope bandsmen represented that perhaps her children's children would one day be able to attend classes there. But except for church services conducted by the Reverend Charles Jones at the Chapel Hill Presbyterian Church, Chapel Hill remained a solidly segregated town.

John Mason

French horn
Durham
Hillside High School

"Just to be on the campus in Chapel Hill was a step towards integration," said bassist Charles Woods. "I knew segregation was wrong, even as a little boy. I just hoped to see it end in my lifetime. I mean, anybody should be able to see that if I pay $1.50 to ride a bus and you pay $1.50 to ride the bus, we ought be able to sit where we wanted. But we always rode in the back of the bus coming home from Chapel Hill to Greensboro, and we never said anything. We knew we were a segregated group, that state laws kept us from staying on campus, that when we rode home we went to the back of the bus. That was the way it was. That doesn't mean we thought it was right."

Not everyone in the band, however, accepted the situation. Abe Thurman, a New Jersey native who had come to A&T for college and to connect with his African-American heritage, simply refused to ride buses at all, a form of protest not often noted but also embraced by Bennett College students in Greensboro at least as early as 1937. Already, the form of protest made famous by Rosa Parks' refusal in December 1955 to move from her bus seat was being employed in North Carolina: two Durham residents were convicted in November 1941 for taking third row seats and refusing to move so that a white man could sit, and a Kannapolis black, James Harper, challenged enforcement of the Jim Crow seating law in July 1942 when he was arrested in High Point, where officers were "temporarily at a loss to know whether Harper had violated any law in refusing to change seats" when ordered to do so by the bus driver. (15)

Still, despite the harsh barriers Jim Crow established and the conditions maintained within that system, once the bandsmen were at home, within the warm and welcoming black community of Chapel Hill, their military experience was softened. William Skinner, the Norfolk native, found life much different in Chapel Hill than it had been while the band trained: "In Norfolk, Navy men were dirt to the people in the community. But in Chapel Hill, we weren't seen as Navy men so much as college men, and we were welcomed into the community there."

Nathaniel S. Morehead

trombone
Greensboro
NC A&T

B-1 finally made its long-awaited formal entrance into Chapel Hill as part of a grand parade. But as it marched down Franklin Street in its official role as an attachment to the pre-flight school, it was also becoming engaged in a much more emotional role in Chapel Hill's black community. At the same time, it was stepping directly into the local struggle against racism that had engaged the Rev. Charles Jones and other locals such as Phillips Russell, Howard Odum, Paul Green, and Frank Porter Graham. Graham and Russell were active members of Jones' Chapel Hill Presbyterian Church (renamed University Presbyterian during the 1960s), which he would later lose, in 1953, because of doctrinal differences with the church's Synod. From the band's arrival only a year into Rev. Jones' Chapel Hill tenure, B-1's integration into his church was publicly obvious and, for some, troublesome. When Rev. Jones appealed his dismissal by the New Hope Presbytery, one of those testifying on his behalf at the Synod's hearing was Graham, who said, "The laws of our state required that [the Negro bandsmen] be housed apart from the whites, but when Sunday came, there was no separate church. They came to our church—a few of them—and they were seated just as you or I would have been. They were not taken to the balcony or stuck in some corner." For the duration of their stay in Chapel Hill, the band would be under the intense scrutiny of those locals who remained intent on maintaining the Jim Crow world that had served them so well, in Chapel Hill as in the rest of the South. (16)

"We were welcome there," Calvin Morrow said of Chapel Hill Presbyterian Church. "That was the only feel of integration I got in Chapel Hill. I went there several times. But you didn't go to any of the other churches."

"That reverend was nice," agreed Raymond Pettiford. "He would bring a few folks from his church over [to the community center] for the movies. He'd bring his youth group over, too."

According to Rev. Jones, B-1 was well suited for the task of advancing integration on a local level, as well as within the U.S. Navy, for several reasons: "They introduced blacks at a level where most folks wouldn't have seen them. They were all out of colleges, they were educated, they were excellent musicians. And they were in places of authority." The men, in turn, thought highly of Jones. "He was the best in Chapel Hill," recalled Arthur Guy. "He was a staunch leader. He'd get all the bigwigs together and point his finger at them, to let them know about humanity. He knew he was white and that we were black. But what was the point, he wanted to know, of us not being allowed to be together?"

James D. Morgan, Jr.

drum major
Comfort
NC A&T

One of the most visible places the band was introduced to, where "most folks wouldn't have seen them," was Franklin Street, down which they proudly marched for the first time on August 1, 1942. The band had arrived the previous day, 42-strong, with Charles E. Dudrow still its official leader. Upon their arrival, the *Chapel Hill Weekly* reported, "the musicians alighted from their special bus, got into parade formation, and marched along the south boulevard, playing as they went." They were welcomed in a brief ceremony at the pre-flight headquarters, Alexander Hall, and "taken to their quarters in the Negro Community Center." B-1's "first really spectacular appearance," the *Weekly* reported, came the next day, a Saturday march down Franklin Street that has occasioned several variant recollections. The *Weekly* noted that the band "marched through the middle of town to the tune of 'Anchors Aweigh' . . . on down Franklin Street and through Raleigh Street to the University grounds. Citizens looked on admiringly from the sidewalks."[17]

James Parsons, who led the band for that Saturday march—and would soon become their official leader for the war's duration—recalled the march much differently in interviews: "I shan't forget it as long as I live. Just outside of town we got off our bus and were met by the officers and three companies of cadets in dress whites, like ours, and we assembled to parade into town. People started coming out on Franklin Street to see what was happening. They started jeering at us, calling us all kinds of ugly names, most of them racial slurs. They were throwing mud and rocks at us. I got cut on my cheek. At least one instrument was dented. My men had mud all over them. But in the midst of all that, they held their heads high. I'd never heard them play better. We played and marched right through that mob."

At their new home, the bandsmen were met by a welcoming committee of a different sort. Local blacks from the community had prepared a wonderful reception, Parsons said, "with great refreshments and lots of pretty women."

Calvin F. Morrow

French horn
Greensboro
Dudley High School

Other recollections of that first march down Franklin Street vary when told from differing perspectives. Some bandsmen remember nothing of the hostility. Thomas Gavin said, "I was in the interior of the band, so I couldn't see if things were being thrown." William Gibson added, "We were reading our music so we couldn't notice much. I did see them throw something. I caught a glimpse out of my left eye of a soda cup being thrown by a girl. Parsons could be right about all that, though, because he was up front and he could see a lot more since he wasn't reading any music, just marching." But Abe Thurman, marching up front without an instrument because the Navy had yet to find him a piccolo, recalled nothing of the hostilities Parsons remembers. Roger Holt recollected the assaults because, he said, he played trombone and thus marched on the front row. But fellow trombonist Richard Jones was just as adamant that nothing of the sort happened.

What transpired on this march remains the most debated memory among B-1 bandsmen. The only historical records of the band's arrival into Chapel Hill are local newspaper articles. On Friday, July 31, 1942, the *Chapel Hill Weekly* announced that B-1 would be arriving "today," and that it "may possibly perform this afternoon." The following week's paper reports on two marches that both wind up with the bandsmen at their new headquarters, one on Friday and another on Saturday. Parsons' account, of the march down Franklin culminating in a public reception at their barracks, seems to conflate the two days' events. So a variant version of these events might suggest that something happened on the first, briefer, less formal march—the incidents Parsons re-calls—but that these would not necessarily be recalled by others as events associated with the larger parade the next day, down Franklin Street, which ended with the public reception. Parsons offers a similar accounting of this first march in his *Unfinished Oral History*, but with some detail added: "I don't remember the march we did but it was one of our favorites. We just did that one over and over. As we paraded through the main part of town, we were booed very heavily. Racial epithets were cast from the sides and younger peoople threw rocks and mud at us. I was hit by a glob of mud. I was right flank to the front row and one of the sou-saphones was hit with a rock and put a dent in it." (18)

Raymond Pettiford

saxophone
Greensboro
Dudley High School

Parsons had been groomed for being the band's leader while they trained in Norfolk; Dudrow's charge had been to get the band trained and to Chapel Hill, so with their safe arrival, his work was essentially done. Between Dudrow's service and the formal appointment of Parsons to be their leader, they were briefly led in Chapel Hill by a Navy bandmaster, Chief Musician Stephen W. McReynolds, who was selected by the Navy as B-1's perma-nent leader, a move which would have relegated Parsons back into the regular band. "This white guy came in and said he was in charge now," said Skinner. "He took Parsons' stick. We were yelling 'Take that stick back! Take that stick back!' And Parsons took it and broke it and threw it at that man. He tried to stay in charge, though, but we wouldn't accept him. When he found out we weren't going to listen to him, there wasn't much of a place for him to stand—surely not in front of a band that might choose to play off-key."

With Dudrow, Parsons worked out the band's regular schedule, which might be altered at any time, depending on the requests being made for their services. "It was carefully ordered and mon-itored," Parsons said. "The entire band was on six days for the flag-raising, after which we had formal drill practice outside the Tin Can. The men were all required to have two uniforms per day, and they had to be kept clean. They wore a work uniform until af-ter lunch; then after rest, they dressed and re-formed for practice."

B-1 wasted little time in getting into its routine. On Monday morning, August 3, they made their first march from their quarters to campus to play for the 8 a.m. "colors," or flag-raising, and from that date until their departure from Chapel Hill in April 1944, their basic routine would be the same: After the flag-raising, the bandsmen would march the pre-flight cadets to class, then practice until 10 a.m., and then march the cadets to class again, then practice and drill and then march them to lunch. "While they changed classes," said Abe Thurman, "we played what you call a grinder—three or four marches played straight through without stopping. You'd have the march, then two cadences and then do another march, then two cadences, then the other march, and so on until they were all seated. Grinders were especially tough on your lips. One time it was so cold that all the valves froze on the trumpets, so you just had the clarinets and piccolo—that was me—playing." After noon, B-1 would march back to barracks for their own lunch, prepared by local women from the black community, and an afternoon of more practicing until 5 p.m. Sundays were abbreviated, with the only regular duty being the flag-raising, which was attended by, Parsons said, "a partial band."

Herbert E. Reeder

clarinet, saxophone

Columbia, SC

South Carolina State

Evenings were usually free time, and bandsmen were allowed liberty to any place within 50 miles of Chapel Hill, a radius that contained Greensboro. "Chapel Hill, all those days in Chapel Hill," Wray Herring recalled, "those were the best of times. That was something else. They were so good, nobody believes it, then or now. We were at war, and we were playing music."

The first dance band that was soon formed out of B-1, the Cloudbusters, would quickly become an area favorite, meaning that the fellows in it worked most nights, performing for officers clubs and smokers, while others went to movies or visited friends in Durham or Greensboro, or courted. A few, like Bennie Laikin, had homes nearby, where they stayed most nights instead of in the barracks. Still, every morning there was the march from barracks to campus for the flag raising, no matter the weather. "Sometimes it was so cold, I couldn't move the valves," said French horn player John Mason.

Richard Jones added: "The Navy had said we didn't have to play if it was below freezing. Parsons said, 'If it's below 26, we won't go.' Even if it was raining, he'd march us, and then he'd march us extra if we messed up."

Parsons, most of the men agreed, was a hard leader who wanted his men to be "better than the best." He freely admitted that the Navy had offered transportation for the men so that they wouldn't have to walk the nearly 3 miles to campus every day, but he declined their offer, wanting instead to drill his men, and to show them off. They would be seen every day by blacks and whites alike as they marched to work. Thomas Gavin, who after the war would organize the marching band at Fayetteville State University, said, "Parsons thought it looked better, more patriotic, to march. Some mornings we marched in the dark."

"Parsons wanted perfection," Gavin added. "He felt he had to do more than was required. Being black may have had something to do with that. He seemed to go just beyond the call of duty. We didn't like it at the time, but later, some of us who worked with bands found that we had unconsciously adopted some of his principles. I know I did. I developed the idea that I would work the hardest, that my bands would work the hardest, that I would always do more than what I had to do. Yet, at the time, I was probably among those who made life miserable for him."

Nathaniel Morehead added, "I know we gave Parsons a lot of those gray hairs, but I don't know that we understood how difficult a role he was in. He wasn't treated fairly. He should've been a petty officer, and had he been white, he'd have been a chief. Still, we expected more from him than he was able to give, and we didn't understand that to the Navy, he was just another black man, not given the respect and consideration he should've been given."

In Chapel Hill's black community, Parsons and his mates were far from being "just another black man." Instead, they became role models and heroes, and their daily marches to campus were watched with great interest, enthusiasm, and pride. And if Chapel Hill wasn't actually home to the bandsmen, it was close to it, both literally and figuratively. Several fellows were from nearby Durham; those already married found homes in Chapel Hill to rent. Over the course of its tenure in Chapel Hill, B-1 would become intricately involved in the community. In addition to the more formal occasions like community concerts and movie socials presented at their quarters, bandsmen taught music to local children, they attended and performed in the local churches,

James B. Scott

bass horn
Greensboro
Dudley High School

dated and in several cases married local women. They secured athletic equipment for the center and taught basic skills to the local youth. They also were a daily inspiration, on their marches to campus, to the many locals who watched their parades with a swelling pride that transcended patriotism. Kids came out to stand on the street as they paraded by; adults, many getting ready to go to work in service jobs at the university, watched from windows with a quiet pride. (19)

Robert E. Sellers

bass horn

Durham

Hillside High School

John and Doug Clark were two local youngsters whose lives were transformed by B-1, especially these daily parades. Doug Clark, who died in 2002, would become founder and bandleader of the renowned party band Doug Clark and the Hot Nuts, in which John Clark also performed. "Doug and I and all the kids in the neighborhood would run out to Robinson Street when we heard the band coming," John Clark recalled, "and we followed them as far as we could. Doug wanted to be just like [John] Morgan [the drum major], and I wanted to play sax like Walter Carlson."

"Yeah, the kids would follow us around," said Carlson. "We participated in events in the black community, and we taught some of them how to play. But what I really remember is how the kids would follow us around town." (20)

The Clarks' mother, Rebecca Clark, recalled vividly 65 years after the fact how wonderful it felt to see "all those handsome and talented young men in their uniforms" marching to campus. "The kids were out at every corner watching them parade," she said. "They were the best thing that could've happened to our community. See, the children hadn't seen a real black band, never, and they made us all so proud."

Edwin Caldwell, 10 years old at the time, recalled: "Anytime you heard the band play, people would stop what they were doing, come running and watch. This band was a show. And they were real role models for the community." (21)

Polly McCauley remembered as a young girl sneaking up to the barracks windows to gaze at the bandsmen's hats lined up. "They were something," she said of the bandsmen. "Good looking men in those hats and uniforms. We'd hear them in the morning starting up the street [marching towards campus] and everybody'd come out and watch. It was like a parade every day. And they influenced so many people. We were just starting music lessons at the school and they came over and taught the lessons personally."

Roland Giduz added: "They were the first uniformed band in town; the white high school's band didn't march. They made Chapel Hill very proud. They definitely changed the town's perceptions of blacks at the time—they had a significant effect."

For their 20-month stay in Chapel Hill, B-1's daily schedule was often altered for special events such as regimental reviews, war bond rallies, and patriotic assemblies throughout the region. They played at cadet football and basketball games, wrestling and boxing matches, and gave concerts at area schools and churches. In addition to the Cloudbusters, B-1 players formed small and large ensembles, brass quintets, and quartets. (22)

Because Parsons was adept at transcribing, transposing and arranging—necessary talents in these days before the Navy began issuing official band books—he arranged most of the music B-1 performed and also scored and wrote original pieces for their concerts. Just a month after their arrival, on August 30, 1942, B-1 performed its first concert in Kenan Stadium. "The fine performance of the band," the *Chapel Hill Weekly* reported, "was enjoyed by a good crowd. It was not yet dark when the concert was given, and the white uniforms of the musicians, against the background of the rich, green turf, made an impressive picture."(23)

Royland V. Siler

trumpet
Newport News, VA
NC A&T

By September, the Cloudbusters had begun playing at weekly smokers held in Woollen Gymnasium for the cadets and for the more elaborate parties given for officers. In October, the whole band was feted by the Navy with a formal dinner at their barracks, with dates brought in from Durham and Greensboro on chartered buses, and they had a triumphant homecoming to A&T for a November Founders Day program at which Governor Broughton delivered the main address. Before the year was out, they had performed with Kate Smith on her regular live radio program; played at a "Negro war bond rally" in Durham that raised $75,000 and netted 232 Navy enlistees; and were featured in an integrated community Christmas sing-along in a program scripted and directed by Paul Green, at which Green's original poem, "A Christmas Prayer," was read. (24)

For Kate Smith's visit, the band performed first with her at a special concert for the cadets, at Memorial Hall. Later, for her radio show, broadcast live from Durham, she sang the pre-flight song arranged by Melvin Wall and James Parsons and her signature song, "God Bless America," to the band's accompaniment. She had "incredible breath control," William Gibson said. "In fact, she didn't even need a microphone." Helen O'Connell, another star of the day, sang with the Cloudbusters at cadet smokers on several occasions. (25)

William E. Skinner

clarinet

Norfolk, VA

NC A&T

B-1 inaugurated a series of Sunday afternoon concerts outdoors in the Forest Theater in September 1943. Featured in their first concert were two white female soloists, a tenor and a soprano from N.C. State in Raleigh, and the Quartones, "a negro girls' quartet from Durham" who sang popular swing songs. A Chapel Hill war bond rally that same month was held on UNC's campus, at Memorial Hall, where "a section of the hall has been reserved for negroes." B-1 was the main entertainment: "the Navy Band sat on the platform at the War Bond Rally in Memorial Hall Tuesday evening, and their playing delighted the assembled company." Another Durham bond rally later that month featured a street parade led by B-1, with the local American Legion, a battalion of the 930th Field Artillery from Camp Butner, Boy Scouts, Elks, and Ushers Union members marching. Keynote speaker James Parsons said in closing that "to participate in bond rallies is part of our way, as musicians, to help win this war until we can get into it, and it is a part of yours." The 2-hour program featured group singing led by Nell Hunter, and B-1 was also a main feature of the event: Encores "kept the Chapel Hill band playing past its allotted time, and extra numbers were offered during the bond purchasing period." (26)

One of the biggest local occasions B-1 performed for was the gala celebration in 1943 that culminated in the presentation of the Army-Navy "E" award for excellence in production of war equipment to the National Munitions Corporation and its employees in Carrboro. Held also on campus in Memorial Hall, the event featured B-1 and speeches by a host of dignitaries, including Governor Broughton, Josephus Daniels, UNC President Graham, and Congressman Carl Durham. For the barbecue luncheon that day, six 90-lb pigs were served with three bushels of slaw, 300 loaves of bread, and 40 gallons of Brunswick stew. (27)

A memorable highlight of B-1's Chapel Hill days included, for William Gibson, meeting Vice-President Henry Wallace, whose December 11, 1943 speech on campus was sponsored by the Carolina Political Union. "Shoot," he said, "me and Filmore Haith played doubles with Wallace and one of the base commanders. Of course, we let them win," he added, laughing. "We sort of felt like we had to!" (28)

Music, of course, would remain the common thread of the bandsmen's experiences throughout their stay in Chapel Hill. But there was more music than what the Navy offered, too. Sometimes, according to several of the bandsmen, they'd sneak out at night to play a gig, either as part of a makeshift combo or, individually, as guests for a traveling performer.

Robert M. Tate

cornet

Durham

Johnson C. Smith Univ.

"Sometimes we'd play a gig in Durham or Greensboro," Huey Lawrence said. "Parsons had apprehensions about that. He was ambitious and didn't want anything going wrong. He didn't like the fellows going off. Fletcher Henderson had come through Durham then. I'd played some with him before. Anytime he'd go on tour, he'd lose fellows to the draft all along. All his guys were going into service. When he got to Durham, we arranged for a couple of guys to go with him to play a gig at Wrightsville Beach. Melvin Wall went, somebody else. Parsons wouldn't let first chairs go. In return, Fletcher gave us a free concert."

"But in Chapel Hill," added Richard Jones, "we never officially played anywhere where we could also have danced."

B-1 played several times in Kenan Stadium for formal Navy regimental reviews, and for visits by dignitaries such as Vice-President Wallace and Lord Halifax. Their performance at the 1943 commencement ceremonies at UNC included a march played while the 1,900 cadets paraded for the students and parents, as well as an open-air concert. But its biggest event in North Carolina was as the featured attraction at the launching in July 1943 of the USS *Merrick* at the Wilmington Shipyards, where 5,300 blacks were employed. This occasion was the most spectacular public event aimed at black participation in the war effort ever staged in North Carolina. James Merrick, one of the founders of North Carolina Mutual Insurance in Durham, was a popular choice for having a ship named for him, an honor championed by NC Mutual's president and co-founder, C.C. Spaulding. The launching itself promised to be a glorious day of celebrating African-American history and heritage. (29)

Over 20,000 attended the launching program (a conservative estimate of the crowd, according to the *Carolina Times*), which was broadcast on the radio in Durham. Spaulding called it "one of the highlights of my life." Governor Broughton, in his keynote address, said that "our honest and determined purpose" is the "assured path toward racial harmony and progress," and he cited as evidence of that progress these achievements for the state's blacks: nine month schools, supplements to teacher pay, construction of a home for delinquent Negro girls, and improvements at the NC College for Negroes. Agitators, he said, "in the guise of seeking only economic opportunity for the Negro" would "flout established and mutually respected conventions and traditions, which cannot in this state, now or ever, be obliterated." He warned against those "seeking to use the war emergency to advance theories and philosophies" that will "result only in a mongrel race—a condtion abhorrent alike to right thinking citizens and leaders of both races." (30)

Abe Thurman

piccolo

Newark, NJ

NC A&T

Few conventions of the time were more pernicious than the one, established by NC law on March 22, 1939, that required blacks to fill a bus from the back while whites filled it from the front and gave "police powers and authority" to bus drivers to enforce the law. Mamie Williamson, a 46-year old black woman who refused to move to the back of a crowded bus en route to the day's celebration, could hardly be called an agitator, and her suggestion that she would leave the bus and find another, provided "the driver would give her money back," hardly qualifies as an action seeking, in the governor's words, "economic opportunity." But her arrest and conviction for violating the state's Jim Crow law attracted considerable attention, partly because in the ensuing scuffle, her false teeth were lost—whether from her being beaten or from her resisting arrest depended on whose story was believed. The Durham *Morning Herald* would editorialize against the police action, which prompted H. Shelton Smith, a Duke Divinity School professor of ethics, to ask for Governor Broughton's intervention. Broughton appears to have been satisfied with Wilmington Mayor Bruce B. Cameron's response to his inquiry, which included copies of the arrest report as well as the results of the police chief's investigation. Cameron, incidentally, notes, "We have had tremendous difficulty with the Jim Crow law as the bus driver has to turn around and drive to the City Hall when there is a case of violation and most times, just before arriving at the jail, the offender jumps up and moves back and then has witness to prove the bus driver wrong." (31)

Williamson was found guilty the following week of violating the Jim Crow law, assault, and resisting arrest. Her sentence, 30 days on a work farm, was suspended, and no fine or court costs were assessed. (32)

This kind of incident, out of context from what was otherwise a peaceful coexistence between B-1 and the white world that surrounded it, would always seem possible. But part of what makes B-1's such a remarkable story is the fact that, when these moments of tension occurred for the bandsmen, they passed without turning into incidents like those being reported regularly in the press.

Huey Lawrence recalls seeing police cars cruising by B-1's barracks whenever Rev. Jones brought white students over. And, according to Parsons, although none blew up into major events, "There were several incidents involving B-1. The worst was when some of my men were accused of accosting while on liberty some white girls. Three or four arresting officers came to the barracks late that night. They wanted a lineup of men so they could be identified. The girls said there were two they could point out. So I said I'd get them up, line them up and put them in formation, but you'll have to wait outside. I went to the lower level and called the officer of the day at HQ of the command base. Within moments it seemed the Marines had arrived. They came through the windows in back of the building, like an invasion, then went out and took the sheriff, the chief of police and several civilians, locked them up in the brig. The governor rushed over the next day. [Acting university President William D.] Carmichael was called in. Charges against my men were dropped." (33)

Still, there were moments that showed the promise of a post-Jim Crow world. At a late September 1942 smoker for the cadets, B-1 bassist Charles Woods performed with three white cadets, in an integrated jive quartet that included Bill Maxted, the former

Melvin L. Wall

clarinet, saxophone
Albemarle
NC A&T

pianist for Benny Goodman's orchestra. "Once," said William Gibson, "we were going to play this show. We got there early and they had these stakes up the middle of the arena, with hooks on them where they were going to put a rope to separate the blacks from the whites. Filmore Haith says, 'Would you look at that?' So we pulled all the stakes up before any people got there and the crowd got mixed up real good." (34)

The steps towards integration throughout the band's tour of duty in Chapel Hill were, like these occasions, small but real ones, more isolated instances than part of any evolving pattern of acceptance. But prior to B-1's arrival on the UNC campus, blacks had been relegated to roles much like what they had been allowed in the Navy: cooks and cleaners. So simply having educated black men on campus was a significant step. "We were hoping [integration] would happen," recalled Rebecca Clark. "But you didn't know if it would. So it was nice to see those fine young men on campus here every day. It gave you hope."

B-1 had so successfully settled into its life and routine in Chapel Hill that the announcement, in February 1944, that they were being shipped overseas was especially shocking. Suddenly, "for the duration of the war" took on a new and frightening meaning. They would be replaced in Chapel Hill by a Great Lakes-trained band about half their size. But they would not be forgotten. (35)

In 2007, B-1 was feted again at their former barracks, now known as the Hargraves Center, where a plaque bearing all of their names hangs above the fire place that used to warm their reception room. A standing-room only crowd heard testimonials from locals whose lives had been changed by B-1's stay in Chapel Hill. In Wilson Library, they were graciously welcomed back onto campus at UNC by Chancellor James Moeser, who also apologized to them for the university's failure to treat them more hospitably their first time on campus, 65 years prior: "I think this is the first time that we have welcomed you on this campus, and it is very, very, very late, but it is never too late. I only regret that we didn't do this many, many, many years ago when we could have had the entire band on campus." Moeser attributed to the band a primary and significant role in transforming Chapel Hill into the progressive community it has become. And in the first return to Kenan

Stadium for most of the surviving members of B-1, they were made
honorary members of the Marching Tar Heels at half-time of the
university's football game against James Madison University on
September 1, 2007. (36)

Said Rebecca Clark at that reunion: "I saw history in the making when they came to Chapel Hill. I saw the same history being
denied for all these years. I'm glad I lived long enough to see that
history being recognized at last." (37)

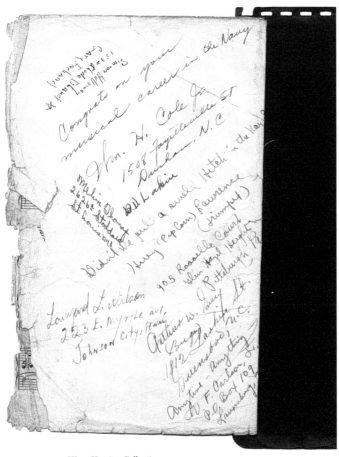

Wray Herring Collection

Special Collections, Joyner Library

East Carolina University

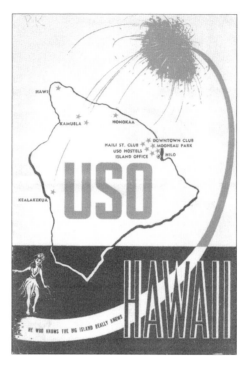

HE WHO KNOWS THE BIG ISLAND REALLY KNOWS

Pearl Harbor: The Biggest Military Band on "the Rock"

"So we went from a college campus in the middle of Chapel Hill right into the war."

— JAMES B. PARSONS

The United States had its sights on Pearl Harbor as a defense stronghold for the Navy as early as 1873, but because the breeching of the reef that shut the harbor off from deep-sea vessels was such a difficult and expensive project, the harbor was not opened until 1911. In 1913, the Navy's first station in Hawaii, at Honolulu, was re-located to Pearl Harbor which, by the end of World War I, had been closed as a commercial fishing harbor; the fishing rights of property owners along the shores of the harbor would disappear during World War II. (1)

Immediately after the bombing of Pearl Harbor, martial law was declared by the governor, and Gen. Walter Short proclaimed himself military governor of Hawaii. Before December 7, 1941 ended, Short had decreed that military police and tribunals would enforce the laws of Hawaii, the U.S., and the military. As early as the summer of 1940, historian Fred Israel writes, military intelligence had been devising plans for controlling what was believed to be a volatile native populace in Hawaii, where "civilian revolts and massive sabotage" were feared once the Japanese attacked. Relieved of his duty less than two weeks after Pearl Harbor, Short was succeeded as military governor by Gen. Delos Emmons, who immediately established that military rule brought with it not just the power to police but also "to punish the offender speedily." Army intelligence admitted that orderly trials were "practically unknown"; they rarely lasted more than 20 minutes and almost always resulted in conviction: in 1942, of 22,480 charges in Honolulu, only 359 defendants were found innocent; and in November alone, of 1,454 charged, none were acquitted. (2)

Jewitt L. White

cornet

Gary, IN

NC A&T

J. Garner Anthony's book *Hawaii under Army Rule* is in places a controlled rant against the injustices martial law brought, illegally, to Hawaii and its citizens. He was Hawaii's attorney general from 1942-43 under U.S. District Court Judge Ingram Stainback; both were harsh critics of martial law, how it was imposed and how it was maintained. Gov. Joseph Poindexter, Anthony writes, "virtually abdicated his office" on December 7, 1941, although he had no such power to do so; under military rule, Hawaii was subsequently governed as though the Constitution and all federal and territorial laws might be "freely ignored or suspended at the will of the commanding general," who substituted "his will" for that of Congress and the legislature of Hawaii. Anthony contends there was no basis in federal or territorial law for a "military governor," a term appropriate only for "areas in rebellion or conquered nations." In April 1944, shortly before B-1 arrived, U.S. District Court held that martial law had been imposed illegally but not until October 24, 1944 did President Roosevelt terminate it. (3)

Nothing in the years before 1942 had prepared the islands, Oahu in particular—with Pearl Harbor and Honolulu within 5 miles of each other—for the upheavals and transformation to come with World War II. The special geography of Oahu made it an ideal place for a Navy base, with those twin ports so close together, both opening to the south. The Army occupied one-third of Oahu's 600 square miles at one time, with 50 "sizable" reservations; the Navy had 26 stations; and the Army engineers had "many more" than 18 bases. The Navy claimed thousands of acres in the Pearl Harbor staging area, which was enlarged at least six times during the war and included four bases in addition to Manana, where B-1 would be stationed. Aiea, which housed 16,000, was the Navy's largest base and until Manana was constructed, between March and September 1944, it also was home to the Navy's African-American sailors. By the end of the war, the Army and Navy owned over 62,000 acres in Hawaii, double their holdings in 1940; the Army also had temporary possession of 210,000 acres; the Navy and Marine Corps, another 118,000 acres. The Navy's construction program became "probably the most stupendous building program ever undertaken in history," burgeoning from initial expense estimates of $31 million to over $200 million—a cost that does not include another $7 million spent in 1940 alone dredging Pearl Harbor, an on-going project that had already cost over $100 million. (4)

Although Hawaii became during the war "one huge military camp," the number of servicemen on the islands at any given time was a closely guarded military secret. Gwenfread Allen notes that in Hawaii a "bewildering variety of Army, Navy, Marine Corps and Coast Guard units came and went, their movements cloaked in secrecy." These were "specialized fighting units and service troops whose duties reflected all the complexity of modern warfare." Some stayed "most of the war; others were here only in transit. Some merely saw the waving palms of Hawaii from offshore." Statistical estimates suggest these peak numbers: for Marines, 79,000 and the Army, 253,000. Navy numbers are more complicated: those based ashore peaked at about 137,200, not counting "men afloat"—another 550,000 in the spring of 1945 prior to the invasion of Okinawa. Most would come ashore at least once, sometimes as many as 35,000 at a time. (5)

Sherman U. Williamson

French horn

Greensboro

NC A&T

Civilian populations rose dramatically during the war, too, Oahu growing from 200,000 in 1940 to 500,000, as "almost overnight, sleepy country villages became beehives of activity seething with defense workers and military personnel." In the process, what had been a paradise of racial tolerance—1940's census identified 8 distinct ethnic populations, with Japanese the most predominant—was also transformed. (6)

Some in military command had recommended that no black troops should be sent to Hawaii, but in the end, military necessity—that is, a shortage of laborers—demanded their presence. The construction of Manana Barracks was part of the Navy's reaction to racial tensions throughout Hawaii that had been documented in "The Negro Problem in the 14th Naval District," compiled by the Navy's counter-intelligence office in August 1943. For the Navy, most trouble had been at Aiea, where the first black sailors in Hawaii had been stationed in quarters separated from those occupied by whites. The black sailors included Seabees (men in the Navy's construction battalion), messmen, and stevedores. The Navy admitted that their discontent was "primarily" because so many were skilled or semi-skilled in some trade and had been led to believe that after enlistment they would be given opportunities for advancement, but had instead been engaged "solely in stevedore work." The Navy documented frequent off-base incidents involving clashes between these men and aggressive whites, too. On base, blacks and whites clashed over recreation and food service issues especially, but even when the fights were over food, "derogatory language seems to have been the spark." A riot in December 1942 arose over segregated seating at a movie when blacks stoned first the auditorium and then the firehouse; three men were court-martialed, one summarily. Through the first half of 1943 conditions deteriorated badly, leading to a situation "so tense" that the military imposed a system of "partial segregation" at social functions, barring blacks entirely from some. But black sailors denied admission to a variety show that starred a traveling black troupe began to riot after a Marine assigned to keep them from entering called them "niggers" and ordered them away from the theater entrance. (7)

Lawyard L. Wilson

saxophone
Johnson City, TN
NC A&T

The Navy's solution in part was to construct a "separate but equal" base to house its African-American personnel, where there would be no chance intermingling of the races at mealtimes or at movies. The Navy said that before the war, Hawaii had no "Negro problem" because only 200-350 people identified themselves as "Negro," although Navy intelligence, investigating that "problem" in 1943, estimated that at least 10,000 more locals would be classified "Negro" had they lived on the U.S. mainland. (8)

Intended to determine the "present status of the Negro problem" in the Hawaiian territory, the Navy's report uses language and methodology similar to that employed in the FBI's better known *RACON: Racial Conditions in the United States During World War II*—which incidentally found little concern regarding racial tensions in Hawaii despite its final draft bearing the same date as the Navy's report. The Hawaii report, like *RACON* (edited by Robert A. Hill), attempted to link Communist and Nazi influences with African-American organizations and thus blame them for individual unrest and militancy, but it added suspicions of Japanese influence to the mix. In the end, Navy intelligence found no Nazi, Communist, or Japanese threats, nor evidence of organizing for subversive activities among the targeted groups. (9)

About 30,000 African-American servicemen and workers were stationed in Hawaii during the war, a relatively small number compared to the million-plus Caucasians, but large numbers of Southern whites brought with them racial intolerance that was often openly directed at anyone who was not white. Servicemen freely called all non-white civilians "gook" and used "nigger," "slant-eyes," "yellow-belly," "Jap," and "kanaky" (derisive slang for native Hawaiians) as circumstance suggested. Carl Clark, a career messman, found Navy life in Hawaii racist and rough when he arrived in 1940, but African Americans there had a solid relationship with locals with whom they identified. Before the war, he wrote, "black folks were treated with respect then, and it was a wonderful place for us to live. . . . But the war changed all that. The Americans, mostly the Southern ones (who were the majority of the military) considered all those who were not white a lower class of people, so now many of the Samoans, Tongans, and Japanese-Americans were considered inferior." (10)

Charles L. Woods

bass, bass viol
Greensboro
NC A&T

Between mid-1942 and 1945, "dozens of fracases occurred between blacks and whites, including four small riots," but the Navy did relatively little to defuse the overall situation and in its investigations found, for example, that black sailors who booed two vaudeville comedians in blackface and then threw peanuts at one of them, chasing him about a theater, were the ones who had "instigated" the ensuing melee. Blacks got mad, the Navy noted, when "nigger" and "darkey" were "innocently used" on a Honolulu radio show. "Promiscuous use" of racial slurs, the Navy found, was the most important single factor in sparking conflict: "Negroes react immediately and frequently with violence when they hear such remarks." But when fault was found, it most often was with the black sailors. (11)

Beth Baily and David Farber chronicle frequent encounters with "imported racism," especially on the "densely packed sidewalks of the Hotel Street district," where variations of the Southern protocol that suggested blacks always make way for passing whites played out but with "very important differences": in Hawaii, white bullies lacked the muscle of their communities to keep blacks frightened of retaliation, and blacks showed increasingly that they were not afraid of direct confrontation. Locals, often disenchanted at how they had been treated by white servicemen, would frequently wind up on the side of the black servicemen; several incident reports indicate that locals would remain disengaged as black servicemen beat up whites who had taunted them. (12)

Continuing the trend of blaming black servicemen for their troubles, the Navy's report concluded that it was "evident that the Negro has brought with him to Hawaii his story of the white man's discrimination against the Negro race." The increased presences of black servicemen in Hawaii seemed "naturally" to increase the friction between "white and colored," as blacks were becoming "more assertive" yet, unused to their new freedoms, more likely to get into arguments and fights. Despite all of its own evidence to the contrary, the Navy determined that racial slurs were not "agitation," even though they were "aggravating to the Negroes" and "a primary cause in bringing about disturbances." Ultimately, the Navy concluded that racial conflicts were not the result of subversive activity although the possibility that they were still existed. The Navy's final blame for unrest: racial prejudice, agitation by blacks, provocation by whites, the influence of "racially inflammatory newspapers" like the *Chicago Defender*, and "possibly" other factors. Andrew Lind in 1947 would suggest that competition for the attention of island women caused most of the race tension during the war, a possibility never addressed in the Navy's report on "The Negro Problem." (13)

But regardless of the causes, tensions between islanders and servicemen and between black and white servicemen had been escalating prior to B-1's arrival. The Navy reported numerous incidents of racially motivated violence and several near riots. "By the time we got there," said William Skinner, "the prejudices were well established. They said we had tails, that you'd get a disease from talking to us, that you had to break a glass after we used it because you couldn't do anything to it to get it clean ever again." He and his fellows could sit down in restaurants, Skinner added, unlike in the South. "But once you got seated, they'd get real busy, so busy they just couldn't find time to serve us. Benny Laikin and I went in to town to get some oysters once, and we sat down about one o'clock. We had to leave to catch the three o'clock truck and they were still too busy to serve us."

:: :: ::

However, as they prepared to leave North Carolina, the men of B-1 had concerns of their own. For many, learning that they would leave Chapel Hill was the worst part of service, in large part because the surprise of the announcement caught them off-guard, but also because of what they would be leaving and the news of where they were headed. "When we found out we were leaving," William Skinner said, "it was hard to accept. I was very sad, hurt, and disappointed. We'd been misled and lied to."

J. Clarence Yourse

trumpet
Greensboro
NC A&T

Charles Woods added, "I felt we'd been betrayed. We felt like Pearl Harbor was going into combat."

"Just getting the news was the worst," said Richard Jones.

But getting there would not be easy, either.

By bus the bandsmen traveled to Durham, where they had a big send-off on April 24, 1944, and boarded two specially outfitted railroad cars that would eventually get them across the United States. "We called them cattle cars," recalled Abe Thurman. "They were set up with bunks, 3 or 4 high." At mealtime, the bandsmen had to pass through white sections of the train. Thurman added: "I was always careful not to bump into anybody. I didn't want to cause any trouble."

At each stop on their weeklong journey across the continental U.S., Wray Herring recalled, "there would be Red Cross workers handing out candy, coffee, and other goodies to the people on the train, but they didn't hand out anything to the black soldiers and the black sailors. That left a bad feeling in us about the Red Cross and the Red Cross mission," which had already been diminished by its practice of keeping blood supplies segregated. That policy of "Jim Crowing" blood, branded as "idiocy" by the black press, caused more resentment among blacks than any single wartime factor "except the Army's own Jim Crow policy." (14)

The Red Cross had first announced in January 1942 that it would not accept Negro blood at all but quickly changed its policy to accept but segregate that blood. Its director said that "the prejudices of individuals to whom transfusions are given should be respected as a symbol of democracy." By July 1942, some Red Cross centers were refusing to label blood sent over-seas though blood collected for domestic use retained its racial designations. Red Cross officials repeatedly defended the policy throughout the war, until the Army eventually took responsibility for it in 1945, when Gen. F. W. Rankin, adviser to the surgeon general, said the policy was the responsibility of the War Department even though there was no scientific basis for it: "I don't think we need debate whether there are people who object" to having Negro blood put into them. The policy was officially in effect for the duration of the war and did not begin to disintegrate until June 1947. (15)

B-1's travel route across the U.S. was documented by Calvin Morrow, who marked each stop and station they passed through on his "Servicemen's Map of the United States." It was so indirect that some believed that they had been lost. The routing may have been a peculiarity of military transport, or caused by "disastrous" flooding in the Southeast, Great Plains, and middle Mississippi valley: from Durham south to Atlanta; then north to Chattanooga, Huntsville, AL, Hopkinsville, KY, and Princeton, IN; then west to St. Louis, where rainfall for April was the most since 1893 and the Mississippi River would crest at 39.1 ft. on April 30. From St. Louis, they traveled north to Chillicothe, MO, then south to Kansas City, then north again to Omaha, from where their travels resumed a more due westerly route.

B-1's transition destination was Shoemaker, CA, where the men were housed for another week of awaiting deployment near thousands of Seabees recuperating from their first Pacific tour and awaiting their own re-deployment. Shoemaker included a Navy hospital as well as a training and personnel distribution center and disciplinary barracks, and with Camp Parks, the area was collectively known as Fleet City. It was an inland compound, 50 miles east of San Francisco Bay, near Livermore, California.

At least a dozen camps were established in the general area so that personnel could have access to the bay. Camp Parks, primarily a Seabees station that could accommodate over 20,000 men at a time, was among the largest. At Shoemaker, B-1 was processed for service outside the continental United States. Shoemaker was, Parsons recalled, the launching pad for regular Navy personnel awaiting transfer into the Pacific Theater. "We were on daily orders," he said, which meant that the bandsmen had to be ready, every day, for shipping out. "We got our gear together and we reported at a set time to the courts awaiting the bus that would drive us to the ship, and we would wait all day and then go back to the barracks. Come back and wait the next day. So it was." (16)

Transitioning troops was always a tactical challenge and delays were not uncommon, but archival evidence of life at these transition stations is scarce. Stafford W. Evans, en route to Manana from Camp Robert Smalls at Great Lakes, was also stuck at Shoemaker, but for much longer—over three months, he wrote to his mentor at Virginia State University, "with hardly anything to do while we are waiting." On the occasions that he got liberty, he found Californians "out for clipping the sailors and giving nothing in return. I don't like this place." His address at Shoemaker changed so frequently during his delay that he thought "they seem as if they don't want to send me over." Evans, a college educated artist traveling with men he hardly knew, was without the peer support that the bandsmen offered each other. His meditations in letters to Amaza L. Meredith, his college art professor and adoptive "mother," are fresher than the recollections of veterans many decades removed from those turbulent days. "The Navy," he wrote, "is no place for a Negro except he is a Tom. . . And I can't fit that picture. However, the Toms make things hard for their own. Some of the boys are so ignorant it is a shame. The only persons I enjoy talking to are a few Jews. Some of them have something worthwhile to say—they too are a minority and are persecuted." The people he encounters in California "won't even speak to you. They try to be hard & get everything they can from the servicemen, rob, cheat, etc, etc, them out of what they can and give nothing in return. The serviceman doesn't expect anything except people being people. . . I don't like this place at all." (17)

But finally, on May 14, 1944, B-1 boarded a transport bound for Pearl Harbor. "I remember the date because it was Mother's Day," said Thurman.

Parsons recalled that their transport was a Dutch cargo vessel that had been converted into a troop carrier while retaining its all-Dutch crew. For most of his men, the ensuing weeklong voyage was bad and made more miserable by seasickness, homesickness, and fear. (18)

"That transport didn't float, it dipped over the waves and through them, up and down, just like this," Raymond Pettiford said, cutting his hands up and down to simulate the sharpness of the waves.

Quarters on the transport were "down in a hole," Skinner recalled.

"Yeah," said Charles Woods. "We were so un-Navy, we'd be asking how to get upstairs." Richard Jones laughed at the memory: "Benny Laikin asked somebody and from then on, all the white sailors laughed at it. They'd keep repeating it when they'd see one of us: 'How do you get upstairs?'"

There were so many men on their transport, Wray Herring said, that "the mess hall was open 24 hours a day, with men constantly around the clock lined up for meals. And people all over the ship were getting seasick. No one was used to this."

Added Skinner: "I stayed sick. A lot of us did. We went to see the doctor, and he was sick, too."

Throughout the voyage, "I was scared to death," said Nathaniel Morehead. "All I knew about Pearl Harbor was the bombing. And as far as I was concerned, we were leaving the United States, so that was frightening, too. I remember thinking that I didn't know there was so much water on the earth."

At times, their transport was in a convoy, some recall; at other times, it had a submarine escort that only surfaced at night. "I never saw it at all," said Pettiford, who added that he felt like they were sailing all alone and thus vulnerable to attack at any time: "Some of the men said they saw that sub at night, and I sure hoped that they did." Thurman insisted that they made the voyage without escort.

Richard Jones remembered being fearful because their transport was also carrying ammunition, a fear made more pressing because of the number of deadly occasions when ammo explosions at bases and on ships would be news. "We spent a lot of time on deck," said Morehead, "thinking about how we'd survive a torpedo attack."

Also on the passage, the bandsmen had the disturbing feeling that they had been betrayed by the Navy and their commander, James Parsons. "From Shoemaker to Hawaii, none of the men would speak to me," recalled Parsons, who understood that most of the men believed that he had been responsible for their re-assignment. "They all hated me. All, one at a time, withdrew from around me."

In early 1944, Parsons had gone to Washington, D.C. to take some classes, for about five weeks, at the Navy School of Music at Anacostia. He had been back only "a short time," he recalled, before the order came through for B-1 to leave. The timing of that order, so soon after his visit to Washington, led some bandsmen to believe that something had happened there to get them shipped to Hawaii. Parsons himself thought that perhaps he had been responsible for the new orders, having complained about the idea of staying in North Carolina for the duration. "I wanted to get into the middle of the action... I spilled this all along, and they all knew that." (19)

"We all thought that his going there had alerted them to our existence," Thomas Gavin said.

Richard Jones added: "We thought he went up there and asked for us to get transferred."

But the real reason, Parsons and his men eventually found, was that their former base commander in Chapel Hill, Commander O.O. Kessing, had requested that they be re-assigned to his command. Kessing's biggest Navy job in a career that spanned both World Wars was as Island Commander of the Ulithi Atoll island of Mogmog, where he was charged with establishing and running recreation for Admiral William F. Halsey's Third Fleet: 11 aircraft carriers, six light carriers, and eight battleships. The five principal islands of the Ulithi, in the Western Carolines, were captured in September 1944 and subsequently developed as the largest fleet anchorage base in the Western Pacific. At full strength, the recreation base at Mogmog had a 1,200-seat theater with accommodations and recreation facilities to handle 8,000 enlisted men and 1,000 officers at a time. It was to this posting Kessing had sought to bring B-1. [20]

Not until Kessing's visit with Admiral Halsey to Manana Barracks would the men discover what had happened to get them transferred to Hawaii. Parsons recalled seeing the admiral and commander arriving in their jeeps and watching as they drove straight to where B-1 was drilling. The bandsmen, Parsons said, "put Kessing on their shoulders and oh how happy they were." Halsey told them that Kessing had tried "very hard a long time to get his band out here" and that they had, in fact, been requested by Kessing. Halsey also confirmed what some had suspected: they had been lost in transit and again in their first days of duty at Pearl Harbor. Kessing had gone to Washington, D.C., twice, to the Navy's Bureau of Personnel, to try to find them. "So, for the first time," Parsons said, "the men discovered that I had not been the one who arranged their shipment out of Chapel Hill." [21]

Several bandsmen recall the Kessing visit in Hawaii and also that he requested that they be assigned to his command. "They told him he could have two 28-piece bands" for Mogmog, said Pettiford, "but not us." However, as soon as Kessing and Halsey left that day, "things picked up," Parsons said. First one, then another fellow offered to buy him a beer. "That day and evening and the next day," Parsons recalled, "I drank 44 beers"—one from every man in the band. "Everybody from then on was 100% with me."

:: :: ::

Despite safe passage, however, the bandsmen were thrust immediately into the dangers of war when, on May 21, 1944 they became eyewitnesses to the unfolding tragedy at West Lock, where 29 LSTs were being prepared for the impending invasion of Saipan. The LSTs, or Tank Landing Ships, were designed to land ashore and deposit troops and stores, ammunition, vehicles, and fuel. A few were being repaired, but most were being loaded with ammo and fuel when the first explosion created a roar "that could be heard all over Oahu and far out to sea." That explosion triggered others on nearby LSTs. "We were docking," said William Gibson, "and these ships started blowing up. We were just getting in and all of a sudden there were these explosions everywhere." (22)

"There were five or six LSTs blown up," said Calvin Morrow. "The Navy said the next day that 18 or 19 had been killed, but that was just propaganda. Those ships were blowing up one by one, and we were watching it, bodies flying in the air." One survivor, alone on the bridge of LST 23, recalled: "We had body parts and metal flying on deck." He estimated seeing "a couple of hundred bodies floating in the water" as he steered his vessel out of the harbor and away from the continuing explosions. News reports said the explosions could be heard in Waikiki, 15 miles away, and that the subsequent fires could be seen for miles. "We thought the Japs were bombing Pearl Harbor again," said another witness. (23)

"They had ambulances going all day and night long for two or three days," added Gibson.

Details of the West Loch explosions remained classified until January 1960. Several weeks after the event—dubbed "the worst mishap of the war"—the toll was still being listed as 27 dead and 100 missing. But in its final accounting, the Navy would officially list 163 killed, 396 injured, seven LSTs lost and three others heavily damaged. (24)

"So we went from a college campus," Parsons said, "right in the middle of Chapel Hill, right into the war."

Not everyone, however, was frightened by the experience. Huey Lawrence said, "The explosions were exciting to me. We'd read all about this stuff. That's why they use young men in war: they get excited about things like that, they don't get scared."

Once on land, however, the bandsmen encountered an incredulous Navy command. No one, it seemed, had expected the in-coming band to be black, and their lack of instruments did not help their case; everyone assumed that because they were black, they were part of the labor force responsible for loading ships and maintaining facilities. So, for the better part of a day, as sirens wailed, they were left in a staging area, until Navy command could figure out what to do with them for the time being. "We arrived at the break of day," said Parsons, "and we were still in the same place at dusk."

"We were supposed to go to Hawaii as the admiral's band," said Morrow, "but then they found out we were black, so they just put us away at Manana Barracks. Somebody met us when we came, I forget who, but he asked where the band was. Man, they were floored. So we were relegated off to the hills."

In "the hills" outside Pearl City, Manana would become the primary base for black seamen in the Pacific and "the largest base of Negro seamen the U.S. Navy has any place in the world." B-1 were the first musician-rated seamen at Manana, where they joined those holding ratings as boatswain's mates, coxswains, specialists, yeomen, storekeepers, carpenters, and motor machinists as well as messmen. (25)

At its peak, Manana housed over 4,000 African-American sailors. Although there were black officers there, none were allowed to take on leadership roles, Ensign Talmadge Neese recalled. It was part of the complex of military bases that surrounded Pearl Harbor. Just outside Pearl City, on a peninsula on the north side of Pearl Harbor, the area for Manana had, literally, been carved out of a cane field. Camps, storage areas, and housing for war workers "replaced cane fields almost overnight" along the main highway that ran from Honolulu to Pearl City and beyond. Manana supplied the labor for loading and unloading all the ships going through Pearl Harbor. Its men operated the Manana Supply Center, a spare parts distribution center that had 18 warehouses with 626,000 square feet of covered storage space and 20 additional supply buildings. (26)

"It was like a small city," Ensign Neece said. He was the last personnel officer to serve at Manana before it was closed down in early 1946 and, ironically, would wind up retiring to Chapel Hill, where he would be a surprise guest at B-1's 2007 reunion. In addition to the supply center, Manana had 20 barracks buildings, a mess hall, a brig, canteen, laundry, barbershop, a baseball field, and the outdoor theater where movies were shown every Friday night at first but eventually on a nightly basis. "We operated 24 hours a day," Neece said. "The mess hall never closed. You could get a meal there any time. We handled everything from beer to battleship propellers, everything but ammunition. I had a fleet of flatbed 10-ton trucks."

At first, B-1 was housed in Quonset huts as the remainder of the base, under the command of Lt. Cmdr. Grady Avant, was constructed. Without instruments, Benny Laikin recalled, they were assigned to kitchen, construction and maintenance tasks such as painting and cutting bamboo on nearby Pali Mountain. To beautify their new outdoor theater, the Tradewinds (with a large mural for its stage backdrop, painted by Stafford Evans), Navy brass decided it should be bordered with bamboo, and the task fell to bandsmen who subsequently spent 16 days climbing Pali, cutting bamboo, and bringing it back to Manana. The band was cited for its "enthusiasm and purposefulness" in accomplishing this task, although none recall this assignment with anything but bitterness. Lacerations and abrasions were common but necessary "sacrifices" made to bring the men of Manana "more pleasure." (27)

Most of the bandsmen vividly recall the harsh landscape and conditions that marked their time at Manana, especially their first weeks without instruments. "I thought I could make two years in prison easy after I did that time," said Willie Currie.

"Living on that hill was the worst experience," said Laikin. "They had flies, mosquitoes, all kinds of bugs."

And dust. "Living there was bad," William Gibson agreed. "It was solid red clay. We had white uniforms, of course, and you could wash them and within a few minutes hanging on the line they'd be pink."

"Once," Skinner said, "me and John and Walter Carlson painted a ship all day. Me and Walter did, anyway. John said he wasn't doing any painting, so he sat there all day and we did the work so he wouldn't have to go to the brig."

"They had us paint the theater," Abe Thurman said. "But instead of taking a brush, we poured the paint on there, especially on the officers' seats. The officers couldn't sit in there for a week. From that point on, we didn't do any more painting."

Wray Herring put his thoughts into a long poem, "To the Boys," written while the bandsmen were still doing stevedore work. It reads in part:

Manana Barracks, the place we are at,
You will even get extra-duty for going without a hat.
The wind blows hard and the red dust flys.
Sometimes I wonder why we all don't die.
At night when I am tired and try to rest,
It's hard to do even though I am the best.
The street lights shine right in my face,
And the noise the planes make is really a disgrace.
The stage shows are bad, the food smells.
In other words, this is a good substitute for hell.
And then when I look around, what do I see?
Thousands of helpless men right here with me.
It's the man that can't and never will
That gets all the ratings and breaks on this red hill.
This is hell, a prison too,
With men in brown suits to watch and guard you.
This is bad, as we all know,
And home is the place we all want to go.
Home, home and people with sense:
Won't that be a relief after being behind a fence?
Just let me hit Frisco on solid ground
And for that I will do anything, even bark like a hound.
But better than that, let me hit my old home state,
And for 30 days the Japs and this war will just have to wait.

But once their instruments finally arrived, life changed for the better, and the bandsmen fell into routines not unlike what they had experienced in Chapel Hill—without the friendly and admiring neighborhood surrounding their barracks, or the long morning marches. With instruments, they could prove themselves. "Going in as specialists," said Morrow, "that elevated us. We rose a little over that. We never got negative feedback as musicians."

"Things definitely picked up once we got the instruments," agreed Gavin. "because we could get off base then. I was in the

Tunesters, a quartet. We were ordered to play at officers clubs almost at will—theirs, not ours."

As in Chapel Hill, the band played for flag raisings daily, for visiting dignitaries, and regimental reviews. They practiced their music and their marching, shined their instruments, and practiced some more. "They were all very good musicians to start with," said Parsons of his men. "But they also practiced regularly, not just for the fun of jamming, but working out, getting it perfect."

The full B-1 band also played for ships embarking for Pacific combat, for wounded troops in hospitals and on hospital ships, and for ships returning home from battle. In March 1945, they played two shows at Aiea Hospital for men returning from combat at Iwo Jima, Tarawa, Leyte, Manila and "possibly Okinawa" and two shows aboard the "very finest aircraft carriers," whose names were withheld from publication for security reasons. One of those was likely aboard the USS *Franklin*, which Thomas Gavin and others recall as one of their most memorable performances. The aircraft carrier *Franklin* was the closest U.S. ship to the Japanese mainland when it was struck by two bombs from a lone airplane on March 19, 1945. The resulting explosions and firestorm killed 724 men and wounded 265; the *Franklin*'s men were presented with more medals and commendations than any unit in the Navy's history. B-1 boarded soon after she docked and played a welcoming concert. "We played before it was cleaned up," said Gavin. "It was a disturbing sight to think what those men had been through." (28)

Melvin Wall's widow, Audrey Wall, recalled that, although her husband loved the music part of his service, "he did not enjoy having to provide the music for sending so many young men off to combat."

Playing for servicemen on the ships, Huey Lawrence said, "was the best part of Hawaii. They really appreciated it and treated us royally. They didn't show any prejudice. We were entertainers."

The full band also played for reviews, football and baseball games, wrestling and boxing matches, parades, bond rallies and concerts, sometimes with a portion of the show featuring one of the two swing bands formed from B-1 in Hawaii. Parsons reported, in a letter back to the *Cloudbuster* at Chapel Hill, that the band had "grown in musical versatility beyond our own expectations." He observed that B-1 was the "largest Navy band ever in the Pacific," and that they had in the last year played for 569,513 people, not including broadcasts. They had organized a 40-voice glee club and a show band of 30 musicians that was regularly backing "one of the best musical variety shows out here, the only Negro show of real worth, adding vocalists, dancers, skits, and stunts to an hour of exciting music." (29)

Much of what is known about life at Manana comes from surviving copies of the base magazine, the *Mananan*, which was published bi-weekly under supervision of the chaplain's office, led by Rev. Bernard E. Heuer. He had just completed Lutheran seminary school at Capital University, in Columbus, OH before arriving, newly commissioned, at Manana in October 1944. The magazine was revamped by Heuer in spring 1945 and covered all aspects of life on the base, reporting on the Manana Maulers, their boxing team; the Bobcats, their basketball team; the Blues, their softball team; and news of the various base companies and departments: education, galley commissary, medical, cranes and rigging, labor and transportation, mess, recreation, athletics, and GSK (general store keeping), which provided clothing, tools, office supplies, whatever supplies might be needed for operation of all departments. (30)

Heuer wrote a regular column about the base's recreation activities, reviewing past shows and activities and promoting future ones. Dubbed "the youthful, popular chaplain," he boasted in one column that Manana had "the finest recreation program on the island." In addition to covering an array of base activities, the *Mananan* connected its readers to the larger complex of military bases spread throughout Hawaii and also to the greater war effort. It ran cartoons and regular features, quizzing its men on such topics as who the most military man on base might be, who the most talented: Parsons was nominated as most military, "not only when directing the band, but even in dungarees," and Walter Carlson as "the most talented cat on the base." Bassist Otto "Peanuts" Harris's "Musically Speaking" column was named more than any other as the magazine's most popular feature. (31)

Harris reported on music news of special interest to its Manana readers from throughout the islands and from stateside as well. In each issue, he profiled a B-1 bandsman, and he regularly reviewed current discs, critiquing the national music scene from an Afro-centric point of view: Buck Clayton and Jimmie Crawford, he reports, are playing in an integrated Army band, the only in service he's aware of. Earl Hines is no longer playing segregated gigs, Count Basie is using white violinists and a white lead trumpeter, and Louis Prima employs "phony Negro dialect" at the end of his latest and "needs to watch himself." Censors in Memphis, Tennessee cut the image of Louis Armstrong performing from *Pillow to Post*, leaving only his music, because seeing Armstrong, the censors said, "tended to corrupt children's morals." Louis Jordan's new show is "the most complete Uncle Tom act put on by a Negro band in recent years [including] just about everything the uninformed ofays expect of this kind." ("Ofays," pig Latin for "foes," was a common term used by black musicians to refer to whites.) (32)

Harris's columns provide perhaps as good an overview as is possible of the extraordinary music scene in Hawaii during the war, where every base boasted at least one band. Some, like the Seaman Raiders, were volunteer performers who took on band work in addition to their regular duty. But the best were made up of outstanding professional jazzmen who had been recruited as entertainers, with the promise that they would be bandsmen for the duration of the war. These included the ever-popular Hellcats, which featured Pee Wee Jackson on trumpet, from the Navy's Barbers Point base. They were handpicked "for zip and sparkle and sizzling heat" and included musicians formerly with Duke Ellington, Fletcher Henderson, Ella Fitzgerald, Lucky Millender, Les Hite, Count Basie, Fats Waller, and Tiny Bradshaw. Jackson, a trumpeter from Cleveland with the nickname of "Gabriel," had played with Fatha Hines' orchestra and Jimmie Lunceford's band before enlisting in the Navy as a bandleader. Other top bands included the Airbase Aces from the Honolulu Air Station; the Skyhawks from the Ammunition Depot at Lualei; the Blackhawks from the Naval Receiving Barracks at Aiea; the Modernaires from Schofield Barracks; and the Jungleers, led by

Reuben Reeves, from the Army Jungle Training Center. Reeves' bio calls him "one of the more exciting trumpeters in jazz" in the late 1920s. He played with Cab Calloway's orchestra for two years in the 1930s, toured with his own band, and freelanced before joining the Army as a bandleader. Arguably the most popular was the Dolphins, a Navy orchestra led by Ray Anthony, who had played trumpet for Glenn Miller and then Jimmy Dorsey before enlisting in 1942. Often winners of the Battle-of-the-Bands competitions staged throughout the islands, the Dolphins were based on the Midway Islands before transferring to Hawaii, where they were the resident band for eight months in 1945 at the Royal Hawaiian Hotel. Anthony organized his first civilian band soon after mustering out of the Navy. (33)

The Manana Meteors, led by Walter Carlson, were the first swing band to form from B-1 in Hawaii. The Meteors proved so popular that formation of a second dance band, the Moonglowers, was necessitated. To keep it fun for the fellows and less competitive, the Moonglowers, led by Otto Harris, was comprised of bandsmen playing on their second instruments. Both bands played for dances, happy hours, entertainments, and radio shows and were featured in several "Battle of the Bands" competitions, usually held at the home bases of the participating bands. At a Schofield Barracks battle staged in March 1945 to "find the most popular band on the rock," the Meteors finished third, besting the Cossacks as well as Marine and Seabees bands. Anthony's Dolphins won, and the Hellcats finished second. The Meteors failed to place at a subsequent battle in April, although Chaplain Heuer reported that, judging from the "sustained applause so terrific that the m.c. practically had to call out the fire department to cool their enthusiasm," they should have gotten 2nd or 3rd. A dance featuring the Meteors at Fuller USO was "best dance ever planned by the recreation Dept." (34)

"We were playing a Battle of Swing in Honolulu the day Roosevelt died," Roger Holt recalled.

Harris in his columns maintained that Reeves' band, the Jungleers, was the best and that the Meteors was second best on the island. Some of the Meteors insist that they could not have won band competitions, even though they were better, because to do so would have shown up the professional jazzmen. Regardless, though, when it came time for ceremonial music, B-1 was always the first pick. (35)

"We were the only regimental band in Hawaii," said Parsons, "and we were Admiral's favorite."

Vice Admiral Robert Ghormley, who was Commander of the 14th Naval District from December 1944 to December 1945, visited Manana for a morning review and inspections on August 12, 1944, spending according to his log over an hour on base. He brought B-1 to at least one major show in Honolulu, to celebrate the 100th birthday anniversary of Henry Berger, who composed the Hawaiian national anthem and was known as the "father of Hawaiian music." The German born Berger was sent to Hawaii in 1872 by Kaiser Wilhelm after King Kamehameha V asked him for a Prussian bandmaster. Berger subsequently led the Royal Hawaiian Band until 1915. He conducted over 32,000 band concerts, arranged more than 1,000 Western musical compositions and 200 Hawaiian songs, and composed 75 Hawaiian melodies, more than 500 marches, and over 100 other compositions and arrangements, including "Hawai'i Pono'i," formerly the national anthem and now Hawaii's state song. For this centennial show, B-1 was one of several Army and Navy bands that joined with the Royal Hawaiian band for a "massed band concert" of "typical Berger music" from the "monarchy period" as well as Hawaiian music, marches, and standard classical pieces. Later in the evening, Ghormley had the Manana Meteors perform at Admirals' Row, the main officers club. It would be through Ghormley, Parsons recalled, that bandsmen would finally get promotions, at least five as high as musician first class: Parsons, William Cole, Herbert Reeder, James Morgan, and Melvin Wall. "Judge [Parsons] should have gotten chief," Holt said. "And more of us should have been upgraded." (36)

"It was very unfair," Parsons agreed.

Because of their extensive performing schedule, B-1 bandsmen had little free time, so their experience with the lively club scene in Honolulu was primarily in performances. The swing bands got gigs in the few USO clubs that catered to blacks, including the Rainbow Club in Honolulu and Fuller's USO in Pearl City; they had repeat engagements at the Lihue-Isenburg and Kalaheo USO clubs on Kauai Island. As in Chapel Hill, they often played for the entertainment of white officers or enlisted men. Some clubs were established in the estates of rich locals for use as officers clubs and R&R centers, and the bands would occasionally get gigs in these, too. Their best were at the Royal Hawaiian Hotel, which had been taken over by the Navy and where enlisted men slept free in "cot-crowded luxury suites." The Breakers, the Navy's rec center on Waikiki Beach, opened in December 1942 and drew up to 4,400 men a day. The "most interesting" of all bars, it had a "more robust atmosphere" than the usual rec spot, with a pavilion overlooking the ocean, a beer garden, and excellent sandwiches and burgers. The "most strenuous jitterbugging seen anywhere" took place on its dance floor. The Army's Maluhia Club, famous for its excellent dance band, the Pipers, and Banyan Court, with an open wall facing Waikiki Beach, were also popular recreation spots. The Maluhia often hosted 10,000 men a day—it packed in 24,700 for a Bob Hope show. (37)

Hotel Street, in the corner of Honolulu's Chinatown, drew over 30,000 servicemen and war workers a day for its attractions: bars, tattoo parlors, and brothels, where 250,000 men a month paid for prostitute services. But it was not the best place for drinking, with its long lines, "terrible liquor" and a 4-drink maximum that was usually served at once, an implicit urging to patrons to "guzzle and move on." Honolulu led the world in tattooing during World War II, with 33 tattoo artists, all Filipinos, at eight Hotel Street parlors needling 300–500 tattoos a day. Brothels were open from 9 a.m. to 2 p.m. daily, with often a 2-hour wait. Workers in them made $30-40,000 a year; madams cleared $150,000 annually. (38)

"Hotel Street?" recalled Huey Lawrence. "Oh, yeah. Now we didn't go down there. But they'd be lined up like you were waiting for a show. Ella Park, she had one of the houses, and we wrote a song about her place. That's where they all lined up to get in. Right next to it, you had a place where the medics cleaned you up. But we stayed away from those places."

When not entertaining, the bandsmen had leave time in the evenings on base and at least one day a week free time to roam. "We had liberty once a week," said Charles Woods. "We'd go to town maybe, to a restaurant, then a USO, but it was still usually a Navy setting. It seemed just as segregated."

Huey Lawrence added: "I was careful there. We all were. Your life was at stake. You didn't want to be out at night. You had to be able to catch a jeep back at Schofield Barracks, and they'd put you off at Manana, but you wanted to get home before dark." Because of their experiences in the civilian world, though, some preferred to spend their leave in their barracks, playing cards. "I think I learned every game of cards there is," said Jones.

"A lot of the guys played cards," said Nathaniel Morehead, "but I liked going down to Hickham Field, talking with the pilots. They were all real nice. I'd chat with them, sometimes fly around the island with one." William Gibson and the Carlson Brothers— three of the bandsmen who had earned pilot's licenses before enlisting —took it a step farther. "Sometimes me and the Carlsons would bootleg a plane," Gibson said. "We weren't supposed to fly, of course, and we could have gotten shot down easily, by our own men, but we'd fly below the radar screen in these little robot planes they used for target practice."

"I never flew with the Carlsons," Morehead said, "but I rode a motorcycle with John Carlson one time. I begged him to let me off, and I never touched one since."

::::

After staying safe and out of trouble, B-1 bandsmen always made music their primary concern, and they appreciated talent wherever they saw it. Abe Thurman recalled that there were a lot of good white musicians and bands in Hawaii. Ray Anthony's band, he said, also played regularly at the Breakers, where first Artie Shaw and then Sammy Donohue had previously been posted with their bands. But these were entertainment bands.

B-1 and its swing bands also played live radio shows and made recordings. "We'd play radio shows once or twice a month," Huey Lawrence said. "They had them every week, and they alternated us [the Meteors] with Ray Anthony's band and with the Hellcats.

They'd be at the YMCA, or sometimes the Royal Hawaiian Hotel or the Breakers, and they'd be remote broadcasts, with us on the stage and with a live audience."

The Manana Meteors also played at the 1945 Hawaiian AAU Outdoor Swimming Championship and other athletic competitions. The most unusual contest at which they performed was a 1945 All-Star baseball game, played between National and American League players who were serving in the Pacific Theater—an especially interesting contest given that this was the only year in the history of Major League Baseball that it did not sponsor its own all-star game. The Hawaii all-star game, sponsored by the 14th Naval District Athletic Association, featured Jonny Pesky and future hall-of-famers Stan Musial, Bob Lemon, Ted Williams (who had trained at the UNC pre-flight school), and Billy Herman as coach for the National League. (39)

Bandsmen recall the Meteors making several recordings for KGU-Honolulu, a member of the Armed Forces Radio Service, which was begun in May 1942. By March 1945, the AFRS network included 154 stations throughout the world, including stations on Saipan, Manila, New Guinea, Guam, Ulithi, Eniwetok, West New Guinea, New Zealand, Noumea, and Guadalcanal as well as KGU. They were divided into the Mosquito Network, in the southwest Pacific, and the Jungle Network, in the central Pacific. Stations received packets of programming that contained an average of 126 separate programs, most specially produced at the Hollywood headquarters. A live performance for KGU in August 1945 at the Tradewinds Theater preceded the screening of *Wonder Man*, starring Danny Kaye. (40)

The full band also made some recordings. One made onstage at the Army-Navy USO Club included "Salute to the Services," Ferde Grofe's "Over There Fantasie," Irving Berlin's "Blue Skies," Ella Fitzgerald's "I'm Making Believe," "Night Special" with featured solos by Arthur Guy on drums and Walter Carlson on trumpet, "God Bless America" with the glee club, and "Navy Blue and Gold." Parsons recalled another: "We spent three or four days making a record at Hickham Field. They let me bring in a couple of singers out of the Great Lakes." Parsons believed that ultimately these recordings were to be distributed via the AFRS. Only one B-1-related recording, however, made by the second swing band, the Moonglowers, for radio station KGU, appears to have survived the war. (41)

Wray Herring sneaked the Moonglowers record home after the war. "We weren't supposed to take anything off the island," he recalled, "but I figured it was worth it to try." Because of that recording and Wray Herring's scrapbook, the Moonglowers are a better documented dance band than the Meteors. Otto Harris and the Moonglowers played their first show on October 8, 1944, opening their program at a BOQ (Batchelor Officer Quarter) with the Ella Fitzgerald hit "Things Ain't What They Used To Be," arranged by Herring. Two days later, they performed at the Fuller USO Club in Pearl City a concert for wounded soldiers "who had just returned from the battle fronts." So popular were their performances at Fuller USO that by October 25, they were back for their 3rd engagement there, at which "they proved to the public that they could 'jump' as well as play sweet music." The Moonglowers performance schedule for April 1945 has them playing for a quiz program on base, before movies three times, at a civilian housing function, and at a Naval housing party, and at Camp Catlin. (42)

For a brief period, B-1 was conducted by Orrin Tucker, a minor big band leader of the day who had joined the Navy, commissioned as a lieutenant. Tucker made his name "playing dance music for the middle-aged crowd," a far cry from what interested the jazz-oriented B-1 fellows. "Tucker tried to take over," said Roger Holt. "He saw a group of talented musicians and he thought up some corny music, arrangements that he'd played with his wife." (43)

"They were really corny arrangements," Thomas Gavin agreed. "When he told us he had two trunks more coming, I volunteered for the fighting zone. But he left as fast he came. While he was there, though, he took us on two or three very high-class engagements. 'Oh Johnny, Oh Johnny Oh!" was his big song (in 1939), and people called him that. They were all coming up to get his autograph. But fortunately he got sent elsewhere. His style wasn't suited for us, or for the people we played for."

"I got Captain's Mess out of that situation," recalled Parsons. "Arrested. I threw him out of my rehearsal and told him to go to hell. I threw him out and he went on over to the administration building, to Grady Avant, and over came some SPs and took me in custody." But, in the end, Parsons resumed control of the band, after pointing out the likelihood, as in Chapel Hill when the outside white bandleader McReynolds had tried to take over, that the band might play off-key at just the wrong moment.

Other celebrities B-1 performed with while in Hawaii included Bob Crosby, Jimmy Durante, and Boris Karloff. Bob Crosby, Bing's younger brother, led successful big bands in the 1930s and early '40s. As World War II opened, his band was depleted by the draft, which in turn got him. He spent his own military tour leading the Bob Cats for the Marines in the Pacific. Durante traveled to Hawaii performing with Garry Moore as part of the Camel Comedy Caravan. Karloff brought his traveling production of *Arsenic and Old Lace* to the Tradewinds Theater—where B-1 bandsmen had planted bamboo and painted the seats—at Manana Barracks in June 1945. After the show, he was photographed autographing dollar bills for the sailors of Manana. Karloff had made his Broadway debut, playing himself, in the 1941 production of *Arsenic* and had subsequently created his own company for traveling productions. The band played before the play was presented, like it would prior to movie screenings. (44)

"They were really good musicians," Ensign Neece said. "The measure of how good they were was this constant demand for them. They had a reputation when I got there as being the sharpest outfit on the island. If the Navy brass wanted a big ceremony down at Pearl Harbor, we'd get a call: 'could we get your band to come Tuesday morning?' So I was in charge of scheduling them for such events, and they kept a busy schedule, a very busy schedule."

In addition to practicing, by the time Neece arrived, bandsmen also were performing nightly on base. "Once we were showing movies every night," said Neece, "we must have shown every B, C, and D movie ever made. So the movies were pretty bad. It was the band that made those movie nights. Before the movie, we'd let the swing band play. It wasn't the same guys each night. But they had a half-hour before the movie to play, and believe me, guys would be jitterbugging in the aisles. They'd be up on the seats jitterbugging when the band would really get going."

"One night," Neece added, "they got to playing on a song—I asked them later what it was, and I'd never heard of it, it was called 'The Honeydripper'—and they really got going that night, like a jam session. They'd pass it around, from the trombone to the trumpet to the sax for their solos. They went on and on and on, and the half-hour lapses. The guy in charge of the movie asks the officer in charge what to do, and he tells him to turn off all the lights to get them to stop playing. But that doesn't stop them. So he came and asked me what to do. I said to tell the operator to start the movie. They're still hitting it. After the movie came on, they slowly faded out. But that was really something, that night, that I've never forgotten."

It was not unusual for the full band to perform at an event that would also feature different small ensembles broken out from the whole to perform specialty numbers. One happy hour at Manana featured the full band, glee club, the Meteors, a visiting novelty vocalist, and a jitterbug contest. At the dedication of Manana's newly renovated theater, the full band performed Parsons' original march, "Drums are Rolling." Featured B-1 performers included "King Cole," B-1's William H. "Lanky" Cole performing a jazz medley, and two quartets: the Harmonizers, with Filmore Haith, and the Tunesters, with Thomas Gavin, Melvin Thomas, Charles Woods, and Maurice "Stubby" Miles, who joined B-1 after it arrived in Hawaii. A comedy skit titled "Expect Anything" was performed by Simeon Holloway, Otto Harris, and James Scott. (45)

In addition to Maurice Miles, three other musicians joined B-1 in Hawaii: Melvin Thomas, Robert Carter, and Robert Holland. Carter and Thomas were from St. Louis; Holland and Miles, from Ohio. Thomas had been playing with the Seaman Raiders, along with Calvin "Boom Boom" Manuel, from New Orleans, who never officially joined B-1 but played drums and sang with the Moonglowers. Manuel was a student in New Orleans of Valmore Victor, who taught elementary school band in New Orleans from 1928-53, counting among his pupils Ellis Marsalis, Thomas Jefferson, and Earl Turbinton. After the war, Manuel would enlist in the Army, where he headlined the 1947 traveling show "Operation Happiness." Carter had been re-assigned to B-1 after he and his Great

Lakes-trained bandmates were arrested for refusing to clean toilets at their posting in St. Louis. Their band was broken up and its members sent back to Great Lakes for re-assignment. (46)

Performance programs were varied; no surviving documents indicate that they were ever repeated. A Happy Hour show featured more pop than jazz while a performance for the Sesquicentennial of Naval Supply consisted of military and patriotic music. For National Negro Week (Feb. 18–24, 1945), B-1's dance bands played nightly, on some nights with touring variety shows and other acts such as the Sixteen Naturals and the Schofield Modernaires. The week's grand finale featured the full band and glee club, speakers, and the singing of "Lift Every Voice and Sing." The VJ Day program at Manana had the band back to work performing jazz prior to the evening's movie. (47)

Manana hosted a range of such entertainments reviewed by Chaplain Heuer in the *Mananan*. A traveling production of *The Man Who Came to Dinner* featured its author, Moss Hart, as one of the characters. Variety shows were especially popular, and the USO services provided many of them. "Shoot the Works" included a juggler who worked with bowling pins, rubber balls and cigar boxes; a "Truth or Consequences" show also included the Meteors; a variety show from Schofield Barracks was highlighted by a quiz show with Parries and his Quizzits—and the Meteors, who also played shows at Manana that featured the Honolulu Men's Glee Club and a Hula Show with the USO's "7 o'clock detail." The "delovely" women vocalists with the Modernaires, also from Schofield, "created in us a sensation hard to satisfy." Even the best of the entertainment bands often had side acts: at least one visit by Ray Anthony and the Dolphins included a magician and a comedian. (48)

Documenting the specific number of these variety shows is likely impossible, but programs collected by bandsmen Wray Herring and Clarence Yourse help give a good idea of their content. One such show, called "Carlson Presents Musical Varieties," was staged at Manana's open-air theater on July 10, 1945. The program includes an Otto Harris drawing of singing sailors. The Meteors opened and closed the show, which featured a variety of acts by bandsmen as well as other sailors stationed at Manana.

Among the Meteors' numbers were "Buck Special," an original composition by Thomas "Buck" Gavin, and a medley of pop tunes arranged by Walter Carlson. The skit "A Visit to Zoot Suit City" starred B-1's Simeon Holloway, James Scott, Otto Harris, and Abe Thurman. "I was the interpreter," recalled Thurman, who said that Holloway scripted their routines, which were heavy on jive talking. "I'll never forget one of them. He'd say he's going to put his deuce of benders under the hash holder, and I'd say, 'What he means is he's going to bend his knees beneath the table.'" (49)

Harris's "Musically Speaking" column often included a bit of jive, such as this number for the first issue after the Japanese surrender: "Pops, the issue that jumped off some brights ago was really solid. The little squares in squint-land finally went down for the count. It'll be a killer when we studs fall onto the turf again in those fine drapes. Some of you will blow your top jumping from lush pads to frolic kiffs and eyeballing the frantic chicks. It shouldn't be much longer so dig this scribe I'm putting down and you'll be in the know, understand!" (50)

B-1 was assigned to Manana because it had become the only barracks housing black sailors, but like in Norfolk, it was not an easy fit. "The band was always an anomaly," said Neece. "Here they were, a bunch of educated musicians placed in with what was basically a bunch of cargo handlers—tote that barge, lift that bale!" While B-1 marched, practiced, played, and shined their instruments as their work detail, their neighbors were engaged in heavy labor, or the brief respite from it. "It was an awkward situation," Neece added. "Nothing that the band had experienced would have prepared them for life at Manana. What they had in Chapel Hill was almost ideal for someone in the Navy. Some of them didn't even have to stay in barracks, which is unheard of. Then, here they are, stuck in the middle of this cane field." His general population, Neece pointed out, was sufficiently uneducated that Manana operated an elementary school to teach basic literacy skills. But his workforce also included college-educated men whose entry into the Navy had been governed by the old system that allowed blacks access only to positions of labor and service.

Service under Grady Avant's leadership was also rough, and his racist nature has been well documented. "Grady Avant ran a concentration camp," Huey Lawrence said. "They had shotgun guards patrolling. They had barbed wire fence up on the pretense he was protecting people from coming in, but the way it leaned in, we knew better. There were two gates, both manned by armed guards. He wouldn't let blacks have beards. He said we looked like monkeys, so a couple of us had to get special permission. I had a goatee because it kept the bottom of my lip from getting chapped. But he was doing the things he knew. He finally slapped a guy— not one of ours—and they broke him down in rank."

Avant, William Skinner recalled, "knew only one thing blacks could do was sing 'Onward Christian Soldiers.' That's all the colored people did down there in Mississippi, he thought."

"But," said Calvin Morrow, "all of the officers were bad. Anytime somebody was sent to be in charge of an all-black camp, it was like being sent down, like going to the boondocks. But we learned to deal with it: if I knew you're an SOB, I learned to deal with it."

Ensign Neece agreed: "Nobody wanted to command a black unit." Yet, Southerners like himself were often placed in charge, because, the Navy believed, they would have had experience dealing with blacks. Citing the number of racial incidents occurring both stateside and in the Pacific, Neece added, "Everybody was afraid there'd be trouble, and then you'd be responsible." Neece, a white man, had been raised near Greensboro by Quaker parents who had early instilled in him a respect for all people. "So I had a different background than a lot of the other white officers," especially the Southern ones.

Avant's racist nature is also recalled by Jesse W. Arbor, one of the first 13 African Americans commissioned as an officer in the Navy. Arbor, the senior black officer at Manana, won a poker game from Avant with a fourth deuce concealed. Avant said, "I should have known there was a goddamned nigger in the woodpile" but got no response from Arbor. The game soon broke up and Avant came to apologize to Arbor, who pretended not to have heard the insult: "He knew I was lying, so it hurt him worse than it hurt me because he had to live with it." (51)

"The entire personnel" at Manana hated Avant, reported Lester Granger, the executive secretary of the National Urban League who was sent to visit black Navy installations in 1944-45 to help implement the Navy's "Guide to the Command of Negro Naval Personnel." Granger, an attorney, and several black newspapermen traveled over 50,000 miles and visited 67 naval installations, meeting with commanding officers and enlisted men alike. They sought to "observe conditions among Negro Naval and Marine personnel, to determine their morale and to appraise the application of the Navy's new and better policy as it relates to the integration of Negro servicemen into an expanded Naval service." The "Guide" he was trying to implement showed how far, at least in theory, the Navy had come: "The Navy accepts no theories of racial differences in inborn ability but expects that every man wearing its uniform be trained and used in accordance with his maximum individual capacity determined on the basis of individual performance." Because he visited Manana near the end of his tour, he had ample comparative data to assert that Avant "carried on the most cruel, discriminatory administration...possible, ordering extremely brutal discipline. After striking an enlisted man with a 'missile,' he shouted, 'This is the first time I've hit a nigger since I left Mississippi.'" It was Avant's order that brought barbed wire and guards to the barracks, and under his leadership, no leaves were granted to officers or enlisted men. One bandsman complained about their bread, said Skinner. "He said 'how come the white boys always got fresh bread and we don't have any.' Word got back that we were complaining about it and Avant wanted to know who it was complaining. He asked us to tell. Parsons said, 'These men will die and go to hell before they'll tell. You might as well put us all in the brig.' So he said he'd think about what to do about it overnight, but we never heard anymore about it." (52)

Granger visited Manana for a week around the end of the war, where he got from the men there "an honest forthright conviction of what has been unfair and unjust in the old navy policy and the subversion by some base commanders of the present more enlightened one." Avant was subsequently transferred from Manana and replaced with Lt. Cmdr. George D. Stern, from Ohio. He had served formerly at Camp Robert Smalls at Great Lakes, so he was prepared to deal "with the special problems created by the very nature of an essentially all-Negro service unit." (53)

A premature radio announcement during the evening of August 13, 1914 of the Japanese surrender led to a spontaneous half-hour celebration that transformed Pearl Harbor into "a mass of color—red, green and white" fireworks produced from flare guns and tracers fired from ships and highlighted with "scores of huge searchlights" crisscrossing the sky. To coordinate the celebration everyone knew was imminent, local officials quickly announced plans that covered six possible scenarios—most based on what time of day the announcement came— for when it was finally and officially known that the terms of surrender had been accepted: this siren announcement would immediately close all businesses except restaurants, taverns and "essential public services" so that celebrations could begin. (54)

The next day, at 1:32 p.m., the siren blasts began, "announcing the arrival of peace." A "wave of exhilaration swept Honolulu," which went "gaily and mildly mad!" Businesses closed immediately, and impromptu parades "sprang up everywhere," with servicemen and civilians crammed into jeeps barely able to negotiate through streets jammed with revelers. The sirens were quickly drowned out by the "thousands of auto horns and sirens and screaming crowds," church bells and steamboat whistles. Firecrackers, which had been banned since war's beginning, "sprang from nowhere. They banged, popped, and cracked throughout the night and far into early morning hours." Countless small parades formed spontaneously, "dwindled away and then reformed again." At the Breakers, the house band "immediately formed and marched" to a nearby park where they played "California, Here I Come" over and over. The officer in charge ordered free beer and hamburgers "on the house for the rest of the afternoon," expecting "to dispense thousands of dollars worth of beer before the day was over." Celebrations continued throughout the night, with the understanding that the real celebration would not come until the peace terms had been signed and President Truman had proclaimed V-J Day. (55)

By far the biggest event B-1 ever played for was the enormous VJ day parade staged in Honolulu as the highlight of the 3-day Labor Day weekend victory celebration in Hawaii. "Never before have these islands seen such a parade," the *Mananan* reported.

Over 200,000 spectators packed the streets of Honolulu to witness the spectacle. "They got every marching unit they could get," said Abe Thurman. "We must have marched for three hours that day. I think we marched through every street in Honolulu. I know it wore the drummers out. We didn't use but two snare drummers and a bass drum, and we really worked them that day." Newspaper reports actually indicate the parade was longer than Thurman remembered: "After three hours, units were still passing the reviewing stand." (56)

More than 30,000 marched in the parade, over 300 airplanes "flashed by at tree-top height," and more than 15 bands performed, including Army and Marine bands, two other Navy bands, a Filipino band, the Royal Hawaiian band, and Chinese, Samoan, and USO bands. B-1 was "acclaimed for top honors by the crowd" and praised by one Honolulu columnist: "None was more of a crowd-pleaser than the Navy's Negro band from Manana Barracks." One of more than 80 military and civilian dignitaries serving as bandstand reviewers, Brig. Gen. L. W. T. Waller, Jr., Commandant of Marines in the 14th Naval District agreed: "They were the outstanding unit in the parade." The general added that, based on his observation and comments of others from the reviewing stand, B-1 was "the best example of appearance and military bearing in the parade." (57)

"When I got out," recalled William Skinner, "I wrote this essay for Kate Smith. She was sponsoring a contest on 'How I won the war.' Mine went something like this: 'I won the war with my clarinet playing a frantic spiel. As we paraded down the street the cats began to dance a jig. The cats was jumping like mad as I put down a mad deuce of bendex on my clarinet.' She sent me a check for $500!"

B-1 and its swing bands continued to perform through August 1945. Their last big show was a Cavalcade of Bands, staged in Manana's Tradewinds Theater, on August 31, with the Airbase Aces, the Barbers Point Hellcats, the Ammunition Depot Skyhawks, the Aiea Blackhawks, the Jungleers, and "Manana's own Meteors and Moonglowers." Soon after, the fellows began mustering out, married men first, based on the military's point system for priority in returning home. By October, a new 17-piece band, the Melody Masters, had replaced B-1. In his column, Otto Harris kept regular tabs on the B-1 bandsmen accruing the most points towards going home: "How many points you got? That's the beginning of every cat's spiel nowadays, ole man, it's really tough for the studs who don't have 44. Yours truly has 41 1/2 and if the system vips a vop, I'll be treading back to the land of the stars and stripes. Let's hope it jumps down within the next thirty—then, maybe many a cat on the compound will be able to give the "Rock" the bye-bye sign. Won't that be something?" (58)

Joe "Frog" Wilson announced in his first "Musically Speaking" column, in the October 30, 1945 *Mananan*, that Otto Harris was "on the shorts, nearly gone," that the Hellcats had been split up "by the point system," and the Jungleers were making one last tour of the states before splitting up. (59)

The last B-1 bandsman, however, would not leave Hawaii until early 1946. Most, like Huey Lawrence, received the Asiatic-Pacific Campaign Medal, a Good Conduct Medal, and the World War II Victory Medal. (60)

B-1 marches
in Honolulu's
VJ-Day parade.

U.S. Navy photo
courtesy of
James B. Parsons

facing page

One of several small
ensembles broken out
from B-1 in Hawaii
was the Tunesters,
photographed on stage at
the Tradewinds Theater,
Manana.
L to R: Charles Woods,
Thomas Gavin, Walter
Carlson, Melvin Thomas,
a stevedore who never
officially joined B-1 but
performed regularly with
several of its ensembles.
U.S. Navy photo courtesy of
James B. Parsons

Self-portrait of
Stafford W. Evans
contemplating the
number of points
he has
accumulated
towards
discharge.
Evans letter to
Amaza Meredith,
8 Oct. 1945
Amaza Lee
Meredith Papers
Virginia State U.

Evans sketch of
Manana Meteors
performing at
VJ Day
celebration.
Drawing from
Mananan
24 Aug. 1945: 5
Courtesy of
James C. Yourse, Jr.

Coming Home

"I thought things would have changed,
but it was the same."

— WILLIAM SKINNER

Most of B-1 became part of the 65,000 African Americans who returned, after World War II, to live in the South. By ones and twos and threes, they made their ways back home to North Carolina, where they found a world whose social structure had not changed at all while they were away. "When we got to Norfolk on our discharge," Bennie Laikin remembered, "we went to a café. The Navy was buying us lunch. Lanky Cole knew what was happening—he never sat down. But I went on over and sat down ready to eat me some ham and eggs. I was the little fool, though. The guy there said, 'I'm sorry, we don't served colored people in here.' That really hit us. I felt real bad. We had to go down two blocks. But that stuff stays with you. It really surprised me. Things seemed to have changed in the Navy. But it was the same back home." (1)

"When I got out," said William Skinner, "I thought things would have changed, but it was the same. We rode at the back of the bus, lived in segregated houses."

"When I was discharged," recalled Calvin Morrow, "I came back by myself, I came across the country with an integrated group, mainly white sailors. When we got to Norfolk, we were all put in the same barracks. I was part of all these guys, see, and being a little light skinned, and it was night—well, the next morning, when they saw me, they came up and said we want you to go over there with this group, and they carried me to a place where there was nothing but blacks. Walked me out of the mess where the German prisoners were eating with the other whites and took me to where the blacks ate. Norfolk after the war, it was still the same."

Messman Carl Clark was bitterly disappointed with the racism still dominant in Norfolk, where he was transferred after the war.

He described a local police scheme to secure black sailors as laborers for local farmers, "a form of modern slavery and political trickery," and narrowly avoided being gunned down by a white policeman. "It is unfortunate," he wrote, "that of all the negative things that have happened to my family and myself in our lives, the most vivid in my memory is Norfolk." (2)

B-1's Nathaniel Morehead said: "I expected to see more of a change than there was. As far as segregation was concerned, I was a little disappointed. As far as the acceptance of people, you expected to find people more receptive, more congenial, in view of the sacrifices service people had made. But we still couldn't go to a theater and sit downstairs.

"One thing, as a child, I always wanted to sit at a counter at Woolworth's and eat a hot dog. But it was so long after we got back that that was possible. To this day, I've never done it. I know in my mind the people today aren't responsible for the sins of yesterday, but something in me just won't let me walk in there and order a hot dog. And it seems like when I was a kid that was just about all I wanted to do."

Skinner concurred: "You remember things like that. Like this man years ago told me he didn't have facilities for niggers. You remember those places, those people. So years later, you might not need to go to the bathroom, but you remember him and you just get your gas someplace else."

Morehead said, "But I was discharged in October and next semester I was back in school, and I began doing the same things. As soon as class ended, I went to work, back at Dudley, helping the janitor clean up. More and more, I thought things were still the same."

Many of the bandsmen, like Morehead, went back to school; others took up trades. Most would eventually wind up with long careers in education. They would be teachers of the young men and women who would eventually integrate North Carolina's lunch counters, including Woolworth's in Greensboro, and school systems—nearly 25 years later—and they would raise children of their own who would graduate from UNC.

"We did a lot for Chapel Hill," Morehead said. "It was still a segregated city. We band members had, to a greater extent, more formal education than most of the black citizens, so we wound up breaking a lot of small barriers in Chapel Hill, in people's attitudes."

"Before us," Calvin Morrow added, "the only image the Navy had of blacks was as servants. Anybody that saw that band, they could say the Navy has made some progress. We could be seen as a role model, so others could say, I can be something more than just a servant. Some of the white sailors'd see our music insignia and wouldn't believe it, but we broke the barrier."

B-1 cut the bamboo used to line the Tradewinds Theater at Manana

The Mananan *illustration by Stafford W. Evans, for "Bamboo Story," 6 Aug. 1945: 6. Courtesy of James C. Yourse, Jr.*

The Rhythm Vets at

WBIG radio

in Greensboro, 1949

L to R:

Jehovah Guy,

Raymond Pettiford,

Richard Jones,

Otto Harris,

Thomas Gavin,

Clarence Yourse,

Walter Carlson,

Jatha Coward,

and Winston Childs

Afterword

After the war, many of the B-1 bandsmen and fellow Navy vets with A&T ties who had trained at Great Lakes and subsequently served as musicians returned to Greensboro, some for school, others for work or to look for it. For many, Greensboro had become their home. The serious musicians from both Navy experiences brought together an interesting mix of musical influences that formed the basis for an exceptional local jazz scene. Nationally, the big bands themselves had shrunken in size but not so much in the sound they sought. The B-1 vets, with their classical and martial music backgrounds, had performed in dance bands that played chart-based material like those big bands, with ample room for solos. The Great Lakes-trained fellows had been heavily influenced by the Chicago bop scene that used smaller combos and relied even more on improvisation. Regardless of where they trained or were stationed, by the time the Greensboro and A&T veterans got home, they were all ready to play.

The Navy vets who stayed active as musicians around Greensboro after the war worked two music scenes. The one for fun jammed at the Artists Guild, a private club, as well as weekend nights on the A&T campus. The other, for funds, was built around the big-band style dance bands scaled down in size and exemplified in local bands such as Max Westerband's and the Rhythm Vets who played for the most part covers of popular R&B songs. The Rhythm Vets would continue playing, with various personnel with A&T and military connections, into the 1960s. The ones who recorded in Greenville, NC one long day and night in July 1947 a soundtrack for Lord-Warner Pictures' musical comedy featurette "Pitch a Boogie Woogie" were B-1 veterans Otto Harris and Walter Carlson on trumpet, Thomas Gavin and Raymond Pettiford on saxophone, Clarence Yourse on piano, and Charles Woods on bass; Great Lakes-trained Lou Donaldson joined them on sax and Jehovah Guy on drums (his brother Arthur played drums in B-1 as well as with the Rhythm Vets). But it was a fluid band, with an ever-ready supply of excellent musicians prepared to

fill in when one or another couldn't make it. Among the most active were B-1 vets Huey Lawrence and Abe Thurman on trumpet
and James Scott on bass, and Great Lakes-trained Carl Foster on
piano, Charlie Morrison and Donnell Cooper on sax, and vocalist
Jake Coward, who also was a popular actor on the A&T and Bennett campuses.

With the opening in Greensboro in 1946 of the after-hours
music club the Artists Guild, Greensboro became a popular place
for traveling musicians to lay over and jam. The Guild was started by visual artists who decorated it with plush carpet and big
New York scenes on the ballroom walls and murals all through
it. "They had African and Spanish and French rooms all in native decor," said Carl Foster, pianist in the house band. "It was
the Mecca between New York and Atlanta, all those musicians
wanting to stay overnight for a chance to play the Greensboro
scene. About 1 a.m. they'd start gathering and we'd jam till 5:00,
5:30 in the morning." Not every night, of course—it depended on
who was in town: Johnny Hodges, Illinois Jacquet, Bud Powell,
J.J. Johnson, Ray Nance, Lionel Hampton, one time Duke Ellington and another time a young John Coltrane who got tricked by
a prearranged chord change on "Cherokee," stumbled on his solo
and put his horn down.

But gradually the young musicians entered their careers, and
by the time B-1 started its biennial reunions in 1956, most of the
fellows also had begun families. As the years sped by and fewer
were left to gather, the reunions became yearly events, but I did
not learn of B-1 until 1985, after a Greenville musician, Bill Shepard, showed me a copy of "Pitch a Boogie Woogie": he pulled several cans of reels of 35 mm nitrate out from a box in his hall clos-
et in a huge, rambling house that only recently, in 2013, burned
down. The American Film Institute would subsequently restore
the film, made with a local cast and two traveling black vaudeville
troupes, by two white brothers from nearby Washington, NC. It
had a soundtrack of original songs written and composed by William Lord, John Warner's brother who was born Walter Warner
and lived in New York in the late 1920s and '30s. He reportedly
performed in the chorus in blackface on Broadway in *Green Pastures* in 1930 and made national news in 1947, just prior to return-

ing South to join his brother in starting their film company, for getting arrested for bringing a black musician up to his New York City hotel room to work on numbers. Lord, who adopted his new name in a Rosicrucian ceremony in the late 1920s, died in Tarboro in 1981, just a few miles from Greenville, where I had that year come to teach English at East Carolina University.

John Warner in the 1930s had run the Plaza Theatre, in Greenville's thriving black business district centered around Albemarle Avenue, only a couple of blocks from where Shep showed me the reels of "Pitch." As he learned to shoot film, Warner began making his own advertisements and short, silent neighborhood scenes he'd show prior to his features. It was in the Plaza that he filmed the Rhythm Vets trying to sync Lord's musical compositions to the lindy hopping, eccentric tap dancing, chorus routines, and grand finale they watched on screen as Warner recorded them over and over again. "It was like playing to the dance," Thomas Gavin recalled, "instead of dancing to the music, we were playing to what the dancers did." Some of the dancers—the Count and Harriet and Cleophus Lyons—had been regulars with Whitey's Lindy hoppers. They were in Greenville as part of Irvin C. Miller's Brown Skin Models, which had been stranded in the Carolinas and rescued by E.S. "Fat" Winstead and his Mighty Minstrels. The chorus numbers in the film are performed by ladies from these two troupes; the orchestra that appears in the film, Don Dunning and His Rhythm All-Stars, was Winstead's. Winstead was white, Irvin C. Miller one of the best-known African-American producers of stage and traveling theater shows from the 1910s up until World War II. By the late 1940s, though, it was hard to keep a show on the road, and his had broken down in North Carolina, where it was rescued by Winstead, who ran a traveling vice show behind the scenes at his small town tent shows.

"Pitch" and all its backgrounds seemed interesting enough to write a book about it, and that's what I started out to do, with a chapter on B-1. But it was a complicated story locally, and the more I learned of its entertainment contexts, the denser they became, too. Some locals didn't like to think about Warner, his theaters and his films—he had, as was not uncommon in small towns of the South, I found out, a sort of second family that he kept in the

Albemarle Avenue neighborhood. And the film itself, with blacks performing some routines in blackface, was horrifying for some contemporary African-American scholars to behold.

By the time I started researching "Pitch," the Warners were dead, as was most of the cast. But most of the Vets were still living, and in the course of developing a UNC-TV documentary about "Pitch," I became well acquainted with several of them. As I learned more about their Navy service, it became increasingly clear that theirs was a story of much greater significance for its unveiling of a previously unrealized achievement in American and Civil Rights history, though not nearly as salacious as that of "Pitch," which also features as part of its back story Most Wanted criminals, counterfeiting and money laundering, drug smuggling, and rescues from 1930s slave farms.

B-1's story has gone through several transformations over too many years, and its publication, finally, comes too late to read for most of the men it's about. First, it was a monograph patterned after Samuel Floyd's *The Great Lakes Experience*. Then it was a heavily illustrated history and then a larger narrative, with chapters instead of sections on each of B-1's periods of service, first with full academic documentation, MLA style, then without it to make it better suited for a general audience. Each version proved unacceptable to the various publishers to whom it was offered. No one, it seemed, thought it a book that could sell—at best it might make an interesting article.

The Forgotten First is my attempt at putting B-1's story into several historical perspectives, with one aspect that has stayed true in all its versions, its North Carolina and A&T points of view.

It could never have been completed without the enthusiastic assistance of so many outstanding men and their families, who were patient with my questions and ignorance of their experiences. They have all been gracious in accepting me into their homes, and my life has been transformed along the way by having known them.

—Alex Albright
Fountain, NC
June 10, 2013

Rhythm Vets reunion
concert, Feb. 8, 1986,
at repremiere of
"Pitch a Boogie Woogie,"
at East Carolina University
L to R:
Carl Foster,
Charles Woods,
Thomas Gavin,
Lou Donaldson,
Abe Thurman,
Walter Carlson, and
Richard Jones.
Not pictured performers:
Jehovah Guy on drums
and Huey Lawrence, who
also played trumpet at
the reunion concert.
Photo by Alex Albright

Notes

Documentation for *The Forgotten First* is with a hybrid of academic styles. Historical, contextual, and background facts are documented with notes at the end of all paragraphs that use a source other than interviews and correspondence with bandsmen and their contemporaries. Endnote text indicates the sources for these facts in the order in which the sources are used within that paragraph; each citation refers readers to an alphabetically arranged "Works Cited" for full bibliographic information. Some notes also include text that augments the narrative. Sources for informational text included in the notes are indicated by parenthetical citations within that text, again keyed to the "Works Cited."

In direct quotations, original spelling and capitalization have been retained without the intrusion of *sic*. Usage otherwise is consistent with the style manual developed by R.A. Fountain for this project.

Much of this story is told through recollections of the bandsmen and others who knew them during their time of service. A separate bibliographic listing details these telephone and personal interviews and correspondence. Use of these sources is indicated by attributive words such as "said" and is not noted in text of notes.

The author is grateful for corrections of facts and direction towards other relevant sources, which will be noted at www.rafountain.com/navy.

Introduction

Epigram: James B. Parsons often referred to his men as "the best, most talented musicians in North Carolina."

1. Charles D. Chamberlain notes that it was not until well after World War II's end that historians started attaching significance to its impact on the South; by 1982, Morton Sosna was suggesting that it may well have been more important than the Civil War in transforming the region.

2. **McWilliams 6; McWhirter 13; Prattis 360.** McWhirter says racial violence was "rampant" between April and November 1919, and that there are no complete and accurate records of this violence (13).

3. **"World War II Facts"; Greene 11; Duval.**

4. **Chamberlain 17, 38.**

5. **McRae; Foster 381. Over a million African Americans also entered civilian employment between 1940-45. (McWilliams 9)**

6. **Marine commandant Maj. Gen. Thomas Holcomb qtd. in MacGregor. (64) Holcomb also said that the interest of African Americans to join the Navy was an attempt "to break into a club that doesn't want them."**

"Notice of Separation from the U.S. Naval Service" documents for B-1 bandsmen John Gilmer, Wray Herring, Huey Lawrence, and Calvin Morrow confirm
newspaper accounts that establish May 27, 1942 as the date of entry into the
service for the first B-1 bandsmen. Lawrence's official records further verify
that they arrived in Chapel Hill on July 31, 1942, that they departed for Hawaii
on April 24, 1944, and arrived there on May 20, 1944.

In black press reports in mid-1942, enlistments for bandsmen to be trained at
Great Lakes are not often distinguished from enlistments at other ranks, but
the several articles about the early development of training centers there make
clear that the first enlistees at Great Lakes did not complete training until after
B-1 arrived in Chapel Hill for service; see, for example, "104 Men."

7. Finkle 131, 145; "Army Forms"; White qtd. in Finkle 160.

8. MacGregor 66-67; Floyd 1; Knox.

9. "104 Men."

Paul Stillwell's *The Golden Thirteen* includes a photo of Secretary of Navy
Frank Knox looking "none too happy" on giving the oath of enlistment to
29-year-old William Baldwin of Washington, DC, who was celebrated as being
the first black to enlist for general-service rating, even though most of B-1
had enlisted as much as six weeks prior (xxi); Raugh.

10. "Navy Band Reports" *Defender*; "Navy Band Reports" *Courier*; "First
    Colored Navy Band Unit"; "First Navy Band Reports"; "Negro Navy Band
    Parades"; Kanter.

11. "Special Tidewater"; MacGregor 67; "About the Bandsmen"; Rondeau.

12. Bell; Rondeau.

13. Floyd 5.

14. Chief of the Bureau, 26 Feb. 1942; Morison vol. 8, 50; Raugh.

15. Chief of the Bureau, 13 Apr. 1942; Buchanan 310.

Official verification of dates relevant to the creation of B-1 would have been
difficult to ascertain without assistance from an astute researcher at the
National Archives at College Park, MD, where official Navy correspondence
pertaining to the band attached to UNC's pre-flight school was discovered only
when, in conversation, I told him about my interest in the pre-flight schools
and my frustration at finding no Navy records pertaining to them. He knew that
cataloging of Navy archives from World War II had not been completed
and, based on a Bureau of Personnel citation I provided him from B-1

bandsman Huey Lawrence's official Navy file, he was able to guess, accurately, where the records might be. Records for UNC's pre-flight school are among a series of RG files at College Park that pertain exclusively to the establishment and day-to-day operations of the pre-flight schools but which at the time of my visit had not been cataloged. They are rich in details that will ultimately allow someone to construct a much more thorough history of how music and the bands that played it were so integral to the pre-flight schools' training.

The black band stationed at the St. Mary's pre-flight school was comprised of older men, all of whom were already professional musicians when they enlisted. They were required to secure their own lodging. Earl Watkins, for example, found his in Berkeley. (Walsh)

16. Musicians in the Navy "ranked just above" messmen; they were recruited and assigned, like messmen, "using criteria significantly different from those applicable to other ratings." (Miller 326)

    Until 1943, the Navy had three enlisted rates for musicians: bandmaster, first musician; musician 1st class; and musician 2nd class. After 1943, these were chief musician, musician 1st class; musician 2nd class; and musician 3rd class. Before 1943, "bandmaster" was an enlisted rating sometimes used as an informal title that did not necessarily designate officer's rank. The first African-American musician bandmaster to serve at officer rank was George Thompson, who was commissioned in 1990. (Bayes, Letter 5 July 2013)

17. **Graff; MacGregor 66. The messman branch of the Navy included officer's cooks, stewards, and mess attendants. (Miller 325)**

18. **Roosevelt qtd. in MacGregor 61; MacGregor 63, 65.**

19. **Knox qtd. in MacGregor 60; Barnes 58–59.**

20. **White 353; Buck qtd. in White 352.**

Backgrounds: Military, Social, Political and Musical

Epigram: **Ellison 15.**

1. **Binkin 11-12; Vardaman qtd. in McWilliams 10; Wynn 3; MacGregor 4; Wynn 3; Binkin 13.**

2. **Wynn 4; Jackson qtd. in Nelson 9; Binkin 13; Nelson 3.**

3. **MacGregor 4; Wynn 5; Sherman; MacGregor 4; Northrup 10; Nalty 43–44.**

    Wynn, like others, describes the dominant segregationist views of the late 19th and early 20th centuries as being primarily "Southern" (5). Woodward counters that, although the South would eventually be responsible for the solidifying of these views into its Jim Crow world, in the early days of this newly re-discovered racism, the Supreme Court laid the groundwork for Jim Crow in several landmark decisions prior to Plessy v. Ferguson, and Northern liberals joined in defending the "Southern view of race"—that blacks were innately inferior and hopelessly unfit for full participation in "the white man's civilization"—with articles in the nation's leading intellectual magazines. (70–71)

4. **Binkin 15–17; Washington. In his letter, Washington also asks "whether it is the intention of the War Department to enlist additional colored soldiers to take the place of the three companies that were dismissed?"**

At Brownsville, TX, riotous conditions blamed on some black soldiers who could not be identified resulted in the dishonorable discharge without trial of three entire black companies—a total of 167 men. Evidence against them was planted by white citizens. Several of the discharged men were career soldiers with citations for bravery; six had won Medals of Honor. Fourteen were re-instated within a year; in 1972, the records of the other 153 were changed to reflect honorable discharges but with no back pay or allowances. By then, most were dead anyway. (Binkin 16–17)

5. **Northrup 11; Weiss 62; Barnett 482; Wynn 6; Weiss 64, 78; Ambrosius 689–90.**

Wilson was a student while at Johns Hopkins of Herbert Baxter Adams, an ardent supporter of the "Teutonic-germ theory," which held that an "institutional germ" developed in German forests had spread to British lands by Teutonic tribes in the 5th and 6th centuries, from where it was transferred to the U.S. at Jamestown. (Rostar 92) In *Congressional Government*, Wilson's PhD dissertation, which was also published by Johns Hopkins Press, he argued that white Southerners had the right to discriminate against blacks and that the white South's best hope was for limits to the power of Congress and a restoration of states' rights. In *The State* (1889) he argued that only whites were ready for democracy. (Ambrosius 692–93)

One of Wilson's classmates in Adams' class was Thomas Dixon, who would urge Wilson upon his inauguration in 1912 to "draw the color line" within the federal government, which he did "deftly," avoiding for the most part any public controversy while pursuing a white supremacy agenda. (Ambrosius 699)

Perhaps Wilson's greatest contribution to the national resurgence of racism was in his showing of *The Birth of a Nation*, the D.W. Griffith film based on Dixon's book *The Clansman*. Although Ambrosius questions whether the verbal endorsement often ascribed to Wilson was ever uttered, he makes clear that the White

House screening and subsequent one to the Supreme Court justices and congressmen had the two-fold effect of blunting NAACP protests against the film's release and of giving it a much needed publicity boost. (Ambrosius 703–04)

Wilson's race philosophy appears, like Jim Crow legislation itself, rife with contradictions and inconsistencies: on one hand he blamed segregationist policies and legislation on the Dixie bloc of Senators; on the other, he proclaimed segregation mutually beneficial to both blacks and whites, insisting that his segregationist policies were not matters of politics but of humanitarianism. (Weiss 69, 77) Although historians and political scientists most often identify Wilsonian diplomacy with liberalism, Ambrosius points out the racist subtext of his liberal democracy and the peace that followed World War I and notes that in Wilson's presidency, "the White South redefined the national agenda in race relations. Its Jim Crow system became public policy throughout the United States, and white supremacy shaped America's international relations" (Ambrosius 689–90).

6. **Nalty 68.**

One military report on the Houston riots—which left 14 whites, including four policemen and a national guardsman, dead—says that black soldiers began causing trouble as soon as they arrived: "Troubles on street cars due to the Jim Crow laws. . . . Segregation signs would frequently be removed and colored men take seats in white section; these men were sometimes profane and abusive [and] soldiers refused to drink from those [drinking water cans] labeled 'colored.'" It concludes: "So long as the people of Houston and the state of Texas maintain their present attitude towards the Negro, troubles more or less aggravated and similar to the affair at Houston are likely to occur at any time Negro troops are stationed within boundaries of the state" (Gross qtd. in Nalty 68, 71).

For more on the Houston riot and courts-martial, see Haynes' *A Night of Violence*, which includes the sad story of Vance County, NC native T.C. Hawkins, who was hanged despite his plea of innocence and conflicting accounts of where he might have been during the initial violence.

7. **Wynn 6–7; Nalty 91; Miller 9–10; Northrup 11; Nelson 7–8; Bayes Letter 15 June 2013; Bayes, Letter 25 June 2013.**

From 1919-1932 the Navy used Filipinos for messmen. As a push was made to re-open the messman rank to African Americans, the head of Navy enlisted personnel training argued that "we ought to hang on to the Filipinos till the last" because they are "cleaner more efficient and eat much less than negros. Negros are capable of being better cooks though even the best require very close supervision or you will find yourself drenched with grease in the cooking.

... Going back to colored men would be a distinct step backward." (Miller 8)

8. Nalty 48–52; Marshall qtd. in Sandler 35.

9. Finkle 45; Wynn 7–9. See also McWhirter and Rucker for more on the "red summer," a term coined by James Weldon Johnson, who was at the time field secretary for the NAACP.

10. Finkle 42–43; Wynn 11-12; McWhirter 253; "Interactive Timeline"; Haley 206; *Thirty Years*; Wolgemuth 173.

11. Haley 207–08; Bickett qtd. in Haley 214.

12. Haley 215; Moton qtd. in Haley 215; Bickett qtd. in Haley 215. For more on Wilmington/1898, see the 1898 Wilmington Race Riot Commission's final report.

13. Among the most prominent of these leaders were James B. Dudley, president of N.C. A&T; the political activist and journalist Charles N. Hunter; Durham businessman C.C. Spaulding; James E. Shepard, founder and first president of the North Carolina College for Negroes, now NC Central University; James E. Seabrook, president of the State Colored Normal School, now Fayetteville State University; and Charlotte Hawkins Brown, founder and first president of Palmer Memorial Institute in Sedalia. Leaders at the state's Negro colleges were especially susceptible to pressures because their boards of trustees were comprised exclusively of white men until Governor Broughton appointed the first black men to A&T's board in July 1942. ("Governor Names")

14. Haley 222, 216; Dudley qtd. in Haley 227; Tyson 14; Haley 276, 279. As editor of the *News and Observer*, Josephus Daniels was also a vocal opponent of lynching from about 1900 on. Bruce Baker notes that the *N&O* was the first major newspaper to publish photos of lynching victims not as a celebration but as a denunciation. (184–87)

15. Haley 247.

16. Binkin 18; Nelson 8; Nalty 94; MacGregor 5; Floyd, "Alton" 179; MacGregor 58; "To Increase"; MacGregor 5, 58; Nelson 12–13.

The case of Alton Augustus Adams, a Virgin Islands native who in 1917 became the first African-American bandleader in the U.S. Navy, is, according to Mark Clague, an "exceptional situation inspired by exceptional circumstances" (7). Adams' military service came about after the United States bought the Virgin Islands in 1917 and got in the process a talented local band. Adams was its bandleader. The Navy recognized the value of this band, which enlisted as a unit and continued to perform throughout the 1920s, touring the U.S during a time when blacks were generally excluded from enlisting in the Navy.

Michael Bayes, the current Navy band historian, agrees that the term "modern Navy" has no set meaning; he uses it to describe the last days in the late 1910s that African Americans were allowed to enlist at any rank, so he considers Adams as the first African American to serve the modern Navy at general rank (Letter 11 Mar. 2013), while I use it to describe the first days, in 1932, that African Americans were once again allowed to enlist in the Navy, although at menial ranks only. (For more on Adams, see Samuel Floyd's "Alton Augustus Adams, " and Adams' own memoir.) Adams, like B-1's first commander, O. O. Kessing, and its first bandleader, C. E. Dudrow, was recalled into active duty at the onset of World War II, when Adams inherited an all-white band in Cuba but added eight African-American musicians from his Virgin Islands band to its roster, thus constructing the first integrated band in the modern Navy. (Clague, "Editor's Note" 233–34)

17. Du Bois 39; Smith, M. 18, 23; Woodward 34.

18. Sitkoff, "Racial" 675; Morrison 66; Sitkoff, "Racial" 675–76.

19. Chafe 5; Greene 238.

In Virginia, Sen. Henry Byrd dominated politics from 1925–65. His machine countered the 1930s liberalism espoused by Virginius Dabney, editor of the Richmond *Times*, and Gov. James H. Price (1938–42), whose administration was brought down by Byrd. (Syrett 437; Henriques 3) Dabney was "the most conspicuous friend of the Negro in Virginia" and one of the first to call for an end to Jim Crow buses because of how impractical they made the process. (Gavins 134; Hughes 212) The editor of the Norfolk *Virginian-Pilot*, Durham native Louis Jaffe, became in 1928 the first white editor in the South to condemn lynching; his editorial "An Unspeakable Act of Savagery" won for him a Pulitzer Prize. (Tarter 177) Two black leaders, educator Gordon Blaine Hancock and Plummer B. Young, the Littleton, NC native who became editor of the Norfolk *Journal and Guide*, the largest circulation black newspaper in the South, remained aligned with conservatives like Spaulding and Shepard. Young's motto was "Build Up, Don't Tear Down," and because he feared that race prejudice would never subside, he was a strong advocate for an independent economy for blacks that would rely on black-owned businesses within black communities for sustenance and growth. (Suggs 169, 167)

Although conditions for blacks in Virginia and North Carolina were far from ideal—and opportunities for education, employment, recreation, transportation, and housing were far from equalized—conditions in the Deep South were much worse by many indicators: by 1944, blacks were still excluded from primaries in the Deep South but could vote in North Carolina and Virginia (and parts of Tennessee). (Foster 268) North Carolina and Virginia had by far the fewest documented lynchings between 1881–1946. (Guzman 306)

Shepard was harshly criticized by black leaders for his refusal in 1933 to release the transcript of a NC College student to UNC so that the student could be considered for admission into the university's pharmacy school (Anderson 368); he subsequently got new buildings and the two new professional schools for his college.

But it remains dangerous to over-simplify any of these leaders' views. Dabney, for example, will later come under attack for claiming that forced integration would result in "violence and bloodshed" (qtd. in Dalfiume 307). Shepard will be called a "misleader and false prophet" by the Norfolk *Journal and Guide* for expressing the opinion that segregation is "realism" and cannot be changed. (Dalfiume 314–5)

20. *Afro-American* qtd. in Finkle 82; Randolph qtd. in Wynn 11; Schuyler qtd. in Dalfiume 301; Finkle 118, 131, 158; Myrdal 1006, 1012. See Miller for a detailed narrative of the 15 sailors' dismissal from duty for writing to the *Courier* about conditions aboard the USS *Philadelphia*.

21. Finkle 61–62; Austin qtd. in Gershenhorn; *New Republic* qtd. in Finkle 559; Myrdal 910, 909.

22. Gershenhorn; *Afro-American* qtd. in Gershenhorn; Broughton qtd. in Gershenhorn.

23. Gershenhorn; *Afro-American* qtd. in Finkle 204. Black leaders were not the only ones who saw the global conflict in racial terms. Charles Lindbergh, for example, saw the coming war as one for white supremacy that threatened the nature of civilization. The real threat, he said, was "by infiltration of inferior blood" (qtd. in Jones, C. 8).

24. Finkle 204; Austin qtd. in Gershenhorn; "An Editorial"; Prattis 360.

Sitkoff points out that most African-American newspapers and leaders, too, softened their rhetoric as the war developed, but he downplays the efforts by military commanders to suppress access to black audience newspapers when he asserts that there were "only a few short-lived bans" on these papers. ("African-American Militancy" 71–73) While it may be true that only a few official bans have been documented, it's clear from surveying the black press during World War II—and from Robert Hill's *RACON* and "The Negro Problem in the 14th Naval District"—that the black press continued to be perceived as a problem throughout most of the war.

25. Finkle 69; Gershenhorn; Finkle 76, 78, 84.

26. Myrdal ii, xxv, 1013, 1012, 1014, 1015, 466, 472, 471.

27. Prattis 360; Wynn 27; Burran 6; Sitkoff, "Racial" 668; Burran 2; Wynn 27; Sitkoff, "Racial" 668; Prattis 355.

Despite seemingly powerful evidence and testimony against him, the white officer accused of blackjacking Pvt. Harold Daniels at the Raleigh bus station was acquitted. Daniels suffered a head gash and the loss of two teeth. ("Soldier Mauled," "Officer Charged," "Capitol City Policeman Acquitted.")

After the killings in Fayetteville, the first major racial incident of the war years, over 500 black soldiers not in their barracks were taken to the base stockade where, some reported, they were beaten; race relations on the base plummeted. The NAACP and Army's Inspector General's Office both sent investigators who found a "general hatred" among black soldiers at Fort Bragg toward the Army's "discriminatory practices in recreation, transportation, and housing, and a complete distrust of the military police." Yet, Secretary of War Henry Stimson claimed that neither the incident itself or its aftermath had "any semblance of a conflict of racial sentiments; and that the occurrence did not arise from, or cause any tendency toward racial discrimination" (Burran 48–50).

Several sources catalog race violence during the war but each includes incidents not included in the others. See Lawrence, McWilliams, and Sandler especially.

Anecdotal evidence supports the belief that acts of racial intimidation and violence were commonplace during the war. One white sailor told a Navy investigator, "We have a race fight down at the mess hall about every night. Just small fights, but it is growing weekly" ("Negro Problem" 30).

Sammy Davis, Jr., writes that he served in the Army's first integrated unit, at Cheyenne, Wyoming, and was in fights frequently, often with several men jumping him, with nothing ever done to protect him from their recurrence. His nose was broken at least twice, and he was painted white in an incident that drew no report nor discipline. (15–16, 18, 22–24)

28. Roosevelt 9.

29. Eppes; Broughton, "John Merrick"; Greene 16.

30. Newkirk; Tursi 180–81; Anderson 386; "Colored Soldiers"; "CCC."

31. Broughton Scrapbooks; "Broughton Tells."

32. Broughton, Letter to Knox; Holmes et al; Cook.

33. "Talmadge Seeks"; "NCU Prexy." For a defense of Talmadge written by one of his contemporaries, see Henson's *Red Galluses*: 223–229.

34. Fairclough 72; "Governor-Elect"; "N.C. Governor Deplores"; "Broughton's Talk"; "Patriotic Rally"; "Broughton Is Speaker."

35. Odum, Letter; Gallagher 76, 178; Odum 4.

36. Yelton qtd. in "State Negro Teachers"; McCulloch; Johnson 31; Myrdal 467.

37. "C.C. Spaulding and Dr. Shepard"; Greene 240; Broughton, Letter to Roosevelt.

From at least the turn of the century, Shepard (1869–1947) and Spaulding (1907–1952) were allies. Shepard, who earned his pharmacy degree from Shaw University and a doctor of divinity from Muskingum College in 1910 ("Negro Educator Succumbs") was one of the six original organizers of North Carolina Mutual Insurance Company, in 1899, for which Spaulding was agent by 1900 and named president in 1923. (*North Carolina Mutual Story*) The Chicago *Defender* referred to Spaulding as "the foremost business leader of the race" ("Spaulding Okays"). When he became Mutual's third president, the company claimed assets of $2.3 million. At his death, they were $33.6 million. (Gloster 207)

Shepard, called by the *New York Times* "one of the country's foremost Negro educators," ("Dr. James E. Shepard") built his reputation as president of the North Carolina College for Negroes, now NC Central University, which in 1925 became the nation's first state-supported liberal arts college for blacks. Its origins are traced to the founding in 1910, by Shepard, Spaulding, and four others, of the National Religious Training School and Chautauqua at White Rock Baptist Church in Durham, where Shepard was a member. (*North Carolina Mutual* 40) It became Durham State Normal School in the early 1920s and then North Carolina College for Negroes in 1925. Its first graduating class was in 1929. ("N.C.C. for Negroes.")

38. "Dr. Shepard's Request"; Jackson qtd. in Gavins 155.

39. Before Eleanor Roosevelt's speech at UNC during her February 1942 visit, Graham introduced her as "the first woman of the world." She had earlier dined with "hundreds of students" at Lenoir Hall and after her talk attended the President's birthday ball for Orange County, also in Lenoir. This was her first return to Chapel Hill since she had been commencement speaker in 1935, when the university also awarded her an honorary degree. ("Mrs. Roosevelt Says Winning.")

Frank Porter Graham's involvement in liberal state and national causes was staggering, as evidenced by a survey of his correspondence housed at the Southern Historical Collection at UNC-CH. In addition to being president of the Southern Council on International Relations and chairing FDR's Council on Social Insurance, he was active in the state Commission on Inter-Racial Cooperation, the Peabody Conference on Education and Race Relations, the Council of North Carolina Women for the Prevention of Lynching, the Association for the Study of Negro Life and History, the State Conference on Employment Problems of the Negro, the Editorial Board of the NAACP, the Volunteer Christian Committee to Boycott Nazi Germany (which asked Graham, as a member of the committee, for his endorsement of anti-lynching legislation that would eventually fail in 1939), the National Association of State Universities, the Council Against Intolerance in America (other members included Josephus Daniels, Reinhold Niebuhr and Alfred E. Smith) and on the Boards of Trustees at two all black schools, Hampton Institute and Palmer Institute as well as the board of the Carnegie Foundation for the Advancement of Teaching.

His appointment by FDR to the National Defense Mediation Board in 1941 and subsequently to the War Labor Board would eventually erode some local support for him, as his detractors would begin to complain that his time away from UNC was hurting the university. (Ashby 174–91) Graham essentially held two full-time jobs for much of the war, shuttling almost every weekend between Washington and Chapel Hill, but he accepted salary only from the U.S. government. (Snider 228)

40. Jones, P. 1; Berger 14 (See also O'Loghlin); Jones, P. 11, 13; Berger 14.

The vital importance of a good band to military command and morale is also illustrated by the manpower issues confronting the Confederacy during the Civil War. With fewer music resources to draw upon than the Union, the Confederacy was not able to assign bands to all regiments. It was not unusual, Ferguson reports, for officers in such regiments to contribute their own personal funds to secure a band. (47)

41. Jones, P. 30; Berger 14; Jones, P. 30; Ferguson 478, 430, 439, 438.

North Carolina produced at least 27 bands, second only to Georgia's 32. Of the 47 Confederate bands that surrendered at Appomattox, six were from North Carolina. (Ferguson 93, 494) The only complete set of Confederate band books still extant is that of the 26th North Carolina Regiment's band, the best documented of the Confederate bands, and with 16 pieces the largest to surrender at Appomattox; see Hall for its story. (Ferguson 32)

42. Jones, P. 68–69, 13, 71.

The first shipboard instruments were the clarionet (an obsolete spelling of clarinet); cornopion (an early name for the cornet); ophocleide (an obsolete bass instrument of the keyed bugle family), the hipocomo, or alto horn; and snare drums. (Jones, P. 70)

43. Jones, P. 26; Bayes, "Navy Pioneers"; Jones, P. 105–6, 112.

Nimrod Perkins was a drummer on the USS *Diligence* and the USS *Accomac* and Cyrus Tiffany a fifer on the USS *Alliance* during the Revolutionary War.

Tiffany also served at the Battle of Lake Erie in the War of 1812, during which another African American, George Brown, also served as a bugler on the USS *Chesapeake*. (Jones, P. 105)

Each of the Army's four African-American regiments in the early 1900s had a band of black musicians with white leaders. President Theodore Roosevelt ordered that they get black bandmasters, which paved the way for the Army's two most famous bandleaders of World War I: Kinston native Lt. J. Timothy Brymn, bandmaster of the 350th field artillery regiment's Black Devils band, and Lt. James Reese Europe of the 15th infantry, later re-designated as the 369th infantry and nicknamed the Hell Fighters. (Jones, P. 43–44)

The only place blacks generally could serve as musicians in the 20th century Navy was in the Caribbean, where Alton Augustus Adams directed three 22-piece bands in the Virgin Islands during World War I. (Jones, P. 106)

44. Jones, P. 72, 73, 96, 76, 385.

The charter of the Navy school of Music, established June 26, 1935, makes no mention of race as being a criterion for admission. Requirements are that the applicant be a natural born U.S. citizen between 18–25 years old, no shorter than 63 inches, and unmarried. (Jones, P. 154, 175)

45. Jones, P. 90, 88; "Navy Musician Trains"; Jones 116, 31. In contrast, the Army had about 500 bands during World War II. (Jones 31)

46. Jones, P. 13, 181. For more on the Navy's recruitment of African Americans for its bands, see, for example, "How About this Band?" "Rehearsing at Savoy," "3 Musical Seamen," "17-Piece Navy Band Is Tops," "Navy Band Is About Set," "Musicians at Hampton to Join Navy," "Lionel Loses Three Key Men," "Les Hite's Band Yields 2," "Navy Calls for Top Musicians," "Navy Takes Over a Tailor-Made Band," and "Doing Their Bit for the War Effort."

47. Jones, P. 60; "Negro Marine Camp"; "Troup, Bobby."

Formation: Greensboro and A&T College

Why the band was designated "B-1"

B-1, says Michael Bayes, U.S. Navy historian and bandsman, most likely stood for Band One because it was the first of its type. (Bayes, Letter 7 Nov. 13) Marshall Hawkins, retired master chief musician who led the Navy's Commodores in 1969–70, thinks it still a mystery as to why it got that designation. B-1, or Band 1, had already been used to designate the U. S. Navy School of Music's first band to graduate, in 1936. Perhaps what the Navy meant was "B-1 (*colored*)." The Navy does not as a general rule keep records on units, and

B-1's history appears to confirm the belief of most of its members that the Navy lost track them and did not catch up with them until late 1943 or early 1944. One surviving document, a muster list prepared while the band was stationed in Hawaii, identifies it as Band #739, which may indicate that it was not officially numbered by the Navy until late in the war. Bayes notes that all black bands in the Navy were numbered in the 700s but that official numbering did not begin until the Great Lakes School of Music began training African-American musicians. Many appear to have gone by their names—Jazz Bombers and Melody Makers, for example—instead of their numbers. (Letters 7 Nov. 2012; 12 Mar. 2012)

1. It remains unclear whether a War Department policy requiring blacks to score higher than whites for enlistment into the armed forces was still in place when B-1 mustered in. (Floyd 2) The Army, however, had been giving "scientific sanction" to the myth of Nordic superiority since the 1920s, when it listed all the races of men in order of their intelligence as revealed by their scores on its Alpha tests. This ranking subsequently became a "fighting document for the KKK" and in 1938 was still "widely cited as an unimpeachable authority" (Gallagher 76, 177).

2. **Hairston 68–69, 99, 101.**

3. **"14 White and Race"; "Bennett College Head"; Chafe 6, 29; Ahearn; McMurtrie.**

    North Carolina's new constitution, adopted during Reconstruction in 1875, made education for black children mandatory but did not dictate how many grades were to be offered. Greensboro's Colored School opened in 1875 and by 1878 it had a black principal. However, no provision was made for a black high school until 1921 (a high school for white students opened in 1899), when students were allowed to take high school courses on the Bennett College campus. Not until 1928-29, when James B. Dudley High was built and opened, did the city offer a standard high school for black students. (Arnett 87–90) Dudley High School, named for A&T's second president, quickly earned a reputation for educational excellence. (Chafe 18) Dudley was president of A&T from 1896 until his death in 1925. ("About A&T")

    Public support for a black library in Greensboro was likewise slow in coming: the Carnegie Foundation offered in 1906 to donate $10,000 to the city for establishing a public library for blacks, so long as the city would maintain it; the library was not built, however, until 1924, when it finally opened with a 150-book collection. (Arnett 98–99)

4. **"Blue and Gold"; "NCC Band Makes Bow"; "Blue and Gold."**

5.　**"Robert Nathaniel Dett" 45.**

Dett was the first African American to earn a B.A. in music from Oberlin
Conservancy. He founded the School of Music at Hampton Institute and
the Hampton Choir, which under his direction performed at Carnegie Hall,
Symphony Hall in Boston, and for both Presidents Hoover and Roosevelt. He
came to Bennett in 1937 ("Dett on Staff") and organized the college's first
orchestra in 1938. ("Bennett College Band") For more on Dett's life outside
North Carolina, see Simpson and also McBrier.

6.　**"Parade Will Open"; "Second Annual Concert."**

7.　**"Arlan Coolidge"; "Bennett Concert"; "Nathaniel Dett's Music"; "A&T's 35-Voice";
"A&T Singing"; "A&T Choir to Sing"; Griffey; "Music Group"; "Await Spelman";
"Oh, Please"; "Pianist, Violinist."**

Greensboro in the 1930s is rife for exploring. One leading proponent of this enriched cultural life was the Greensboro *Daily News*, which under the editor-
ship of H. W. Kendall maintained a policy regarding news about blacks that was
quite liberal for a Southern paper of its time. Kendall was "progressive as such
views went in the Tar Heel politics of that era" (Yoder 113).

While Dett was nearing the end of his life, Lawson was just beginning his career. He would soon leave A&T and, with Bernard Mason, join the Howard
University faculty, where they would together make it one of the most important music programs in the U.S.

　　Howard's president, Dr. Mordecai W. Johnson, a former preacher from
West Virginia who became the first African-American president of Howard
University in 1926, delivered the baccalaureate sermon at Bennett College
on June 1, 1941. Within a year, he had hired both Lawson and Mason.
("Bennett's Finals")

　　Lawson, a Hartford, CT native, graduated from Fisk in 1924 and from Yale
School of Music in 1928, where he studied with his father, the "well-known
R. Augustus Lawson." Before joining the faculty at Fisk in 1930, he studied in
Paris and in Germany with the legendary Beethoven specialist Artur Schnabel.
At Fisk, Lawson was piano accompanist for the famed Fisk Jubilee Singers and
in 1933 was named chair of the music faculty. ("Fisk to Graduate"; Allen, C. "In
Gay Paree"; "Fisk Singers;" Griffey) By 1936, he was director of the department
of music at A&T. ("A&T Choral Units") He became the first dean of music at
Howard in April 1942. ("Warner Lawson Named")

　　Mason, a Des Moines, IA native who earned his M.A. in music from Oberlin
College, was director of instrumental music and assistant instructor of band

at A&T as early as 1935. At Howard, he directed its symphony orchestra, continued his active concert performance career, and established himself as one of the best-known violin teachers in the area. (Brawley 316; "College Band"; "Artists Trio"; "Long Tradition")

8. "Palmer Students Hear"; "Concert Pianist Heard"; "Pankey Concert." For more on Jackson, see Stevens.

9. "Bennett Hears"; Powell qtd. in "New York Negro"; "Hastie Begs Question."

10. "Soloist to Appear"; "Miss Burge"; "Queen of Swing"; "Lincoln Players"; "N.C. College Chorus"; "Eight Choirs."

11. "Drama Group."

12. "A&T Debate"; "Debate Teams Meet"; "Famous Play"; "Life of Christ"; "A&T Choir to Give."

Richard Harrison, born to runaway slaves in 1864 in Ontario, Canada, joined the A&T faculty after meeting president James Dudley. He began a dramatics school for black teachers as part of A&T's summer curriculum and subsequently became a full-time professor. After he was selected to play De Lawd in Richard Connelly's Pulitzer Prize-winning play *Green Pastures*, he moved to New York, where he starred in it until his untimely death in 1935. (Daniel; Tabranor 45) A&T's college players were named for him soon after his death, and later, the school's auditorium would be named for him. (Arnett 300) His understudy, Charles Winter Wood, assumed the role of De Lawd and then, in 1936, he began a 2-year stint as director of dramatics at Bennett College. Wood next joined the faculty at Florida A&M, where he modernized the theater arts program and its theater was later named in his honor. ("FAMU Essential")

13. "First Colored Navy Band"; "Warner Lawson Named."

14. In his "Unfinished Autobiography," Parsons identifies the others who enlisted with him as "Bill Goldsboro who taught political science at Lincoln U. and Ernest Fry, and one other" (34). "Navy Lets Down"; "Class Orator."

15. "Sub Is Sighted"; "Third Air Raid"; "59,319 Gas Masks"; "58 White Men"; "Draft Board 1."

16. "A&T Supplies 13."

17. "A&T Instructor"; "A&T Sets up"; "A&T Training"; "A&T Keys."

J. Archie Hargraves (1917–2003) was also director of publicity for the college. A Greensboro native and graduate of both Dudley High and A&T, he would become a nationally renowned pioneer of nonviolence, civil rights and community organization, first as co-founder of the East Harlem Protestant Parish and then as pastor of Chicago's South Shore Community United Church of Christ. He was also president of Shaw, vice-president of the Association of American Colleges, and president of the Institute for International Development. ("Hargraves Dies")

The other colleges granted 4-year ROTC programs were West Virginia State in field artillery; Hampton Institute in coast artillery, and Prairie View State Normal and Industrial in infantry. A&T's program was to prepare infantry officers. ("A&T Gets.")

18. **"Story of the Band."**

The Navy's *Bluejackets' Manual* states, "All enlistments are made for general service. No promise or assurance can ever be given an applicant that he will be assigned to any particular detail or duty" (147). Still, the promise of service in Chapel Hill "for the duration" was heard by virtually every member of the band and appears to have been a recruiting tactic. When Robert Carter, who would join B-1 in Hawaii, enlisted at St. Louis, he was told that St. Louis would be his only duty station and that playing music would be his only job. Later, when he and his bandmates refused to clean toilets, they were put under house arrest and the band was broken up. He was re-assigned then to Manana and B-1.

19. **Jones, P. 177. Dudrow was the son of Jon C. Dudrow, a drummer with the Union army, and a skilled trap drummer himself. He enlisted in the Navy in 1907 at Baltimore and earned over his career seven gold re-enlistment stripes. ("Navy Bandsman Is Moved")**

20. **"Oldest Negro Navy Band"; Broughton, Telegram.**

F. D. Bluford became A&T's third president, succeeding James B. Dudley in 1925 and serving until his death in 1955. Bluford was a Virginia native and had been at A&T for over 10 years at the time of his appointment. He was educated at Virginia Union and Howard in English and psychology. ("Elect Dean Bluford") His tenure was marked by considerable unrest in the late 1930s as some black leaders in the state appear to have fought a move by A&T to shift focus from industrial education to liberal arts after plans were announced to eliminate programs in plumbing, carpentry, bricklaying and plastering. Citing the "much muddled condition existing" at A&T, the *Carolina Times* called for his firing in 1937. ("The A&T College Muddle") Liberal arts degrees, the paper said, are not working for the "thousands" of blacks in colleges like Hampton and Tuskegee who lack the capacity to "get what those colleges have to offer" when "they could do well in mastering a trade of some kind." In fact, liberal arts degrees can "handicap" their future. ("A&T College") In 1939, over 200 students marched on his home to protest the firing of the school's athletic director. ("Riot Quelled")

J. W. Seabrook (1880–1973), the son of former slaves who became teachers and Presbyterian ministers, grew up in South Carolina learning that "white power was overwhelming and that blacks in the South had no dependable friends" (Fairclough 74). He was the fifth president (1933–1956) of Fayetteville State. ("Guide to the James Ward Seabrook")

21. Dates for Lampley's service are impossible to reconstruct, as a fire destroyed Chapel Hill Presbyterian Church's session records in 1957. (Brown, T.) Born March 4, 1924 in Dunn, he graduated from A&T and served in the Army's 364th regiment in World War II, after which he studied at Julliard School of Music. He taught at the Peabody Conservatory and made his Carnegie Hall debut on piano in 1950. He subsequently went to work as a producer for Columbia Records, where one of his first projects was Miles Davis' *Miles Ahead*. He also produced records for Dave Brubeck, Louis Armstrong, Leonard Bernstein, Duke Ellington, Mahalia Jackson, and Judy Garland, among many others. He taught piano and composition at Morgan State University for 18 years. ("Cal Lampley")

22. **Place of origin for original B-1 recruits is identified with their individual photos in** *United States Pre-Flight School.*

23. **Parsons, "Unfinished" 35.**

Training at Norfolk: No Day at the Beach

Epigram: B-1 clarinetist William Skinner recalled these drill instructor's words.

1. **"Navy Pre-Flight School"; "UNC Navy School"; Linder 186; Stone. Date of entry into service is noted in "Notice of Separation from U.S. Naval Service" documents for John Samuel Gilmer, Wray Herring, Huey Lee Lawrence, Calvin Frank Morrow, and James Benton Parsons.**

2. **Linder 171.**

3. **Stone.**

4. **Manning 1: 262; Stewart 382–83; Miller 12; Manning 1: 173; Stewart 384; Linder 187; Stewart 385, 378, 395.**

The Navy's first base, established in 1883, was at Newport, RI, and could train 2,000 sailors at a time. The Great Lakes bases, established in 1911, could handle 50,000 men. The San Diego base, established during World War I, had a 5,000-sailor capacity. (Manning 1: 261–62)

5. **Linder 205; Miller 79; Stewart 385–86.**

    Carl E. Clark's memoir *Pieces from My Mind: A True Heartfelt Journey in Black American History* is about his 22 years of service in the Navy, from 1936-58. He along with twelve other African Americans did basic training as a segregated group in San Diego, in 1936, before traveling by transport via the Panama Canal to Norfolk for training as messmen. He had enlisted with the mistaken notion that he would serve as an electrician. Unit K West at Norfolk, where his fellow messmen were trained, was isolated from the rest of the white population and encircled with a 10' fence with controlled access: "The white boys were in a nice brick barracks and could come and go as they pleased" (51).

6. **"Charge Navy"; "Navy Yard." Both articles are based on a speech given by Dr. Charles S. Johnson, at a meeting in Chicago of the Society for Social Research, that repudiated recent claims made by the *Reader's Digest*, *Saturday Evening Post* and *Life* that the Norfolk Navy yard had become an example of a "government establishment where democracy and equal rights for the Negro are rapidly becoming realities."**

7. Beginning pay rate is noted in Huey Lawrence's records. William Skinner said pay went to $66 a month within a few weeks and some men were making $98 a month before long, while Parsons was bumped up to $114. Skinner added, "They'd told us at A&T we'd be lucky to make $85 a month to start at a job after we graduated."

8. **Turner qtd. in Miller 81.**

9. **"Sailors Are Taught"; Miller 81.**

10. *The Bluejackets' Manual* **238.**

11. **"Naval Band Ordered to Chapel Hill"; "All-Negro Navy Band."**

    The wait for appropriate accommodations also delayed the opening of the Great Lakes training camps for African Americans. The Navy, meanwhile, was "negotiating" with other locations for advance training. ("Negro Volunteers Have to Wait")

12. **"Enjoy Breeze."**

13. **Dallam 61–62.**

    Marcelino Manuel da Graca (1881–1960), from the Cape Verde island of Brava, immigrated to the U.S. in 1903, where he changed his name to Charles M.

Grace. By 1922, he had established the United House of Prayer for All People in Charlotte, and by 1926 he had moved into the Hampton Roads area, first in Newport News and then in Norfolk on Elmwood Avenue, just off Church Street. Dallam describes the United House of Prayer as a mix of Holiness, Pentecostal, and Nazarene traditions. Historically, one of the House of Prayer's biggest attractions was its extensive use of music—most of its churches had both a concert band, with over a dozen instruments as well as flag carriers and majorettes, and a shout band, typically comprised of a sousaphone, drums, and half a dozen or more trombones. It was not unusual for services to last all night, nor for House of Prayer churches to be cited for noise violations. (Dallam 61–62)

By the time of his death in early 1960, Daddy Grace had built a church empire that would continue to flourish. Today, the church has over 130 temples in 26 states. After World War II, Daddy Grace opened a Greensboro temple on Dudley Street, near the A&T campus, and its lunchroom today remains a popular gathering place. The church now has two temples in Newport News and two in Norfolk. ("Location Directory")

14.   **"American Heroes."**

Chapel Hill: "The Best of Times"

1.   **"Population"; Cohn 327-28; "Board To Investigate;" Parsons, "Unfinished" 135.**

The *Daily Tar Heel* ran a series of articles and editorials on the race question in late 1942. Coverage of a December 1938 incident "brought to mind the Carrboro race riot" from the late summer of 1937. ("Negro Problems"; "Posse Searches"; "SAE House Boy"; Levin; "Aldermen to Investigate"; "Why We"; Kamisaruk)

Both Junius Scales and Daphne Athas (pp. 33–38) in their memoirs detail a racially tense pre-World War II Chapel Hill. Scales recalls a 1937 riot, after which "sheer terror reigned in the Negro community for three days" and reports several near-lynchings from the late 1930s. (Scales 44, 48) Robinson also recounts, in 2002, the 1937 riot.

During his North Carolina stay, Richard Wright also addressed a "spellbound, racially mixed audience" at North Carolina College, attacking most black leaders for going hand-in-hand with "the powerful whites" in order to keep "their groaning brothers in line, for that is the safest course of action" (Tuck).

2.   **Bauer 527–28; Campbell 21; Athas 38; Bauer 528.**

3.   **"Governor Broughton Orders"; "Two Killed"; "Sixty-day Reprieve"; "Governor Frees Doomed"; "Plan for More."**

4.   Gavins 124–26, 153.

Some national black leaders were angered because they were invited to attend the Durham meeting but as participants, not leaders. The conference unanimously elected as leaders three conservative blacks, including Gordon Blaine Hancock of Virginia Union Seminary as director, and Norfolk *Journal and Guide* editor Plummer Young as chairman. Hancock said that the "real problem" national leaders had was that Southern blacks had taken matters into their own hands. (Gavins 131–32)

5.   "Quarters Built"; "Minstrel Show Casting"; "Minstrel Show Given"; "Smoker Features."

6.   A&T's civilian pilot training in March 1942 included 8 other students in addition to the Carlson brothers ("A&T Training"); it was moved to Reidsville in July, after the Army took over facilities at the Greensboro airport. ("A&T Flight")

7.   Barnes 52–53; Cooper 75.

8.   Henderson 194; Lackey; Davis, J.

Graham was in Puerto Rico as part of a committee appointed by FDR when John P. Davis, National Secretary for the National Negro Congress, wrote to him asking for evidence that cities farther South than DC had allowed blacks use of facilities at white schools. The issue at hand involved Marian Anderson being denied a Washington venue: Eleanor Roosevelt would resign from the Daughters of the American Revolution after that organization refused to allow Anderson to perform in Constitution Hall, which made the ensuing controversy front-page news across the U.S. Anderson's performance, subsequently arranged as a free open-air "Freedom Concert" at the Lincoln Memorial, drew 75,000 and a national radio audience. (Black 725–26, 735)

9.   "Negro Boys"; "Dusky Gridders"; "Bennett College Theatre"; "WPA Chorus"; "Negroes to Sing"; "Nell Hunter Singers"; "14 White"; "Interracial Forum"; "Presides at Interracial Meet"; "CPU Panel."

10. Brown, D; Henderson 325.

11. Brown, D.

12. Wynn 16, 31, 27.

13. "ODT Told."

14. Graff; "Citizen's Committee's"; Graves.

15. McMurtrie; "Two Convicted"; "Negro May Test."

16. Graham qtd. in Pryor 236–37.

More than half of Mark Pryor's biography of Charles Jones (pp. 143–290) is devoted to the events and testimony surrounding the controversies and church hearings that resulted, ultimately, in Rev. Jones' resignation from the Chapel Hill pastorate, a story that is still locally debated. Pryor makes clear that Jones ultimately resigned but also that the resignation was forced, and that he had until the end of his tenure at Chapel Hill Presbyterian the near full support of the local church officers and his congregation. Contemporary accounts may have over-emphasized the role his racial attitudes played in his dismissal, probably because the first move to oust him, in 1945, was clearly related to his integrationist views. However, in 1945, the Orange Presbytery "protected and supported him and, at least implicitly, defended his activism" (Monroe, Letter to Schultz).

By the time actions began anew in 1952 to oust him, those behind that first effort had left the church. Except for Graham's comments about Rev. Jones' friendship with B-1 bandsmen, there is no mention in Orange Presbytery records of race being interjected into the proceedings that would eventually result in Rev. Jones' resignation. With Jones as its pastor, Chapel Hill Presbyterian "was essentially a Unitarian enterprise and only nominally Presbyterian," recalled Thad Monroe. The move to oust Jones, he says, was really a petition to the Presbytery to establish a new church, one that abided by Presbyterian doctrine. "None of the 1945 petitioners were a part of this group," said Monroe, who believes "this effort was motivated by doctrinal issues rather than racial animus" (Monroe, Letters to author). Jones' replacement, it should be noted, was called from Charleston, SC, where he was known as a "staunch integrationist" (Dunham). Jones would subsequently found the Community Church in 1953 and Chapel Hill Presbyterian would be re-named in the 1960s as University Presbyterian.

Monroe also provided the author a copy of his six-page letter to Mark Schultz, editor of the *Chapel Hill News*.

Jones himself told an interviewer in 1990 that he believed race to be part of the cause of his troubles, although he also admitted, "I did not believe in the Confession of Faith" (Egerton). The Community Church webpage maintains that Jones would not have had charges of doctrinal heresy brought against him "had he not threatened the social structure" of segregation in Chapel Hill, a belief also shared by Chapel Hill historian Roland Giduz. (Kast)

17. **"Navy's Negro Band Is Now Established."**

18. **"Navy's Negro Band Is Coming"; "Navy's Negro Band Is Now"; Parsons,** *Unfinished* **134–35.**

19. "Community House at Carrboro."

20. Carlson qtd. in Brown, D.

21. Caldwell qtd. in Brown, D.

22. This summary of B-1 performance activities is based on interviews with bandsmen, a review of event programs, and a survey of copies of the Cloudbuster, the pre-flight school's weekly newspaper, which was edited by Pierce O. "Kidd" Brewer.

23. "Negro Band's Concert."

24. "Pre-Flight Colored Band"; "Founder's Day"; "Kate Smith"; "Community Song"; "Negroes to Hold"; "Big Bond Rally"; "Negro War Bond"; "Big Parade"; "232 Men"; Green.

25. Hilliard.

26. "Band to Play"; "War Bond Rally Tuesday"; "The War Bond Rally."

27. "There'll Be a Big Celebration Today."

28. "Vitality for All."

29. "Review of Naval"; "Service Units"; "People of the Village"; "5,300 Negroes."

    At least seven other Liberty ships named for prominent African Americans were launched during World War II: the *Booker T. Washington*, the *George Washington Carver*, the *Paul Laurence Dunbar*, the *Frederick Douglass*, the *Robert L. Vann*, the *James Weldon Johnson*, and the *John Hope*. One warship was named for Leonard Roy Harmon, a black mess attendant who was killed in battle near Guadalcanal. (Johnson 75–76)

30. "Merrick To Be Launched"; "20,000 at Merrick"; Broughton, "John Merrick." See also "Broughton Points Way."

31. North Carolina General Statues. (A copy of this statute is included, along with correspondence cited elsewhere in this and succeeding paragraphs, in Gov. Broughton's file on the Williamson case. Wolfe; Smith, H.; Broughton, Letter to Smith; Cameron.)

32. "Negress Found Guilty"; Meyland.

    Williamson initially appealed her guilty verdict, despite its lack of an active sentence, but on July 15, 1943, she accepted the judgment without explanation.
    Another account notes that witnesses said "the well known woman was the victim of the prejudice of the driver" and gave accounts much different from the official ones quoted below. Significantly, they claimed there were no seats available for Mamie Williamson to occupy had she given up her seat. ("N.C.

Woman, Beaten") North Carolina's Jim Crow bus law appears not to take into consideration a situation in which a bus is filled beyond its seating capacity—it even allows for blacks and whites to occupy the same bench, side by side, if they are occupying the last seats remaining. (North Carolina General Statute)

The incident's drama is captured chillingly in the police chief's summary report to the mayor, "When she [Williamson] got off the bus she was fighting and kicking and when she attempted to bite [the driver] on the hand he slapped her in order to keep her from biting his hand as he did not want to strike her with the police club. At that time [the arresting officer] got there and took hold of her other arm and when he did she bit him on his hand breaking the skin and [he] stated that he had to slap her to keep her from biting him again as he did not want to strike her with his club. During all this time she was rearing and trying to kick the officers. During the scuffle she got down on the sidewalk and the officers stated they picked her up and carried her in the front door of the Court House. [The arresting officer] went back and got her purse and umbrella and carried it to her. [When he] was out on the sidewalk she started rearing again and [the driver] was attempting to hold her by the wrist and her watch band broke and fell on the floor in front of the elevator and [the arresting officer] told her that if she would stop rearing that she could pick it up which she did. Then she claimed she lost some bridgework out of her mouth during the scuffle. Later the bridge-work was recovered and [the bus driver] took it to her at her home at night as she was out on Bond" (Casteen).

Some variations between the chief's summary and the actual arrest record are apparent in the arresting officer's report, upon which, supposedly, the chief's summary had been based: "I told her she would have to go with me and she asked where and I told her to jail. She got up and I preceded her out of the bus. When I was on the sidewalk I looked back and saw her hitting at the bus driver with her umbrella. I reached through the door and caught her by the arm and pulled her out of the bus. She started fighting and trying to get away. She then tried to bite me on the hand I was holding her with and I had to slap her to make her turn my hand loose. Leitch then grabbed her other arm and she bit him, breaking the skin on his hand. He then slapped her. She continued to fight, kicking and biting and had to be slapped again. She then slipped on the sidewalk and fell flat. I told her to get up but she refused. Leitch and I then got her by each arm and picked her up and took her inside the court house. Leitch then returned to the sidewalk to get her purse, hat and umbrella which she had dropped. She continued to try to get loose while we were waiting on the elevator. I had her by both arms and her watch band broke and her watch fell to the floor. She picked it up and said that she had lost her teeth on the sidewalk... They were later found by a negro man who said he saw them fall and he picked them up... I delivered them to her at her home" (Wolfe).

33. No public record of the incident Parsons recounts exists; no B-1 bandsmen
     were aware that it had occurred.

     Another incident involving the band that in May 1944 replaced B-1 proved
     more publicly troubling and may have been the spark that eventually led to the
     dismissal, a decade later, of Rev. Charles M. Jones from the pastorate of Chapel
     Hill Presbyterian Church. On July 2, 1944, some of the replacement bandsmen
     attended a picnic sponsored by the church at Battle Park at which some bands-
     men were observed walking with white co-eds. Rumors were rampant, some
     repeated in the campus newspaper and throughout the state in newspaper
     accounts, and some in Jones' congregation were riled up again. So volatile was
     the situation that the War Department prepared a confidential memo
     entitled "Commingling of Whites and Negroes at Chapel Hill, N.C.," a document
     that Mark Pryor says was based on "inaccurate accounts" provided primarily
     by Police Chief W. T. Sloan and two other officers, who warn that "serious trou-
     ble could result" unless Jones was "dismissed at once." (Pryor 98–108).

     Both Rebecca Clark and Roland Giduz remember this incident and its
     aftermath. Giduz believed it was what led eventually to Jones' dismissal.
     Whether that's the case or not, it clearly marked an escalation of public trou-
     bles for Jones. Prior to this event, his difficulties had primarily been within
     the Presbyterian congregation. Rebecca Clark said, "When that second group
     arrived, they were older. They weren't from around here and they didn't know
     how it was. They'd go to Durham, go to the bars, and the police would be wait-
     ing for them at the bus station to arrest them when they got back. Dr. Jones'd
     be there waiting, to protect them. He stood up for them. He wanted integra-
     tion. The local whites, they yelled at him, they egged his house, they egged the
     church. Then, when he started the Community Church, it was integrated from
     the beginning."

34. **Flavelle.**

     Goodman's pianist, Bill Maxted of Racine, WI, had also played for Jimmy and
     Tommy Dorsey. Among the tunes he performed with the jive quartet that in-
     cluded Woods was a tribute to the pre-flight cadets' training: "20 Mile Hike at
     Fast Cadence." Maxted made several recordings after the war and became a
     regular performer at Nick's in Greenwich Village. He moved to Ft. Lauderdale,
     FL, in 1961, where he died in 2002. ("Maxted")

35. **This replacement band, trained at Great Lakes, is also likely the source of some his-
     torical confusion concerning B-1. They were in place soon after B-1 left and their
     service is fully documented by the Navy as part of the mass training of bandsmen at
     Great Lakes. For a list of those replacements, see "Pre-Flight Band Leaves."**

36. Moeser; DeConto.

37. Rebecca Sellers Clark, who died in 2009 at the age of 93, was revered in Chapel Hill as a "champion for justice, community leader and political organizer." B-1's Robert Sellers was her cousin. ("Rebecca Clark Dies") See also Bob Gilgore's interviews with Clark.

Pearl Harbor: The Biggest Military Band on the Rock

1. Melendy 436, 439; *Administrative History* 39–40.

2. Anthony ix; Israel 244; Emmons qtd. in Israel 247; Israel 248.

3. Anthony 191, x.

4. Melendy 432; Allen, G. 221–222; "Island of Oahu" 132; Anthony 3; *Administrative History* 48.

   Aiea was built to accommodate enlisted personnel who were staging through Pearl Harbor. Construction on it began during the summer of 1942 and Aiea continued to grow in size for most of the war. It included 117 single-story barracks, two large mess halls, and four recreational halls that were part of a recreational area developed on a 25-acre site across the street from the barracks. ("Island of Oahu" 135)

5. Grier 92; Allen, G. 219; Bailey and Farber 43, 36.

6. Anthony 3; Schmitt 120.

7. Byers 236; "Negro Problem" 33, 23, 31, 28.

8. Bailey and Farber 141; "The Negro Problem" 2. Unlike the Army, which employed Japanese-American laborers, the Navy wanted to employ only Caucasians for its civilian work, an impractical wish given the dearth of whites on the islands. Thus the Navy's demand for African-American laborers was increased. (Israel 245)

9. Hill 2, 6; "Negro Problem" 6, 35.

10. Lind 253; Bailey and Farber 158; Miller 161.

11. "The Negro Problem" 25, 33.

12. Bailey and Farber 151–52, 161.

13. "The Negro Problem" 20, 29, 31, 32, 35; Lind 253. Blacks intentionally provoked whites, the Navy said, by leaving copies of the Defender and other black audience newspapers around recreation halls where whites could see them and then think

that they had been left on purpose to "cause trouble" over their reports of state-side lynchings, race riots and "other instances of Negro-white strife" ("The Negro Problem 35).

14. "Navy Blames Blood"; "Red Cross Chief."

15. "Red Cross Solves"; "Red Cross Turns Down"; "Army, Navy Differ"; "Army Takes Full Blame"; "Segregated Blood."

16. Blevins; Karoly; Parsons, *Unfinished* 139–140.

17. Evans 2 Sept. 1944; 10 Sept. 1944; 31 Oct. 1944; 10 Oct. 1944; 3 Oct. 1944.Stafford Evans stayed in limbo at Shoemaker from September 1, 1944 until early January 1945, when he left for "some island in the Pacific." Some of his letters are heavily censored: "the white man has spread [censored] too ignorant to think of them-selves" (1 Feb. 1945).

18. Parsons, *Unfinished* 140.

19. Parsons, *Unfinished* 139.

20. Parsons, *Unfinished* 36; Morison vol. 8, 49, 50–51; Braisted 540.

21. Parsons, *Unfinished* 142.

22. Morison vol. 12, 171.

23. Roth; "Pearl Harbor Blast"; "Marine Private."

24. Roth; "Ammunition Explosions" (Casualties in this article combine the May 21 event totals with those from another explosion on Oahu on June 11); Morison vol. 12, 171.

25. "Men from Manana."

26. Allen, G. 225; Manning vol. 2, 132.

27. "Bamboo Story."

28. Harris, 17 Mar. 1945: 9; Harris, 2 April 1945; "USS Franklin." See Hoehling for the complete story of the USS *Franklin*, whose men were presented with more medals and commendations than any unit in the Navy's history.

29. "Old 'Buster Band."

30. "Aloha Chaplain."

31. "Aloha Chaplain"; Heuer, "New Movie Set-up"; Frost; Bailey, Bill.

32. Harris, "Musically Speaking" 2 April 1945; 4 July 1945; 6 Aug. 1945; 3 Oct. 1945.

33. "17-piece"; "Star Musicians"; Mosbrook; "Reuben Reeves"; "Ray Anthony."

34. Harris, 2 Apr. 1945; Heuer "Meteors Compete Well"; "National Negro Week" 7.

35. Harris, 2 Apr. 1945.

36. "Robert L. Ghormley"; Ghormley; "Massed Bands"; "Berger, Henry."

37. Herring, Scrapbook; Bailey and Farber 50; Grier 99, 98; Bailey and Farber 50–51, 95.

38. Bailey and Farber 95, 97, 100–101, 105.

39. "1945 Hawaiian"; "American vs. National League Program"; "All-Star Game"; Hilliard.

40. Sklaroff 950; *History of AFRTS* 61–64; "Tradewinds Presents."

41. "Broadcast Transcription Readied." The V-disc on which this Moonglowers' performance was recorded was donated to East Carolina University's special collections by Herring and preserved and re-recorded by the Southern Historical Collection, Wilson Library, UNC-CH, in preparation for B-1's return to Chapel Hill for its 2007 reunion.

42. "Otto Harris and the Moonglowers"; "Moonglowers Keep Glowing"; "Dates for April."

43. "Orrin Tucker."

44. "Bob Crosby"; Fiddler 369; "Scenes from the Arsenic"; "News of the Stage"; "Troupers Are Carrying."

45. "Happy Hour"; "Happy Hour: Dedication."

46. Harris, 6 Aug. 1945; 4 July 1945; "Robert Carter."

47. "Happy Hour"; "Sesquicentennial"; "National Negro Week"; "V-J Day."

48. "The Man Who"; Heuer, "News"; Heuer, "Recreation" 17 Mar. 1945; Heur, "Recreation" 14 Apr. 1945; Heur "News"; "Scenes from the Ray Anthony."

49. "Carlson Presents."

50. Harris, 24 Aug. 1945: 7.

51. Arbor 184–185.

52. Byers 234, 236; "Lester Granger Group"; Byers 232; Avant qtd. in Byers 236.

53. "Lester Granger Group"; Byers 236; "On the Cover."

54. "Pearl Harbor Glows"; "Honolulu to Have Holiday."

55. "Bedlam Reigns"; "Waikiki Turns"; "Parade Due."

56. "Manana Outstanding" 8, 10. First news reports estimated the parade audience at 135,000. ("135,000 See Victory Parade")

57. "Floats Included"; "300 Planes"; "Manana Outstanding" 8.

58. "Cavalcade of Bands"; Harris, 13 Sept. 1945: 7.

59. Wilson.

60. Wray Herring, for example, was cleared for transfer from Manana to the states for mustering out on Sept. 29, 1945; he was honorably discharged on Oct. 25, 1945. (Clour)

Coming Home

1. Foster 381.

2. Clark 133–34.

Wray Herring Collection

Bandsmen
in work uniforms,
Chapel Hill,
L to R:
John Carlson,
Warmouth
Gibbs, Jr., and
Thomas Gavin
Wray Herring
Collection

B-1 comedy
routine
L to R:
James Scott,
Simeon Holloway,
and Otto Harris
Wray Herring
Collection

I. Interviews and Correspondence

Personal and telephone interviews and correspondence with B-1 veterans and their contemporaries, and historical documents provided and/or produced by bandsmen.

Carlson, Walter, Jr.

• Personal interviews. Greensboro, NC. 23 May 1985; 15 July 1987.

• Telephone interview. 24 Sept. 1985.

Carter, Robert

• Personal interview. Chapel Hill, NC. 31 Aug. 2007.

• Remarks. Wilson Library, UNC-Chapel Hill, NC. 31 Aug. 2007.

• "Robert Carter, Musician, Singleton Palmer's Dixieland Six; President, Local 197, American Federation of Musicians." *Lift Every Voice and Sing: St. Louis African Americans in the Twentieth Century*. Doris A. Wesley, ed. Columbia, MO: U of Missouri P, 2000: 24–25.

• U.S. Navy B-1 Survey. 1 Apr. 2001. Collection of the author.

Clark, John

• Personal interview. Chapel Hill, NC. 17 July 2008.

Clark, Rebecca

• Personal interviews. Chapel Hill, NC. 30 Aug. 2007; 17–18 July 2008.

Currie, Willie, Jr.

• Personal interview. Fayetteville, NC. 13 June 1986.

Foster, Carl

• Personal interviews. Greensboro, NC. 6 Apr. 1986; 15 July 1987.

• Telephone interview. 5 Apr. 1986.

Gavin, Thomas

• Personal interviews. Fayetteville, NC. 18 Feb. 1985; 12 June 1986; 7 July 1987.

• Telephone interviews. 10 Sep. 1985; 23 Apr. 1986.

Gibbs, Warmouth T., Sr.

• Personal interview. Greensboro, NC. 15 Dec. 1988.

Gibson, William

• Personal interview. Durham, NC. 10 July 1986.

Giduz, Roland

• Personal interview. Chapel Hill, NC. 16 July 2008.

Gilmer, John

• Notice of Separation from U.S. Naval Service. 11 Jan. 1946.

• Personal interview. Greenville, NC. 25 Oct. 2002.

• U.S. Navy B-1 Survey. 30 Apr. 2001. Collection of the author.

Guy, Arthur

• Personal interview. Greensboro, NC. 8 Oct. 1986.

Guy, Jehovah

• Personal interview. Greensboro, NC. 15 July 1987.

Haith, Filmore

• Personal interview. Chapel Hill, NC. 2 Sept. 2007.

Herring, Wray

• Honorable Discharge from the U.S. Navy. 25 Oct. 1945.

• Notice of Separation from the U.S. Naval Service. 25 Oct. 1945.

• Personal interviews. Gloucester, VA. 29 June 1987; Greenville, NC. 25 Oct. 2002.

• Remarks. Wilson Library, UNC-Chapel Hill, NC. 31 Aug. 2007.

• Scrapbook. Wray Herring col.

• Telephone interview. 3 Jan. 2008.

• "To the Boys in B-1." Manuscript, 3 pp. [Manana Barracks, HA, 1944]. Wray Herring col.

• U.S. Navy B-1 Survey. 19 Feb. 2001. Collection of the author.

• Wray Raphael Herring Collection. Manuscript Collection 810. Greenville, NC. Joyner Lib., ECU.

Holloway, Simeon

• Notice of Separation from the U.S. Naval Service. 8 Jan. 1946.

• Personal interview. Greenville, NC. 25 Oct. 2002.

• Telephone interview. 10 June 2013.

Holt, Roger

• Personal interview. Chicago, IL. 11 Aug. 1985.

Jones, Richard

• Personal interviews. Fayetteville, NC. 13 June 1986; 6 July 1987; Greenville, NC. 25 Oct. 2002.

• Letters to the author. 12 May 2006; 13 Apr. 2008.

Laikin, Bennie

• Personal interview. Durham, NC. 10 July 1986.

• Letter to the author. 1 Oct. 1986.

Lake, Roy

• Personal interview. Greenville, NC. 19 Oct. 2003.

Lawrence, Huey

- Notice of Separation from the U.S. Naval Service. 26 Jan. 1946.

- Personal interviews. Ayden, NC. 9 Apr. 1985; 13 Aug. 1986; Greenville, NC. 25 Oct. 2002.

- Telephone interviews. 9 Feb. 1985; 1 Aug. 1990; 3 Aug. 2005; 13 Jan. 2009; 23 Feb. 2011; 18 July 2011; 3 Jan. 2012.

McCauley, Polly

- Personal interview. Chapel Hill, NC. 16 July 2008.

Mason, John

- Personal interview. Durham, NC. 10 July 1986.

Morehead, Nathaniel

- Personal interview. Greensboro, NC. 7 Oct. 1986.

Morrow, Calvin

- Notice of Separation from the U.S. Naval Service. 25 Oct. 1945.

- Personal interviews. Greensboro, NC. 25 July 1986; Greenville, NC. 25 Oct. 2002.

- Remarks. Wilson Library, UNC-Chapel Hill, NC. 1 Aug. 2007.

- Telephone interviews. 29 Feb. 2008; 15 Mar. 2011.

Neece, Talmadge

- Personal interview. Chapel Hill, NC. 9 Jan. 2008.

Parsons, James B.

- Personal interviews. Chicago, IL. 10–12 August 1985; 18 July 1990.

- "The Unfinished Oral History of District Judge James Benton Parsons." Typescript. Chicago: U of Chicago, DeAngelo Law Library Law School. May 1996 .

Pettiford, Raymond

- Personal interviews. Greensboro, NC. 16 July 1986; 25 July 1986.

- Telephone interview. 5 Apr. 1986.

Thurman, Abe

- Letter to author. 21 Apr. 2006.

- Personal interviews. Greenville, NC. 25 Oct 2002; WTEB-Radio, New Bern, NC. 6 Oct. 2011.

- Remarks. Wilson Library, UNC-Chapel Hill, NC. 31 Aug. 2007.

- Telephone interviews. 3 Jan. 2008; 1 Mar. 2008; 8 Apr. 2008; 25 May 2008; 18 Mar. 2010; 25 Mar. 2011.

Wall, Audrey

- U.S. Navy B-1 Survey. Collection of the author. 1 Apr. 2001.

Woods, Charles

- Telephone interviews. 5 Nov. 1986; 11 Nov. 1986.

- Personal interviews. Rocky Mount, NC. 11 July 1987; 6 Nov. 1986.

II. Works Cited

"A&T Choir to Give Operetta at 8:30 Tonight." Greensboro *Daily News* 30 Apr. 1942, sec. 2: 4.

"A&T Choir To Sing at NC College." *Carolina Times* 3 May 1941: 3.

"A&T Choral Units Schedule Holiday Carols." Chicago *Defender* 19 Dec. 1936: 5.

"A&T College." *Carolina Times* 18 June 1938: 4.

"The A&T College Muddle." *Carolina Times* 24 July 1937: 8.

"A&T Debate Team Clashes with Bluefield." Greensboro *Daily News* 10 Apr. 1942, sec. 2: 4.

"A&T Flight Students Using Reidsville Field." Greensboro *Daily News* 22 July 1942: 2.

"A&T Gets Four-Year R.O.T.C. Unit." Greensboro *Daily News* 1 May 1942, sec. 9: 2.

"A&T Instructor Given Post in Capital." *Carolina Times* 9 Aug. 1941: 2.

"A&T Keys Program for Defense." Greensboro *Daily News* 12 Apr. 1942, sec. 2: 5.

"A&T Sets up Program for Defense." Greensboro *Daily News* 28 Jan. 1942: 2.

"A&T Singing Groups Heard over CBS Hook-up." Chicago *Defender* 28 Dec. 1940: 1.

"A&T Supplies 13 Musicians for Navy Aid School." Greensboro *Daily News* 10 May 1942, sec. 3: 9.

"A&T Training Civilian Pilots." Greensboro *Daily News* 21 Mar. 1942: 11.

"A&T's 35-Voice Choir Goes on Tour." Chicago *Defender* 24 Feb. 1940: 3.

"About A&T: History." North Carolina A&T State U. Web. 8 Nov. 2011.

"About the Bandsmen: Dr. Roger Holt." "A Little Known Legacy": 17-24.

Adams, Alton Augustus. *The Memoirs of Alton Augustus Adams, Sr.: First Black Bandmaster of the United States Navy*. Mark Clague, ed. Berkeley: U of California P, 2008.

Administrative History of the Fourteenth Naval District and the Hawaiian Sea Frontier, vol. 1. Historical Section, Fourteenth Naval District [Hawaii, 1945].

Ahearn, Lorraine. "'37 Boycott Was Ahead of Its Time." Greensboro *News and Record*. 4 Feb. 1994. Web. 13 Oct. 11.

"Aldermen to Investigate DTH Charges." *Daily Tar Heel* 19 Nov. 1942: 1.

"All-Negro Navy Band to Perform in State." Raleigh *News and Observer* 9 July 1942: 3.

"All-Star Game." All-Star Game History. MLB.com. Web. 7 Mar. 2012.

Allen, Cleveland G. "Music." Chicago *Defender* 15 Dec. 1928: 10.

Allen, Gwenfread. *Hawaii's War Years: 1941-1945*. Honolulu: U of Hawaii P, 1950.

"Aloha Chaplain Heuer." *Mananan* 24 Aug. 1945: 6.

Ambrosius, Lloyd E. "Woodrow Wilson and *The Birth of a Nation*: American Democracy and International Relations." *Diplomacy and Statecraft* 18 (2007): 689-718.

"American Heroes Day in Norfolk." Norfolk *Journal Guide* 25 July 1942, sec. 2: 13.

"American vs. National League 1945 All-Stars." Program. Honolulu, HA. Wray Herring Col.

"Ammunition Explosions Take Toll of 137 at Pearl Harbor." Los Angeles *Times* 15 June 1944: 1.

Anderson, Jean Bradley. *Durham County*. Durham: Duke UP, 1990.

Anthony, J. Garner. *Hawaii under Army Rule*. Palo Alto, CA: Stanford UP, 1955.

Arbor, Jesse W. "Run My Mouth and Boss Like Hell." Stillwell 171-191.

"Arlan Coolidge to Play His Violin at Bennett." Chicago *Defender*. 6 Nov. 1937: 15.

"Army Forms 2 Jim Crow Units, and New Air Squad." Chicago *Defender* 31 Jan. 1942: 13.

"Army, Navy Differ on Blood Ban." Chicago *Defender* 18 July 1942, sec. 1: 2.

"Army Takes Full Blame for Jim Crow Blood Bank." Chicago *Defender* 28 April 1945: 3.

Arnett, Ethel Stephens. *Greensboro, North Carolina*. Chapel Hill: U of NC P, 1955.

"Artists Trio to Albany, Ga." Washington *Afro-American*. 7 Apr. 1953: 7.

Ashby, Warren. *Frank Porter Graham: A Southern Liberal*. Winston-Salem, NC: Blair, 1980.

Athas, Daphne. *Chapel Hill in Plain Sight: Notes from the Other Side of the Tracks*. Hillsborough, NC: Eno, 2010.

"Await Spelman Recital." Chicago *Defender* 25 Jan. 1941: 8.

Bailey, Beth and David Farber. *The First Strange Place: The Alchemy of Race and Sex in World War II Hawaii*. New York: Free P, 1992.

Bailey, Bill. "Questions & Answers" *Mananan* 24 Aug. 1945: 7.

Baker, Bruce. *This Mob Will Surely Take My Life: Lynchings in the Carolinas, 1871-1947*. New York: Continuum, 2008.

"Bamboo Story." *Mananan* Aug. 1945: 6.

"Band to Play in Forest Theatre at 4:30 Sunday." *Chapel Hill Weekly* 13 Aug. 1943: 1.

Barnett, Claude. "The Role of Press, Radio, and Motion Picture and Negro Morale." *Journal of Negro Education* 12.3 (Summer 1943): 474-489.

Barnes, Samuel E. "Living a Respectable Life." *The Golden Thirteen: Recollections of the First Black Naval Officers.* Paul Stillwell, ed. Annapolis, MD: Naval Inst. P, 1993: 46-74.

Bauer, Margaret. "Call Me Paul: The Long, Hot Summer of Paul Green and Richard Wright." *Mississippi Quarterly* 61 (2008): 518-537.

Bayes, Michael. Letters to author. 10 Mar. 2010; 11 Mar. 2011; 12 Mar. 2012; 7 Nov. 2012; 25 June 2013; 5 July 2013.

- - -. "Navy Pioneers: A History of African Americans in the Navy Music Program." Smithsonian Institute Videos. 29 Nov. 2010. YouTube. 20 July 2011.

"Bedlam Reigns in Honolulu as Peace News Sets off Historic Celebration." Honolulu *Star-Bulletin* 15 Aug. 1945: 3.

Bell, Terrence. Introduction. "A Little Known Legacy," 2.

"Bennett College Band Makes Its Initial Bow." Chicago *Defender* 10 Dec. 1938: 4.

"Bennett College Head Takes Seat." Chicago *Defender* 14 May 1927: 5.

"Bennett College Theatre Guild Wins Drama Award." Chicago *Defender* 9 April 1938: 5.

"Bennett Concert." Chicago *Defender*. 25 Feb. 1939: 11.

"Bennett Hears Bishop Purcell in Vesper Talk," Greensboro *Daily News* 5 Jan. 1942: 9

"Bennett's Finals to Begin with Address by Leading Minister of Philadelphia." *Carolina Times* 17 May 1941: 3.

"Berger, Henry." Oxford Music Online. Biographies. Web. 7 Mar. 2012.

Berger, Kenneth. "Military Bands of History." *Music Journal* 15.7 (Sept. 1957): 14, 76.

"Big Bond Rally Is Conducted by Durham Negroes." Durham *Morning Herald* 25 Sept. 1943: 2.

"Big Parade Will Feature Navy Day Activities Here." Raleigh *News and Observer* 25 Oct. 1942: 12.

Binkin, Martin and Mark J. Eitelberg. *Blacks and the Military.* Washington, DC: Brookings Inst., 1982.

Black, Allida M. "Championing a Champion: Eleanor Roosevelt and the Marian Anderson 'Freedom Concert.'" *Presidential Studies Quarterly* 30.4 (Fall 1990): 719-736.

Blevins, Lea. "Lab Sprouts Population Growth in Livermore." Oakland *Tribune* 7 Apr. 2006. Web. 5 Mar. 2012.

"Blue and Gold Marching Machine: History." NC A&T State U. Web. 3 Aug. 2011.

The Bluejackets' Manual. U.S. Navy, 10th ed. Annapolis, MD: US Naval Inst., 1940.

"Board to Investigate Charges against Police.*" Chapel Hill Weekly* 20 Nov. 1942: 1.

"Bob Crosby." *Solid: The Encyclopedia of Big Band, Lounge, Classic Jazz and Space-Age Sounds*. Web. 6 Mar. 2012.

Braisted, William R. "Ulithi Atoll, Carolina Islands, U.S. Advanced Fleet Anchorage, 1944–1948." *United States Navy and Marine Corps Bases, Overseas*, ed. By Paolo E. Coletta. Westport, CT: Greenwood, 1985: 341–42

Brawley, Benjamin Griffith. *The Negro Genius*. New York: Dodd, Mead, 1937.

"Broadcast Transcription Readied." *Mananan* 17 Mar. 1945: 9.

Broughton, J. Melville. "John Merrick: Pioneer and Builder." Typescript of speech. Wilmington, NC: 11 July 1943. Raleigh: State Archives of NC. Broughton papers, box 82: "Race Relations."

---. Letter to Frank Knox. 11 Feb.1942. Raleigh: State Archives of NC. Broughton papers, box 59: "Navy Department."

---. Letter to Franklin D. Roosevelt. 9 May 1942. Raleigh: State Archives of NC. Broughton papers, box 17: "S" 1942 miscellaneous.

---. Letter to H. Shelton Smith. 7 Oct. 1943. Raleigh: State Archives of NC. Broughton papers, box 82: "Race Relations."

---. Scrapbooks. Raleigh: State Archives of NC. Broughton papers. RG 2143.

---. Telegram to Spaulding et al. 16 April 1942. Raleigh: State Archives of NC. Broughton papers, box 17: "S" 1942 miscellaneous.

"Broughton Is Speaker Here." Greensboro *Daily News* 10 Apr. 1942: 5.

"Broughton Points Way to Future of Negroes," Wilmington *Star-News*. 12 July 1943: 3.

"Broughton Tells F.D.R. Tar Heels Back Program." Raleigh *News and Observer* 21 Feb. 1941: 1.

"Broughton's Talk to Negro Group Praised." Greensboro *Daily News* 15 Aug. 1942: 10.

Brown, Tom. Letter to Thad Monore. 8 Nov. 2011. Collection of the author.

Brown, David E. "The War Years." *Carolina Alumni Review* Sep.–Oct. 1995. UNC Alumni Assoc. Web. 16 Feb. 2012.

Buchanan, A.R., ed. *The Navy's Air War, A Mission Completed*. New York: Harper, 1946.

Burran, James Albert. *Racial Violence in the South During World War II*. Diss. Knoxville, TN: U of Tennessee, 1977.

Byers, Jean. *A Study of the Negro in Military Service*. [Washington, DC: Dept. of Defense] 1950.

"Cal Lampley, 82, Producer of Records, Music Educator." Knight-Ridder *Tribune Business News*. 8 July 2006: 1. Web. 22 Nov. 2012.

Cameron, Bruce B. Letter to Broughton. 11 Aug. 1943. Raleigh: State Archives of North Carolina. Broughton papers, box 82: "Race relations."

Campbell, Ouida. "Bigger Is Reborn." *Carolina Magazine.* Oct. 1940: 21-23.

"Capitol City Policeman Acquitted in New Hearing on Brutal Arrest of Soldier." *Carolina Times* 19 Apr. 1941: 1, 8.

"Carlson Presents Musical Varieties." Program. Manana Barracks. 10 July 1945. Wray Herring Scrapbook. Wray Herring Col.

Casteen, Charles H. Letter to Bruce B. Cameron. 6 Aug. 1943. Raleigh: State Archives of NC. Broughton papers, box 82: "Race Relations."

"Cavalcade of Bands." Program. Manana Barracks. 31 Aug. 1945. Wray Herring Scrapbook. Wray Herring Col.

"CCC Camp Boys May Be Proved Innocent of Part in Mob Violence as Governor Sends Investigator." *Carolina Times* 2 Aug. 1941: 1.

"C.C. Spaulding and Dr. Shepard Appointed to National Defense Council by Gov." *Carolina Times* 21 June 1941: 1.

Chafe, William H. *Civilities and Civil Rights: Greensboro, North Carolina, and the Black Struggle for Freedom.* Oxford: Oxford UP, 1980.

Chamberlain, Charles D. *Victory at Home: Manpower and Race in the American South during World War II.* Athens, GA: U of Georgia P, 2003.

"Charge Navy Yard 'Reels' with Jim Crow." Chicago *Defender* 12 Sept. 1942: 5.

Chief of the Bureau of Navigation [Acting Chief L.E. Denfield]. Memo to Sec. of the Navy. 26 Feb. 1942. National Archives, College Park, MD. RG 24, box 1172.

Chief of the Bureau of Navigation. Memo to Chief of the Bureau of Aeronautics. 13 Apr. 1942. National Archives, College Park, MD. RG 24, box 1172.

"Citizen's Committee's Tentative Plan for Raising Funds for Negro Community Center." *Chapel Hill Weekly* 21 Feb. 1941. N.p. Clipping file. Chapel Hill: NC Collection, Wilson Library, UNC-CH.

Clague, Mark. "Editor's note." Adams 233–34.

---. "Introduction: the Soul of Alton Adams." Adams 1–18.

Clark, Carl E. *Pieces from My Mind: A True Heartfelt Journey in Black American History.* Berkeley, CA: Creative Arts, 2001.

"Class Orator." Chicago *Defender* 29 June 1929: 4.

Clour, E.C. Memo to Wray R. Herring. 29 Sept. 1945. Wray Herring Col.

Cohn, David L. "Chapel Hill." *Atlantic Monthly* Mar. 1941: 322-328.

"College Band to Make Tour." Chicago *Defender* 23 Mar. 1935: 9.

Coletta, Paolo E., Ed. *United States Navy and Marine Corps Bases, Domestic*. Westport, CT: Greenwood, 1985.

---. "Livermore, Calif. Naval Air Station, 1928-1946." Coletta: 289-90.

"Colored Soldiers Under Fire in Wilmington. *Carolina Times* 30 Aug. 1941: 2.

"Community House at Carrboro Used by Navy Bandsmen." Durham *Morning Herald*. 14 Feb. 1943. N.p. Clipping file. Chapel Hill: NC Collection, Wilson Library, UNC-CH..

"Community Song Celebration Will Be Held Sunday Night in Memorial Hall." *Chapel Hill Weekly* 11 Dec. 1942: 3.

"Concert Pianist Heard at A&T." Greensboro *Daily News* 29 Jan. 1942, sec. 2: 2.

Cook, James F. "The Cocking Affair." *New Georgia Encyclopedia*. Web. 12 Aug. 2002.

Cooper, George C. "Producing Something the World Wants to Buy." Stillwell: 73-95.

"CPU Panel Slated to Debate Problem of Negroes in War." *Daily Tar Heel* 22 Oct. 1942: 1.

Dalfiume, Richard M. "The Forgotten Years of the Negro Revolution." Sternsher: 298-316.

Dallam, Marie W. *Daddy Grace: A Celebrity Preacher and His House of Prayer*. New York: New York UP, 2007.

Daniel, Walter C. "Richard B. Harrison." *Negro History Bulletin* 50.1 (1987): 9.

"Dates for April." [Manana Barracks, Pearl Harbor] n.d. Wray Herring Scrapbook. Wray Herring Col.

Davis, John P. Letter to Frank Porter Graham. 7 Apr. 1939. Chapel Hill. UNC-CH, Southern Historical Collection. Frank Porter Graham Papers. Correspondence.

Davis, Sammy, Jr. *Why Me? The Sammy Davis, Jr. Story*. New York: Farrar, 1989.

"Debate Teams Meet at A&T Tonight." Greensboro *Daily News* 15 Apr. 1942, sec. 1: 2.

DeConto, Jesse James. "WWII Band Back on Campus." Raleigh *News and Observer* 1 Sept. 2007, sec. 1: 9.

"Dett on Staff of Bennett College." Chicago *Defender* 6 Mar. 1937: 3.

"Doing Their Bit for the War Effort." Chicago *Defender* 28 Apr. 1945: 17.

"Dr. James E. Shepard, Negro Educator, 72." *New York Times* 7 Oct. 1942: 27.

"Dr. Shepard's Request." *Carolina Times* 6 Aug. 1938: 6.

"Draft Board 1 Picks Negroes for Induction." Greensboro *Daily News* 12 Feb. 1942: 6.

"Drama Group Hears Dett." Greensboro *Daily News* 12 Apr. 1942: 9.

Du Bois, W.E.B. "Race Relations in the United States, 1917-1947." Sternsher: 29-52.

Dunham, Bob. Letter to author. 29 Oct. 2010.

"Dusky Gridders Clash Here in Chocolate Bowl Tomorrow." *Daily Tar Heel* 20 Nov. 1942: 1.

Duvall, John S. "North Carolina's Training Camps." NC at Home and in Battle in World War II. NC Museum of History. Web. 11 Dec. 2012.

"An Editorial." Chicago *Defender* 18 Apr. 1942: 1-2.

Egerton, John. Interview with Charles M. Jones. 21 July 1990. Interview A-0335. Oral Histories of the American South. Documenting the American South. Web. 29 Dec. 2010.

"Eight Choirs Will Present Concert Today." Greensboro *Daily News* 8 Feb. 1942, sec. 4: 3.

1898 Wilmington Race Riot Commission. "1898 Wilmington Race Riot, Final Report." NC Dept. of Cultural Resources. 31 May 2006. Web. 12 Feb. 2013.

"Elect Dean Bluford Head of North Carolina A&T." Chicago *Defender* 27 June 1925: 3.

Ellison, Ralph. *Invisible Man*. New York: Random, 1950.

"Enjoy Breeze at City Beach." Norfolk *Journal-Guide* 18 July 1942: 8.

Eppes, C. M. Letter to J. Melville Broughton. 29 Apr. 1942. Raleigh: State Archives of NC, Broughton papers: box 5, folder E.

Evans, Stafford W. Letters to Amaza Lee Meredith., Petersburg, VA: Virginia State U. Amaza Lee Meredith Papers. Series II B, box 4, folders 38–49.

Fairclough, Adam. "The Black College Presidents Who Tried to Thwart the Racial Integration of Higher Education." *Journal of Blacks in Higher Education* 55 (Spring 2007): 71–75.

"Famous Play Presented at A&T." Greensboro *Daily News* 13 Mar. 1942. 8.

"FAMU Essential Theatre History." Florida A&M. Web. 5 Aug. 2011.

Ferguson, Benny Pryor, III. *The Bands of the Confederacy: An Examination of the Musical and Military Contributions of the Bands and Musicians of the Confederate States of America*. Diss. Denton, TX: U of North Texas, 1987.

Fiddler, Jimmy. "The Jimmy Durante Show." *On the Air: The Encyclopedia of Old-Time Radio*, John Dunning, ed. New York: Oxford UP, 1998. 368–370.

"58 White Men, 38 Negroes Are Drafted." Greensboro *Daily News* 11 Feb. 1942, sec. 8: 1.

"59,319 Gas Masks Are Allotted Here," Greensboro *Daily News* 6 Mar. 1942, sec. 2: 4.

"5,300 Negroes Employed at Shipyard Where S.S. John Merrick is Launched." Cleveland *Call and Post* 24 July 1943: 2B.

Finkle, Lee. *Forum for Protest: The Black Press during World War II.* Rutherford, NJ: Fairleigh Dickinson UP, 1975.

"First Colored Navy Band Unit Drawn from These." Norfolk *Journal-Guide* 13 June 1942, sec. 2: 17.

"First Navy Band Reports at UNC School." Raleigh *News and Observer* 1 Aug. 1942: 9

"Fisk Singers Will Be Heard on Air." Chicago *Defender* 14 Nov. 1931: 3.

"Fisk to Graduate 102 on June 10." Chicago *Defender* 6 June 1931: 4.

Flavelle, Robert. "Former New York Cop (Irish, Too) Steals Spotlight at Station Smoker." *Cloudbuster* 3 Oct. 1942: 1, 8.

"Floats Included as Feature of Honolulu's Victory Day Parade." Honolulu *Star-Bulletin* 16 Aug. 1945: 1–2.

Floyd, Samuel A., Jr. "Alton Augustus Adams: the First Black Bandmaster in the U.S. Navy. *Black Perspective in Music* 5.2 (1977): 173-187.

---. *The Great Lakes Experience, 1942– 1945.* Carbondale, IL: Black American Studies Program, 1974.

Foster, Vera Chandler and Robert D. Reid. "The Negro in Politics." Guzman: 258–291.

"Founder's Day." Program. Greensboro, NC: NC A&T, Harrison Auditorium. 2 Nov. 1943. Wray Herring Col.

"14 White and Race Colleges in 'Y' Meet." Chicago *Defender* 13 May 1939: 19.

Frost, Frenchy. "Questions & Answers." *Mananan* 19 July 1945: 7.

Gallagher, Buell G. *American Caste and the Negro College.* 1938. New York: Gordian P, 1966.

Gavins, Raymond. *Perils and Prospects of Southern Black Leadership: Gordon Blaine Hancock, 1884–1970.* Durham, NC: Duke UP, 1977.

Gershenhorn, Jerry. "Double V in North Carolina." *Journalism History* 32.3 (2006). Web. 13 Oct. 2011.

Ghormley, Robert L. Admiral's Log. Greenville, NC: East Carolina U, Joyner Lib. Robert L. Ghormley Papers. Series 6, folder E.

Gilgor, Bob. "Interview with Rebecca Clark." 21 June 2000. Documenting the American South. Oral Histories of the American South. Interview K-0536. 4007. Web. 6 May 2013.

Gloster, J.E. *North Carolina Mutual Life Insurance Company: Its Historical Development and Current Operations.* Diss. Pittsburgh, PA: U of Pittsburgh, 1947.

"Governor Broughton Orders Release of Men Accused of Near Lynching." *Carolina Times* 1 Aug. 1942: 1

"Governor-Elect Speaks at Shaw U. Jubilee." Chicago *Defender* 9 Dec. 1940: 5

"Governor Frees Doomed Man." *Carolina Times* 24 Apr. 1943: 1.

"Governor Names Negro Trustees." Raleigh *News and Observer* 29 July 1942: 14.

Graff, John P. Letter to the Recreation Commission, Town of Chapel Hill. 21 Apr. 1942. Chapel Hill: UNC-CH. University Archives, Manuscripts Dept. VP and Controller Files, Series 1, subseries 1.

Graves, Louis. Letter to Frank Porter Graham. 13 Apr. 1942. Chapel Hill: UNC-CH. Southern Historical Collection. Frank Porter Graham Papers. Correspondence.

Green, Paul. "A Christmas Prayer." *Chapel Hill Weekly* 18 Dec. 1942: 2.

Greene, Christina. *Our Separate Ways: Women and the Black Freedom Movement in Durham, North Carolina.* Chapel Hill: U of NC P, 2005.

Grier, Edward F. "Stationed in Paradise." *General Magazine and Historical Chronicle* Winter 1946: 93–102.

Griffey, William A. "Warner Lawson Is Great in Recital." Chicago *Defender* 25 March 1933: 5.

Gross, Col. C.C. Memo to Brig. Gen. James Parker. 13 Sept. 1917. Nalty: 68–71.

"Guide to the James Ward Seabrook Collection, 1880-1973." Chestnutt Library Archives and Special Collections. Fayetteville, NC: Fayetteville State U. Web. 15 Mar. 2012.

Guzman, Jessie Parkhurst, editor. *Negro Year Book: A Review of Events Affecting Negro Life, 1941-46.* Tuskegee, AL: Tuskegee Inst., 1947.

Guzman, Jessie P. and W. Hardin Hughes. "Lynching—Crime." Guzman: 302–319.

Hairston, Otis L. *Greensboro, North Carolina.* Charleston, SC: Arcadia, 2003.

Haley, John H. *Charles N. Hunter and Race Relations in North Carolina.* Chapel Hill, UNC P, 1987.

Hall, Harry H. *A Johnny Reb Band from Salem: The Pride of Tarheelia.* 1963. Rev. ed. Raleigh: NC Office of Archives and History, 2006.

"Happy Hour." Program. Manana Naval Barracks 919, Hawaii. 22 Sept. 1944. Wray Herring Scrapbook. Wray Herring Col.

"Happy Hour: Dedication of New Theater." Program. Manana Naval Barracks 919, Hawaii. 28 July 1945. Wray Herring Col.

"Hargraves Dies at 86." Transitions. United Church of Christ. Web. 16 Mar. 2012.

Harris, Otto. "Musically Speaking." *Mananan.* 17 Mar. 1945: 5; 2 Apr. 1945: 5; 13 May 1945: 7; 4 July 1945: 7; 6 Aug. 1945: 7, 10; 24 Aug. 1945: 7; 3 Oct. 1945: 7.

"Hastie Begs Question on Army Bias." Chicago *Defender* 24 Jan. 1942: 5.

Hawkins, Marshall. Personal interview. Greenville, NC 19 Oct. 2013

Haynes, Robert V. *A Night of Violence: The Houston Riot of 1917.* Baton Rouge, LA: LSU P, 1976.

Henderson, Archibald. *The Campus of the First State University.* Chapel Hill: U of NC P, 1949.

Henson, Allen Lumpkin. *Red Galluses: A Story of Georgia Politics.* Boston: House of Edinboro, 1945.

Henriques, Peter R. "The Byrd Organization Crushes a Liberal Challenge, 1950–1953." *Virginia Magazine of History & Biography* 87.1 (1979): 3–29.

Heuer, Bernard. "Meteors Compete Well" *Mananan* 2 April 1945: 8; "New Movie Set-up Liked": 8; "News." *Mananan* 3 Mar. 1945: 7; "Recreation."

Mananan 3 Mar.1945: 7; 17 Mar. 1945: 9; 14 Apr. 1945: 3.

Hill, Robert A., ed. *The FBI's RACON: Racial Conditions in the United States During World War II.* Boston, Northeastern UP, 1995.

Hilliard, Jack. "An Infamous Day: Campus Prepares for War." 21 May 2010. "A View to Hugh: Processing the Hugh Morton Photographs and Films." Blog. Stephen Fletcher. Chapel Hill, NC: UNC-CH. Web. 17 Feb. 2011.

History of AFRTS: The First 50 Years. Armed Forces Network Online. Web. 15 Mar. 2012.

Hoeling, A. A. *The Franklin Comes Home.* New York: Hawthorn, 1974.

Holmes, Harold M., Albert Register et al. Telegram to Broughton. Chapel Hill, NC 20 Apr. 1942. Raleigh: State Archives of NC. Broughton papers, box 5: folder 2.

"Honolulu to Have Holiday When Surrender Terms Are Accepted." Honolulu *Star-Bulletin* 14 Aug. 1945: 4.

"Honolulu Goes Wild as the War Ends, Here Are Highlights of Celebration." Honolulu *Star-Bulletin* 15 Aug. 1945: 4.

"How About This Band?" Chicago *Defender* 15 May 1943: 19.

Hughes, W. Hardin. "The Race Problem and Race Relations in the United States." Guzman: 197–231.

"In Gay Paree." Chicago *Defender* 12 July 1930: 4.

"Interactive Timeline." NAACP.org. Web. 2 Aug. 2011.

"Interracial Forum Sends Resolution to Legislature Regarding Race Education." *Carolina Times* 18 Feb. 1939: 1, 8.

"Island of Oahu." US Navy Base Construction in World War II. The Navy Department Library: 121-150. Web. 31 Mar. 2013.

Israel, Fred. "Military Justice in Hawaii, 1941-1944." *Pacific Historical Review* 36.3 (Aug. 1967): 243-67.

Johnson, Charles S. *Into the Main Stream: A Survey of Best Practices in Race Relations in the South.* Chapel Hill: U of NC P, 1947.

Jones, Claudia. *Jim Crow in Uniform.* New York: New Age, 1940.

Jones, Patrick M. *History of Armed Forces School of Music.* Diss. State College, PA: U of Pennsylvania, 2002.

Kamisaruk, Paul. "We Wanted to See What Police Had to Say about Our Story." *Daily Tar Heel* 19 Nov. 1942: 2.

Kanter, Fred. "Navy Negro Band Is First to Be Recruited Since '18." *Daily Tar Heel* 23 Sep. 1942: 4.

Karoly, Steve. "Brown Grass and Rolling Hills: Camp Parks Continues Its Military Training Mission." Seabee Log 4 (Fall 1998). Seabeecook.com. Web. 16 Feb. 2011.

Kast, Charlie. "The Community Church Story." 5 Feb 2006. Community Church of Chapel Hill. Web. 29 Dec. 2010.

"Kate Smith Is Here," *Chapel Hill Weekly* 13 Nov. 1942: 3.

Knox, Frank. Memorandum to Rear Adm. Randall Jacobs. 21 Apr 1942. Nalty: 144.

Lackey, Katherine. Letter to John P. Davis. 14 April 1939. Chapel Hill: Southern Historical Collection. Frank Porter Graham Papers. Correspondence.

Lawrence, Charles R. "Race Riots in the United States, 1942–1946." Guzman: 232–257.

"Les Hite's Band Yields 2 Members to U.S. Navy." Pittsburgh *Courier* 31 Oct. 1942: 21.

"Lester Granger Group Visits Manana." *Mananan* 30 Oct. 1945: 3.

Levin, Bob. "Reporter Worked on Story for Over Three Weeks." *Daily Tar Heel* 18 Nov. 1942: 1.

"Life of Christ Is Portrayed in Song Here." Greensboro *Daily News* 23 Mar. 1942: 3.

"Lincoln Players to Appear at Bennett College." Greensboro *Daily News* 30 Jan. 1942, sec. 10: 1.

Lind, Andrew W. "Service-Civilian Tensions in Honolulu." *Community*

Forces in Hawaii: Readings from Social Process in Hawaii, Bernard L. Hormann, ed. Honolulu: U of Hawaii P, 1947: 248–253.

Linder, Bruce. *Tidewater's Navy: An Illustrated History*. Annapolis, MD: Naval Inst. P, 2005.

"Lionel Loses Three Key Men to the Navy." Pittsburgh *Courier* 10 Oct. 1942: 21.

"A Little Known Legacy: The Great Lakes Experience: A Salute to African American Navy Bandsmen at the Great Lakes Naval Base, 1942-1945, A Weekend of Nostalgia, Feb. 28–Mar. 2, 2003" [Chicago, IL], [Feb. 2003]. Collection of Carl Foster.

Location Directory. United House of Prayer for All People. Web. 2 Jan. 2012.

"A Long Tradition." Music at Howard. Howard U. Web. 18 Nov. 2011.

McBrier, Vivian Flagg. *R. Nathaniel Dett: His Life and Works*. Washington: Associated Pub., 1977.

McCulloch, Margaret C. Letter to Broughton. 29 Sept. 1943. Raleigh: State Archives of NC. Broughton papers, box 82: "Race Relations."

MacGregor, Morris J. *Integration of the Armed Forces, 1940–1965*. Washington, DC: Center of Military History, U.S. Army, 1985.

McMurtrie, Beth. "Bennett Activism a Tradition." Greensboro *News and Record* 11 Oct. 1998: B1.

McRae, Bennie J., Jr. "African Americans in World War II." African American Military History. Web. 11 June 2013.

McWhirter, Cameron. *Red Summer: The Summer of 1919 and the Awakening of Black America*. New York: Holt, 2001.

McWilliams, Tennant S. *The New South Faces the World: Foreign Affairs and the Southern Sense of Self, 1877–1950*. Baton Rouge, LA: Louisiana State UP, 1988.

"The Man Who Came to Dinner." *Mananan* 2 April 1945: 3.

"Manana Outstanding in V-J Day Parade." *Mananan* 13 Sept. 1945: 8–10.

Manning, J. J., ed. *Building the Navy's Bases in World War II: History of the Bureau of Yards and Docks and the Civil Engineer Corps, 1940–1946*. 2 vols. Washington: U.S. Government Printing, 1947.

"Marine Private Sees Big Hawaii Ship Explosions." Chicago *Defender* 1 July 1944: 11.

"Massed Bands Will Play for Berger Ceremony." Honolulu *Star-Bulletin* 10 July 1944: 6.

"Maxted, Billy." Requiem. Allegro Archives: Local 802 News." 102.1 (Jan. 2002) Web. 12 Dec. 2011.

Melendy, H. Brett. "Pearl Harbor, Hawaii, and Support Bases." Coletta: 431-463.

"Men from Manana." N.d., n.p. Wray Herring Scrapbook. Wray Herring Col.

"Merrick To Be Launched Today," Wilmington *Star-News* July 11, 1943: 5.

Meyland, A.L. Record of Judgment. July 15, 1943. Raleigh: State Archives of NC. Broughton papers, box 82: "Race relations."

Miller, Richard E. *The Messman Chronicles: African Americans in the U.S. Navy, 1932–1943*. Annapolis, MD: US Naval Inst., 2004.

"Minstrel Show Casting Ends Tomorrow." *Daily Tar Heel* 23 June 1942: 1

"Minstrel Show Given for Cadets at UNC." Raleigh *News and Observer* 8 July 1942: 5.

"Miss Burge in Recital." Chicago *Defender* 15 Jan. 1938: 2.

Moeser, James. Remarks. Chapel Hill, NC. Wilson Lib., UNC-CH. 31 Aug. 2007.

Monroe, Thad. Letter to Mark Schultz [editor of Chapel Hill *News*] 3 Oct. 2005. Collection of author.

Monroe, Thad. Letters to the author, 2 Nov. 2010, 4 Nov. 2010.

"Moonglowers Keep Glowing." *Mananan* N.d. Wray Herring Scrapbook. Wray Herring Col.

Morison, Samuel Eliot. *History of United States Naval Operations in World War II: New Guinea and the Marianas, March 1944–Aug. 1944*. Vol. 8. Boston: Little Brown, 1953.

- - - . *History of United States Naval Operations in World War II: Leyte, June 1944–Jan. 1945*. Vol. 12. Boston: Little Brown, 1958.

Morrison, Alan. "The Secret Papers of FDR." Sternsher: 66–77.

Mosbrook, Joe. *Jazzed in Cleveland* 29 May 1996. Web. 5 Mar. 2012.

"Mrs. Roosevelt Says Winning War Is First." Greensboro *Daily News*. 1 Feb. 1942: 1, 2.

"Music Group to Convene at Institute." Chicago *Defender* 20 Apr. 1940: 12.

"Musicians at Hampton to Join Navy." Chicago *Defender* 24 Oct. 1942: 20.

Myrdal, Gunnar. *An American Dilemma: The Negro Problem and Modern Democracy*. 1944. New York: Harper, 1962.

Nalty, Bernard C. and Morris J. MacGregor. *Blacks in the Military: Essential Documents*. Wilmington, DE: Scholarly Resources, 1981.

"Nathaniel Dett's Music to Be on CBS Sunday." *Carolina Times* 1 Oct. 1938: 3.

"National Negro Week at Manana." *Mananan* 3 Mar. 1945: 7–8.

"Naval Band Ordered to Chapel Hill." Chicago *Defender* 18 July 1942: 2.

"Navy Band Is about Set with Name Aces." Chicago *Defender* 15 Aug. 1942: 23.

"Navy Band Reports." Chicago *Defender* 8 Aug. 1942: 7.

"Navy Band Reports." Pittsburgh *Courier* 22 Aug. 1942: 20.

"Navy Bandsman Is Moved after Work at Carolina." Raleigh *News and Observer* 29 Nov. 1942: 6.

"Navy Blames Blood Ban on Red Cross." Chicago *Defender* 24 Jan. 1942: 1, 2.

"Navy Calls for Top Musicians in New York Band Campaign." Pittsburgh *Courier* 1 Aug. 1942: 20.

"Navy Lets Down Bars, Wants Men." Greensboro *Daily News* 23 Dec. 1941, sec. 2: 7.

"Navy Musician Trains Over 100 Bands." Chicago *Defender* 25 Aug. 1945: 14.

"Navy Pre-Flight School Commissioned." *Daily Tar Heel* 24 May 1942: 1.

"Navy Takes over a Tailor-Made Band." Pittsburgh *Courier* 8 Aug. 1942: 2.

"Navy Yard Articles Refuted." Pittsburgh *Courier* 12 Sept. 1942: 12.

"Navy's Negro Band Is Coming to Town Today." *Chapel Hill Weekly* 31 July 3 1942: 1.

"Navy's Negro Band Is Now Established." *Chapel Hill Weekly* 7 Aug. 1942: 1

"Negress Found Guilty of Resisting Arrest." Wilmington *Star-News* 16 July 1943: 12.

"Negro Band's Concert." *Chapel Hill Weekly* 4 Sep. 1942: 5.

"Negro Boys to Play at 2." *Daily Tar Heel* 3 Dec. 1938: 1.

"Negro Educator Succumbs at 72." Raleigh *News and Observer* 7 Oct. 1947: 1.

"Negro Marine Camp." Raleigh *News and Observer* 10 Nov. 1942: 1.

"Negro May Test 'Jim Crow' Law." Greensboro *Daily News* 11 July 1942: 9.

"Negro Navy Band Parades in Initial Appearance." *Daily Tar Heel*. 4 Aug. 1942: 1.

"The Negro Problem in the Fourteenth Naval District"(report prepared by the Counter-Intelligence Section, District Intelligence Office, 15 Aug. 1943). San Francisco: National Archives. RG 181. General Correspondence (Formerly Classified), 1940–1946, Box 52, Records of the Office of the Commandant, Pearl Harbor Naval Shipyard. Records of Naval Districts and Shore Establishments.

"Negro Problems Demanding Immediate Consideration. "*Daily Tar Heel* 21 Oct. 1942; 2.

"Negro War Bond Rally Here Results in $75,000 Business." Durham *Morning Herald* 18 Dec. 1942, sec. 2: 4.

"Negro Volunteers Have to Wait While Navy Builds Jimcrow Barracks at Great Lakes Base." *Carolina Times* 16 May 1942: 8.

"Negroes to Hold Big Parade and Rally on Friday." Durham *Morning Herald* 19 Sept 1943, sec. 1: 4

"Negroes to Sing Sunday." *Chapel Hill Weekly* 19 July 1940: 1.

"Nell Hunter Singers Are Organized Permanently." *Carolina Times* 18 Feb. 1939: 1, 8.

Nelson, Dennis D. *Integration of the Negro into the U.S. Navy*. New York: Farrar, Straus, and Young, 1951.

"New York Negro Minister Heard in Local Speech." Greensboro *Daily News* 13 Feb. 1942, sec. 2: 6.

Newkirk, Vann R. *Lynching in North Carolina: A History, 1865–1941*. Jefferson, NC: McFarland, 2009.

"News of the Stage: Boris Karloff Opens this Evening in 'Arsenic and Old Lace.'" *New York Times* 10 Jan. 1941: 22.

"1945 Hawaiian AAU Outdoor Swimming and Diving Championships for Men and Women. Program. Honolulu, HA: 29–30 June 1945. Wray Herring Scrapbook. Wray Herring Col.

"NCC Band Makes Bow." *Carolina Times* 3 Feb. 1940: 5.

"N.C. College Chorus Units Give Recital." Chicago *Defender* 21 May 1938: 5.

"N.C.C. for Negroes Surges Ahead, Called Fastest Growing Institute in Nation." *Carolina Times* 20 May 1939: 7–8.

North Carolina General Statues Chapter 147, section 1: 3537. Raleigh: State Archives of NC. Broughton papers, box 82: "Race relations."

"N.C. Governor Deplores Evil of Lynchings." Chicago *Defender* 25 July 1942: 8.

The North Carolina Mutual Story. [Durham, NC] North Carolina Mutual Life Insurance Co., 1970.

"NC Woman, Beaten by Cops, Convicted by Court." Raleigh *News and Observer* 7 Aug. 1943: 6.

"NCU Prexy Raps Dixie 'Fascists.'" Pittsburgh *Courier* 19 Sept. 1942: 2.

Northrup, Hebert R., John A. Brinker, Steven M. Diantonio, and Dale F. Daniel. *Black and Other Minority Participation in the All-Volunteer Navy and Marine Corps*. Philadelphia: Industrial Research Unit, Wharton School, 1979.

Odum, Howard W. Letter to Broughton. 14 Aug. 1942. Raleigh: State Archives of NC. Broughton papers, box 13: folder "O, Miscellaneous."

———. *Race and Rumors of Race*. Chapel Hill: U of NC P, 1943.

"ODT Told Negro Travel Creates Serious Problem." Chicago *Defender* 1 Jan. 1944: 8.

"Officer Charged with Brutality in Soldier's Case." *Carolina Times* 12 Apr. 1941: 1.

"Oh, Please May We Have Your Autograph?" Chicago *Defender* 25 Jan. 1941: 7.

"Old 'Buster Band Success in Pacific." *Cloudbuster* 27 July 1945: 8.

"Oldest Negro Navy Band at Manana." *Mananan* [n.d.]. Wray Herring Scrapbook. Wray Herring Col.

O'Loghlin, Michael. *Frederick the Great and His Musicians: the Viola da Gamba Music of the Berlin School.* Burlington, VT: Ashgate, 2008.

"On the Cover." *Mananan* 3 Oct. 1945: 3.

"104 Men Are Praised by Commander." Chicago *Defender* 15 Aug. 1942: 1.

"135,000 See Victory Parade." Honolulu *Star-Bulletin* 3 Sept. 1945: 1, 4.

"Orrin Tucker." Solid: The Encyclopedia of Big Band, Lounge, Classic Jazz and Space-Age Sounds. Web. 6 Mar. 2012.

"Otto Harris and the Moonglowers Makes Debut." *Mananan*. N.d. Wray Herring Scrapbook. Wray Herring Col.

"Palmer Students Hear Address by James Jackson." Greensboro *Daily News* 26 Feb.1942, sec. 2: 4.

"Pankey Concert Pleases Large A&T Audience." Greensboro *Daily News* 26 Feb. 1942, sec. 2: 4.

"Parade Due When V-J Day Designated." Honolulu *Star-Bulletin* 15 Aug. 1945: 3.

"Parade Will Open Negro Trade Week." Greensboro *Daily News* 20 May 1942, sec. 2: 2.

Parsons, James B. "The Unfinished Oral History of District Judge James Benton Parsons." Typescript. Chicago: U of Chicago, DeAngelo Law Library Law School. May 1996.

"Patriotic Rally Held at Bennett." Greensboro *Daily News* 13 July 42: 12.

"Pearl Harbor Blast Shakes Navy Yard." *New York Times* 26 May 1944: 7.

"Pearl Harbor Glows in Victory. " Honolulu *Star-Bulletin* 14 Aug. 1945: 4.

"People of the Village Invited to Attend 2 Military Ceremonies in Stadium this Week-end." *Chapel Hill Weekly*. 21 May 1943. 1

"Pianist, Violinist Please Big Audience." Chicago *Defender* 10 July 1937: 7.

"Plan for More Interracial Cooperation Presented at Recent Meeting in Atlanta." *Carolina Times* 26 Dec. 1942: 1.

"Population: Characteristics of the Population, part 5: New York–Oregon." *Sixteenth Census of the United States.* Washington: U.S. Gov. Printing, 1941.

"Posse Searches Nearby Area of County Following Assault on Local High School Girl." *Daily Tar Heel* 7 Dec. 1938: 1.

Prattis, P.L. "The Morale of the Negro in the Armed Services of the United States." *Journal of Negro Education* 12.3 (1943): 355–63.

"Pre-Flight Band Leaves for Duty Outside Country." *Cloudbuster* 29 Apr. 1944. 1, 3.

"PreFlight Colored Band Has Made-to-Order Party." *Cloudbuster* 24 Oct. 1942: 3.

"Presides at Interracial Meet." Chicago *Defender* 19 Nov. 1938: 5.

Pryor, Mark. *Faith, Grace, and Heresy: the Biography of Rev. Charles M. Jones.* Lincoln, NB: iUniverse, 2002.

"Quarters Built for Negro Band of Navy School." *Daily Tar Heel* 23 June 1942: 1.

"Queen of Swing." *Carolina Times* 17 May 1941: 4.

Raugh, James P. Letter to Frank Porter Graham. 22 June 1945. Chapel Hill: UNC-CH. University Archives, Manscripts Dept. VP and Controller Files, Series 1, subseries 1.

"Ray Anthony." Swingmusic.net. Web. 5 March 2012.

"Rebecca Clark Dies." Carrboro *Citizen.* 8 Jan. 2009. Web. 6 May 2013.

"Red Cross Chief Won't Change Jim Crow Blood Policy." Chicago *Defender* 12 Aug. 1944: 1.

"Red Cross Solves Problem: Will Accept and Segregate Negro Blood." Chicago *Defender* 31 Jan. 1942: 1.

"Red Cross Turns Down Negro Blood." Chicago *Defender* 17 Jan. 1942: 1.

"Rehearsing at Savoy Every Afternoon." Chicago *Defender* 15 Aug. 1942: 23.

"Reuben Reeves." AllMusic. Biography. Web. 5 Mar. 2012.

"Review of Naval Aviation Cadets Will Be Part of University Commencement Program." *Chapel Hill Weekly* 28 May 1943. 1.

"Riot Quelled at A&T but Students Ask Breaux's Reinstatement." *Carolina Times* 20 May 1939: 1.

"Robert Carter." *Lift Every Voice and Sing: St. Louis African Americans in the Twentieth Century.* Ann Morris, ed. Columbia, MO: U of Missouri P. 1999.

"Robert L. Ghormley." Naval Historical Center. People. Web. 5 Mar. 2012.

"Robert Nathaniel Dett." *Negro History Bulletin* 7.2 (1943): 45, 47.

Robinson, Matt. "Race Riot," Indyweek.com. 31 July 2002. Web. 5 Feb. 2012.

Rondeau, A.E. Letter to the First U.S. Navy African American Musicians, 28 Feb. 2003. Insert. "A Little Known Legacy."

Roosevelt, Eleanor. "If I Were a Negro." *Negro Digest* Oct. 1943: 8–9.

Rostar, James T. "Johns Hopkins University and the Teutonic Germ." *North Carolina Literary Review* 2.1 (1994): 92.

Roth, Amy. "The 'Other' Pearl Harbor Horrific Explosions Burned in Former Signalman's Memory." Aurora, [IL] *Beacon News* 20 May 2001. Web. 16 Feb. 2011.

Rucker, Walter and James N. Upton. *Encyclopedia of Race Riots.* 2 vols. New Haven, CT: Greenwood, 2007.

"Sailors Are Taught to Swim by Navy." Greensboro *News and Record* 18 Dec. 1941, sec. 1: 2.

Sandler, Stanley. *Segregated Skies: All-Black Combat Squadrons of World War II*. Washington, DC: Smithsonian Inst. P, 1992.

Scales, Junius Irving and Richard Nickson. *Cause at Heart: A Former Communist Remembers*. Athens, GA: U of Georgia P, 1987.

"Scenes from the 'Arsenic and Old Lace' Stage Production Starring Boris Karloff." *Mananan* 4 July 1945: 5.

"Scenes from the Ray Anthony All-Navy Variety Stage Show and Arthur Donovan's USO Overseas Troupe." *Mananan* 6 Aug. 1945: 5.

Schmitt, Robert C. *Demographic Statistics of Hawaii: 1778–1965*. Honolulu: U of Hawaii P, 1968.

"Second Annual Concert." Program. Dudley High School Band Concert, Greensboro, NC, Dudley High School, 3 Mar. 1942. Wray Herring Scrapbook. Wray Herring Col.

"Segregated Blood Bank." Chicago *Defender* 21 June 1947: 14.

"Service Units Parade for Lord Halifax." *Cloudbuster* 18 Dec. 1943: 1.

"Sesquicentennial of Naval Supply." Program. [Honolulu] 23 Feb. 1945. Wray Herring Scrapbook. Wray Herring Col.

"SAE House Boy, Two Others Beaten by Police." *Daily Tar Heel* 18 Nov. 1942: 2.

"17-Piece Navy Band Is Tops." Chicago *Defender* 29 July 1944: 14.

Sherman, W. T. Letter to J.D. Cameron. 21 Feb. 1877. Nalty: 48–49.

Simpson, Anne Key. *Follow Me: The Life and Music of R. Nathaniel Dett*, Metuchen, NJ: Scarecrow, 1993.

Sitkoff, Harvard. "African-American Militancy in the World War II South." *Remaking Dixie: The Impact of World War II on the American South*. Neil R. McMillen, ed. Jackson: UP of Mississippi: 1997. 70–93.

---. "Racial Militancy and Interracial Violence in the Second World War." *Journal of American History* 58:3 (1971): 661–681.

"Sixty-day Reprieve Granted Wellman by Gov. Broughton." *Carolina Times* 12 Dec. 1942: 1.

Sklaroff, Lauren Rebecca. "Variety for Servicemen: the Jubilee Show and the Paradox of Racializing Radio During World War II." *American Quarterly* 56.4 (2004): 945–973.

Smith, H. Shelton. Letter to Broughton. 18 Oct. 1943. Raleigh: State Archives of NC. Broughton papers, box 82: "Race relations."

Smith, McNeil, A.T. Spaulding et al. *Statutes and Ordinances Requiring Segregation by Race*. [Raleigh] NC Advisory Committee to the U.S. Commission on Civil Rights. 9 Mar. 1962.

"Smoker Features Band, Orchestra." *Cloudbuster* 12 Dec. 1942: 2.

Snider, William D. *Light on the Hill: A History of the University of North Carolina at Chapel Hill*. Chapel Hill: U of NC P, 1992.

"Soldier Mauled at Bus Station." Raleigh *News and Observer* 6 Apr. 1941: 4.

"Soloist to Appear at A&T College." *Carolina Times* 7 Mar. 1941: 3.

Sosna, Morton. "More Important than the Civil War? The Impact of World War II on the South." *Perspectives on the American South: An Annual Review of American Society, Politics and Culture* vol. 4, James C. Cobb and Charles R. Wilson, eds. New York: Gordon and Breach, 1987.

"Special Tidewater Black History Concert Honoring Unit Band #1 and All Black Musicians Who Served in the U.S. Navy in World War II." Program. 14 Feb. 1981. Norfolk: Naval Amphibious Base Theater, Little Creek. Wray Herring Scrapbook. Wray Herring Col.

"Spaulding Okays Roosevelt." Chicago *Defender* 26 Oct. 1940: 6.

"Star Musicians Triumph in a South Pacific Orchestra." Chicago *Defender* 15 July 1944: 6.

"State Negro Teachers to Get Salary Raises." Raleigh *News and Observer* 12 June 1942, sec. 1: 12.

Sternsher, Bernard, ed. *The Negro in Depression and War: Prelude to Revolution, 1940–45*. Chicago: Quadrangle, 1969.

Stevens, Charles. "J.A. (Billboard) Jackson and the News: Pioneer in Black Musical Entertainment and Journalism." *Western Journal of Black Studies*. 16.1 (1992): 30–38.

Stewart, Peter C. "Norfolk, Va., Naval Air Station, 1917 -." Coletta: 377–379.

---. "Norfolk, Va., Naval Operating Base, 1917 -." Coletta: 379–387.

--- "Norfolk, Va., Naval Shipyard, 1767 -." Coletta: 387–397.

Stillwell, Paul, ed. *The Golden Thirteen: Recollections of the First Black Naval Officers*. Annapolis, MD: Naval Inst. P, 1993.

Stone, Steve. "Hampton Roads Goes to War — Again; the Huge Military Buildup Brings Jobs, Sailors and Overcrowding to Norfolk." Norfolk *Virginian-Pilot* 25 July 1999. Web. 19 Nov. 2011.

"Story of the Band." *United States Pre-Flight School Band*: 2.

"Sub Is Sighted off Hatteras." Greensboro *Daily News* 3 Feb. 1942. 10.

Suggs, H. Lewis. "Black Strategy and Ideology in the Segregation Era: P.B. Young and the Norfolk *Journal-Guide*, 1910–1954." *Virginia Magazine of History and Biography* 91.2 (1983): 161–190.

Syrett, John. "The Politics of Preservation: The Organization Destroys Governor James H. Price's Administration." *Virginia Magazine of History and Biography* 97. 4 (1989): 437–62.

Tabranor, Mae. "Richard B. Harrison." *The Negro History Bulletin* 5.2 (1941): 44–45.

"Talmadge Seeks Re-election." Pittsburgh *Courier* 20 June 1942: 1, 12.

Tarter, Brent. "The Making of a University President: John Lloyd Newcomb and the University of Virginia, 1931–1933." *Virginia Magazine of History and Biography*. 87.4 (1979): 473–481.

"There'll Be a Big Celebration Today When "E" Is Given to Carrboro Plant." *Chapel Hill Weekly* 22 Jan. 1943. 1.

"Third Air Raid Alarm Test Set for Noon Today." Greensboro *Daily News* 12 Feb. 1942.

Thirty Years of Lynching in the United States, 1889-1918. New York: Negro Universities P, 1919.

"3 Musical Seamen Join Band in West." Chicago *Defender* 21 Aug. 1943: 10.

"300 Planes in Aerial Parade." Honolulu *Star-Bulletin* 3 Sep. 1945: 4.

"To Increase Navy Enlistment of Negroes." *Carolina Times* 23 Sep. 1939: 5.

"Tradewinds Presents." *Mananan* 4 July 1945: 10.

"Troup, Bobby [Robert William]." Obituary. Oxford Music Online. Web. 29 Apr. 2013.

"Troupers Are Carrying 'Arsenic and Old Lace' Across the World." Washington *Post* 21 Feb. 1943: 12.

"20,000 at Merrick Launching, First Ship in South to Bear Negro's Name Is Christened at Wilmington." *Carolina Times* 17 July 1943: 1.

"Two Convicted on Jim Crow Charge." *Carolina Times* 22 Nov. 1941: 1.

"Two Killed in Fort Dix Riot; MP Jailed for Shooting Soldier in N. Jersey Camp." *Carolina Times* 12 Dec. 1942: 1.

"232 Men Enlist in Navy Program." Raleigh *News and Observer* 28 Oct. 1942: 1.

Tuck, William A. "Wright Attacks Leaders." *Carolina Times* 3 Aug 1940: 1.

Tursi, Frank. *Winston-Salem, A History*. Winston-Salem: Blair, 1994.

Tyson, Timothy B. "The Ghosts of 1898: Wilmington's Race Riot and the Rise of White Supremacy." Raleigh *News and Observer*. 17 Nov. 1996, sec. H.

"USS Franklin (CV-13)." *Ships of the World*. Boston: Houghton-Mifflin, 1997. Credo Reference. Web. 5 Mar. 2012.

United States Pre-Flight School Band: The Cloudbuster Band in Pictures. [Chapel Hill, NC: U.S. Navy], 1944.

"UNC Navy School Put in Commission." Greensboro *News and Record* 24 May 1942: 1.

"V-J Day Program at Manana." Manana Barracks. [30 Aug. 1945] Clarence Yourse Scrapbook. Collection of James C. Yourse, Jr.

"Vitality for All." Papers of Henry A. Wallace. Series X: Writing, Speeches by Wallace 1943. Series X: box 55. Iowa City, IA: U of Iowa Libraries.

"Waikiki Turns into Bedlam of 'Hey, Fellas, We are Going Home!'" Honolulu *Star-Bulletin* 15 Aug. 1945: 3.

Walsh, Alex. "Earl Watkins: Mr. Lucky." Local 6 Archives. Musicians Union Local Six, San Francisco, CA. Web. 9 Mar. 2011.

"The War Bond Rally." *Chapel Hill Weekly* 17 Sept. 1943. 6.

"War Bond Rally Tuesday Evening." *Chapel Hill Weekly* 10 Sept. 1943: 1.

"Warner Lawson Named Music Dean at Howard." Chicago *Defender* 25 Apr. 1942: 7.

Washington, Booker T. Letter to William H. Taft. 20 Nov. 1906. Nalty: 61–62.

Weiss, Nancy J. "The Negro and the New Freedom: Fighting Wilsonian Segregation." *Political Science Quarterly* 84.1 (1969): 61–79.

White, Walter. "Race Relations in the Armed Services of the United States," *Journal of Negro Education* 12.3 (1943): 350–354.

"Why We Raised the Issue." *Daily Tar Heel* 19 Nov. 1942: 2.

Wilson, Joe. "Musically Speaking." *Mananan* 30 Oct. 1945: 7.

Wolfe, N. J. "Complaint Report: Woman Taken Off Bus." Wilmington Police Dept. 11 July 1943. Raleigh: State Archives of NC. Broughton papers, box 82: "Race Relations."

Wolgemuth, Kathleen L. "Woodrow Wilson and Federal Segregation." *The Journal of Negro History* 44.2 (1959) 158–73.

Woodward, C. Vann. *The Strange Career of Jim Crow*. 1955. New York, Oxford UP, 2002.

"WPA Chorus Will Sing Here Today." *Daily Tar Heel* 4 Dec. 1938: 1.

"World War II Facts and Figures." NC at Home and in Battle in WWII. NC Museum of History. Web. 11 Dec. 2012.

Wynn, Neil A. *The Afro-American and the Second World War*. Rev. ed. New York: Holmes and Meier, 1993.

Yoder, Edwin M. *Telling Others What to Think: Recollections of a Pundit*. Baton Rouge: LSU P, 2004.

Program for VJ celebration
at which B-1 performed

Wray Herring Collection, Special Collections

Joyner Library, East Carolina University

Alex Albright, a native of Graham, NC, earned a BA in English/journalism from UNC-CH in 1972 and an MFA from UNC-Greensboro in 1975. He worked in bookstores in Greensboro, Winston-Salem, Gastonia and Athens, GA and taught high school English and history at Chalmette (LA) High School before joining the English faculty at East Carolina University in 1981.

He was founding editor of the *North Carolina Literary Review*, which he edited from 1991-96, with Eva Roberts as its art director. He wrote and co-produced two music programs: the UNC-TV documentary *Boogie in Black and White* (1988), about the making and restoring of the 1947 black cast musical comedy *Pitch a Boogie Woogie,* and for the North Carolina Department of Cultural Resources the one woman show *Coming into Freedom: The End of the Civil War in Eastern North Carolina,* which was performed in 1990 by the North Carolina Symphony and Louise Anderson at Somerset Plantation.

He edited *The North Carolina Poems* (2010) by A.R. Ammons and *The Mule Poems* (2010), also by Ammons; *Dreaming the Blues: Poems from Martin County Prison* (1984); and with Luke Whisnant *Leaves of Greens: The Collard Poems* (1984).

He won the 1991 Jack Kerouac Literary Prize, from the Lowell (MA) Historic Preservation Commission; the 1998 R. Hunt Parker Award for lifetime contributions to NC literature, from the NC Literary and Historical Association; and the 2007 Roberts Award for literary inspiration (with Eva Roberts and Keats Sparrow), from East Carolina University.

Albright lives in Fountain, NC with his wife, Elizabeth Edgerton, and son, Silas James, where they operate R.A. Fountain, General Store.

Eva Roberts was born in Washington, DC but has deep roots in NC and earned her undergraduate and graduate degrees from NC State School of Design. Designer and typographer of this edition, she always enjoys working with Alex Albright. Her work has won numerous awards and, with editor Albright, *NCLR* earned honors that include Best New Journal, CELJ, 1994; Best in Show, *Aldus* magazine, 1993; American Center for Design 100 Show, 1994; Creative Club of Atlanta; Applied Arts Awards Annual design excellence, 1995, 1996; as well as 13 other design awards and distinctions 1992–1996.

Roberts is department chair and professor of Visual Communication Design at Herron School of Art + Design in Indianapolis. She has two daughers, Morgen Burzynski, who lives and works in Greenville, NC, and Callan Burzynski, who is a graduate student in New Orleans.